A Mother's
Nightmare -
Incest

*To all protective parents
and my own dear children,
Willie and Eric*

A Mother's Nightmare- Incest

A Practical Legal Guide for Parents and Professionals

John E. B. Myers

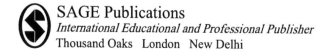

SAGE Publications
International Educational and Professional Publisher
Thousand Oaks London New Delhi

For information:

SAGE Publications, Inc.
2455 Teller Road
Thousand Oaks, California 91320
E-mail: order@sagepub.com

SAGE Publications Ltd.
6 Bonhill Street
London EC2A 4PU
United Kingdom

SAGE Publications India Pvt. Ltd.
M-32 Market
Greater Kailash I
New Delhi 110 048 India

Printed in the United States of America

Library of Congress Cataloging-in-Publication Data

Myers, John E. B.
    A mother's nightmare—incest: A practical legal guide for parents and professionals / author, John E. B. Myers.
       p. cm.
    Includes bibliographical references and index.
    ISBN 0-7619-1058-1 (pbk.: acid-free paper). — ISBN 0-7619-1057-3 (cloth: acid-free paper)
    1. Incest—United States. 2. Incest victims—United States.
3. Sexually abused children—United States. 4. Custody of children—United States. 5. Mothers and daughters—United States. I. Title.
HV6570.7.M94   1997
364.15'36—dc21   97-4759

This book is printed on acid-free paper.

97 98 99 00 01 02 03 10 9 8 7 6 5 4 3 2 1

Acquiring Editor:	C. Terry Hendrix
Editorial Assistant:	Dale Mary Grenfell
Production Editor:	Astrid Virding
Production Assistant:	Karen Wiley
Book Designer/Typesetter:	Christina M. Hill
Cover Designer:	Candice Harman
Print Buyer:	Anna Chin

Contents

Preface

This book by John Myers, a renowned law professor and authority on child abuse evidence, is a valuable resource for parents grappling with the dilemma of suspected child sexual abuse. It is clearly written and illustrated with compelling case examples. Myers reviews what is known about child sexual abuse, about child sexual abusers, and about how the legal system handles allegations of child abuse. This information can assist parents to carefully consider what to do, and what not to do, in response to their concerns about possible sexual abuse of their children. It could help prevent cases of misperceived concerns from escalating into full blown court battles. It could prevent concerned parents from engaging in repeated interrogations of their children that may ultimately undermine the ability of professionals and the courts to accurately discern the true nature of their children's statements. In situations where there is or has been child sexual abuse, this book can help guide parents to protect their children. It could also help persons who find themselves falsely accused of child sexual abuse; they also need to understand the current knowledge about child sexual abuse and how the legal system works.

A suspicion of child sexual abuse in the context of separated parents is one of the most difficult situations parents, children, and professionals face in today's effort to confront and stop the abuse of children. The determination of whether or not our society has progressed enough to maintain its present concern and awareness of the serious and widespread problems of childhood sexual abuse and other forms of childhood maltreatment will depend on how well professionals and courts handle these most complex and troubling cases. These situations are difficult for the parents who come to suspect or believe that their children have been sexually abused by other parents or someone affiliated with those parents. They are stressful to the children and to the parents who are suspected or accused. The feelings of safety, beliefs about justice, and the very future of these parents and their children all depend on how accurately and fairly these concerns are resolved.

Proving that child sexual abuse has occurred is difficult. It is even more difficult in the context of parental separation, where the counter charge of indoctrination, manipulation, or fabrication by the parent who is seeking to limit the other parent's access to their child or children may be easier to believe than the fact that sometimes adults who appear to be normal may sexually abuse children. Further increasing the challenge for parents seeking to protect their children from other parents is the fact that courts are justifiably cautious in restricting the rights of parents to participate in the raising of their children. Unfortunately, this problem has been made even worse by misleading claims that the vast majority of these cases are false and other equally erroneous assertions that they are nearly all true. The reality, most research suggests, is someplace in between these extremes. The research also indicates that most cases of suspected sexual abuse between separated parents are based on sincere and justifiable concerns by parents who are only trying to do what they believe is best for their children.

Bonafide cases of child sexual abuse can surface at the time of parental separation and divorce. Some parents separate and divorce after discovering the abuse. In some cases, the secrecy of ongoing incest is broken by the fracture of the parents' marriage. In other cases, the stress, loss of sexual and emotional intimacy, and psychological regression associated with marital problems and divorce appear to contribute to the first occurrence of child sexual abuse. There are even situations where it appears that children are abused as retaliation by angry ex-spouses. False cases can arise from reasonable concerns or from misperceptions and appear to do so more frequently than as a product of outright fabrication. In what appears to be a small minority of cases, dishonest or very disturbed parents have sought to gain advantage in child custody contests by knowingly pursuing false claims of child sexual abuse. The act of falsifying a charge of abuse against an innocent person is a criminal offense that causes great suffering to the wrongfully accused party and to the children involved. This kind of deceit is legally and morally wrong. It is also foolish. As Myers points out in the pages that follow, even honest, sincere parents with legitimate concerns and professionals who support their beliefs sometimes fail to convince courts that they are right. These concerned parents can lose custody to the parent they have accused and can even be ordered to have virtually no contact with the children they have sought to protect.

The perpetrators of child sexual abuse are more often male than female. But there are also some women who sexually abuse children, although they are outnumbered eight or nine to one by males among perpetrators of this crime. Child victims can also be male or female. The problem of child sexual abuse allegations between separated parents is too complicated to characterize as simply one of mothers accusing fathers of sexually abusing their children.

Parents who sincerely believe that their children are being abused by another parent, or any other person, have a moral and legal responsibility to protect their children from such abuse. This book and the information it contains can assist parents to understand the legal system and to advocate for their children's safety. It can also assist parents who find themselves falsely suspected or accused of child sexual abuse. Both of these are important objectives for promoting justice for children and parents.

There are two worst possible outcomes of alleged child sexual abuse between separated parents. The first is failure to affirm actual abuse, leaving victimized children unprotected or even, in the worst scenarios, awarding their full custody to abusing parents. The second is erroneously affirming false allegations against innocent parents and depriving them and their children of normal relationships. This book can help prevent both of these tragic outcomes. All non-abusive parents caught in these terrible situations are served by Myers' courageous effort to come to their aid.

—DAVID L. CORWIN, M.D.
The Childhood Trust
Children's Hospital Medical Center
University of Cincinnati College of Medicine

A Note to Readers

This book is written for two audiences: first, parents—primarily mothers—who suspect their child has been sexually abused; and second, professionals who work with sexually abused children and their parents. Many parents who open this book are in tremendous pain and turmoil, and I hope in these pages to communicate as directly as possible with them. To communicate directly, many portions of the book are written as though I was engaged in one-on-one conversation with a parent. I write of "Your child," "Your worst nightmare," "Your rights," "Your child's safety," and so on. My hope is that this more personal style will feel comfortable to parents.

Professionals who read this book are accustomed to reading the professional literature, which speaks not of "Your child," but "The child." Not "Your worst nightmare," but "A parent's worst nightmare." At first, professionals may find the one-on-one conversational style of this book a bit awkward. I hope professionals will understand my motivation for writing as I have. My hope is to communicate directly with parents at a very difficult time in their lives. Also, I hope to avoid the somewhat dry and academic style of much of the professional literature. That said, I hope professionals will approach the text with understanding and patience for what I'm trying to accomplish.

As I mention above, most parents who read this book are women. The reason is simple: The vast majority of sexual abuse is committed by men. Because most readers are women, the book is addressed primarily to a female audience. If you are a man, however, please don't feel left out. I realize there are many protective fathers out there. For example, some divorced fathers suspect that their child is being sexually abused by the mother's boyfriend or new husband. This book is as much for protective dads as it is for protective moms—it is dedicated to protective *parents,* regardless of their gender.

—JOHN E. B. MYERS

1

One Mother's Nightmare

In the United States, we grow up believing that the legal system is just and fair and that judges make correct and wise decisions. Most of the time, our beliefs are confirmed. There are times, however, when the legal system fails, when it backfires. This book is about the frightening fact that in some cases the legal system turns its back on parents—primarily mothers—who are desperately trying to protect their children from sexual abuse.

To introduce this troubling subject, in this chapter I describe the true story of one woman's struggle to protect her children. The names and places have been changed to protect the confidentiality of the mother and the children.

Sue's Story

Sue grew up in a middle-class suburb. After high school, she attended a local college but interrupted her studies to become a flight attendant. Three years later, she quit flying and moved to Hawaii, where she returned to college and worked as a sales representative. In Hawaii, Sue met Roger, who was then a medical student. Roger was as handsome as Sue was beautiful, and they quickly fell in love. They lived together while Roger finished medical school and began his training as a brain surgeon. Two years later, they married.

When Roger finished his surgical training, the couple moved to a midwestern city and Roger began practicing medicine. Sue stayed home, and it wasn't long before their first child arrived, a boy they named Eric. Two other children followed in quick succession, Nancy and Trent. Sue loved being a full-time mother, and Roger buried himself in his work. Before long, the family was living in a beautiful home and enjoying the affluent lifestyle that comes with a successful medical practice.

The first time Sue noticed something odd about Roger was on a visit to his parents' home. Several of Roger's brothers were there with their children, including a ten-year-old girl. Roger and the ten-year-old were playing badminton in the backyard. The shuttlecock flew into the bushes, and Roger and the child went looking for it. Sue was standing inside, watching from a window. She saw Roger come up behind the girl, grab her by the shoulder, and push his crotch against her bottom. It only took a moment, and Sue didn't think much of it. She turned away from the window thinking, "That's odd. I wonder why he did that? Oh well, it's probably nothing."

Time went by. Eric, the first born, was a toddler, and Nancy was just two months old. One evening, Roger was lying on his back on the couch. The baby was lying on top of him, right over his crotch, and Roger's hand was down the front of her diaper. When Sue entered the room, Roger jerked his hand away. This time, Sue was worried, but she was afraid to ask Roger anything. He had a hot temper and could fly into a rage.

From the time the children were babies, Roger found ways to press them against his genital area. He didn't hug his children like other fathers—he didn't put his arms around them and hug face to face. Roger resisted normal hugs. He embraced his children by pulling them against his crotch. For example, when he read to the children he'd lie on his back and place the child on his crotch. If the child moved, Roger would carefully put the child back on his crotch. Sometimes, he'd lie on his side and press the child's bottom against his crotch. At the time, Sue didn't think much of it. Yes, it was odd, it didn't seem quite right, but Sue couldn't bring herself to think that her husband—a doctor and a community leader—could be a pervert.

Roger's sexualized touching of the children continued, but when Eric was six and Nancy four, things got worse: The children started touching their father's crotch. One night Sue said, "Roger, why don't you tell the children to stop. It's not right." Roger became furious. "I have my own style," he snarled. "Just shut up!" Sue persisted; they had numerous arguments, but Roger wouldn't stop.

The inappropriate touching was not the only source of friction in the marriage, and Sue and Roger started seeing a marriage counselor. Sue was talking to the counselor by herself one day when she described how Roger touched the children. Sue mentioned a recent episode where Roger had been lying on his side on the couch. He greeted Eric, now seven, by pulling him down onto the couch and positioning the child's bottom tight against his own genitals. Then, Roger lifted his leg over Eric to pull him tighter. The counselor said, "That's sexual abuse. Your husband is sexually abusing your son." Sue was shocked. Sexual abuse? She knew the behavior was odd, but it had gone on so long it seemed almost normal. It was just Roger's "style," as he put it. The counselor said, "I'm scheduled to see Roger tomorrow, and I'll tell him how inappropriate this is." Sue asked if she should call child protective services, but the counselor said, "No. Getting protective services involved will ruin the family, and all that will happen is Roger will be ordered to see another counselor. I've got some experience with men who do this. Let me talk to him." As Sue drove home, the counselor's words began to sink in: "sexual abuse." The nightmare had begun.

That evening, Sue said nothing, and Roger went to his appointment the next day. When he came home, his face was purple with rage. He hissed between clenched teeth, "I hope it was worth it, telling the counselor those things, because it cost you your marriage." From that moment, Roger was cold and distant. He opened a new bank account in his own name. He started seeing a different counselor and refused to let Sue talk to the counselor. He talked to a divorce lawyer. When he got angry—which was often—he'd walk up to Sue and hold his thumb and finger a fraction of an inch apart while he seethed, "You're this close to a divorce."

Finally, Sue couldn't stand it anymore. She told Roger she was leaving, but before she was out the door, Roger was begging her to stay. "Don't go, honey. Let's not throw everything away. We can work it out." But Sue was determined. She took the children and moved to a city two hours away.

During the separation, the children lived with Sue and visited Roger on weekends. One Sunday afternoon, Roger returned the kids to Sue's house. Roger said, "I think I'll take Eric to a movie before I drive home." It was late when Roger dropped Eric off and drove away. The two younger children were already asleep. Sue was getting Eric ready for bed when he said, "Mom, I know what teenagers do on dates." Sue replied, "What, honey?" Eric explained, "Dad told me all about it on the way home from the movie. They take off their clothes and screw." Sue stared in disbelief as her seven-year-old son went on, "Dad showed me how to get a hard-on. See?" Eric put his hand down the front of his pajamas and rubbed his penis. Then he started masturbating. Sue said, "Did your daddy show you that?" Eric replied, "Yeah." Sue removed Eric's hand from his pj's and gently told him, "Honey, it's not okay to do that in front of other people. Daddy shouldn't have told you that. You're too young. Go to bed now. Mommy loves you." Sue tucked Eric in, gave him a good-night kiss, and turned out the light before she let herself cry. In a daze, she walked to the kitchen and slumped into a chair. Tears fell like rain.

Other disturbing incidents piled up, such as the time five-year-old Nancy traced her hand seductively over Sue's breast, across her stomach, and between her mother's legs. When Sue told her to stop, Nancy replied, "But Daddy does it to me." Nancy also described how her father lay on top of her, crotch to crotch. Eric said his dad and his new girlfriend walked around the house naked. Roger made the children sleep on the floor in his room while he and his girlfriend occupied the bed. When the alarm went off in the morning, Roger and the girlfriend had sex while the children pretended to sleep.

During the separation, Sue was seeing a counselor. She asked if there was anything she could do about the sexual behavior. The children didn't like it and they were confused. The counselor suggested that the children write a letter to their father, but the children were afraid, so they told the counselor the things they didn't like and the counselor wrote the letter. What a sad letter: Two little children pleading with their father to stop touching them inappropriately and to respect their privacy. The letter had a place for Roger to agree by signing his name. He refused.

When Nancy learned that Roger refused to sign the letter, she called him and left a message on his answering machine. Sue was in the next room and she heard her daughter's angry words, "Daddy, I want you to sign that letter. You should sign it 'cause you got off easy in the letter, and you know what I mean." For several months, Sue had suspected Nancy wasn't telling her everything her father did, and Nancy's words—"You got off easy"—confirmed her fear.

Later that night, Sue talked to Nancy about what her father did. Nancy said, "Things happened, Mommy, but I can't remember. I can't talk about those things 'cause they're in a black dot in my head. When the dot moves in front of my eyes, I can see inside it and then I remember, but before I can say anything the dot moves away and I can't see inside it anymore, so I can't remember."

Sue talked to her attorney about the sexual behavior. The attorney prepared a document for Roger to sign in which Roger agreed to stop having sex with his girlfriend while the children were in the bedroom and to stop walking around the house naked. The document didn't say anything about inappropriate touching—Roger was too smart to admit that. This time, Roger signed, and for a while things calmed down. The children seemed safe, although Eric and Nancy still expressed tremendous anger toward their father.

Up to this point, Sue hadn't worried much about the little one, Trent. After all, he was barely three. Yet, following visits to his dad's house, Trent began acting strangely. He started having nightmares and he became afraid of the dark. Over and over again, he pushed his face into his mother's crotch. Sue gently pushed him away, but he persisted. Two or three times, Trent tried to pull Sue's head down to his crotch. He did the same to his big brother, who in typical big brother fashion punched him. Then, in the car one day, Sue looked in the rear view mirror to see Trent sitting with his eyes half closed slowly pushing three fingers in and out of his mouth and sucking. Trent never sucked his thumb or fingers. Sue said, "Honey, what are you doing?" Trent removed his fingers and said, "Somebody hurt Trent," but he wouldn't say more.

A week later, Sue was busy getting the kids packed for a weekend visit with Roger. They were leaving after school. Trent walked quietly up to Sue and whispered in her ear, "Somebody go pee-pee in my mouth." Sue asked who, but Trent said, "Nobody." He wouldn't talk about it. Sue tried to figure out what he meant. Her son went to preschool during the morning, and Sue thought maybe an older boy at preschool had urinated on him. She decided to talk to him again, but getting a three-year-old to hold still long enough to answer questions is not easy, so Sue dropped the older children at school and took Trent for a drive. Strapped in his car seat, Trent was a captive audience. Sue took a tape recorder. She said, "Remember when you told me somebody went pee-pee in your mouth?" Trent said, "Yes." Sue asked, "Who's been going pee-pee in your mouth?" Trent answered, "Daddy." He said it with such sadness in his little voice that Sue knew he was telling the truth. Trent picked up a small plastic sword and slowly pushed it in and out of his mouth while he made sucking sounds. Then he said, "Me kill Daddy."

Sue drove straight to child protective services (CPS) and asked to speak to a social worker. (See Chapter 10 for a discussion of CPS.) She'd called CPS several times before, but no one there had been any help. After half an hour, a social worker came out and escorted Trent into a stuffy little office with no windows and nothing to make him feel comfortable. Sue was not allowed to go with him. Trent wouldn't say a word, and the social worker told Sue there was nothing CPS could do. Sue said, "I've got a tape I just made. On the tape, he says what happened. Will you listen to it?" The social worker said she was too busy to listen to the tape, and she started back to her office. Sue followed, saying, "Oh please, it'll just take a minute. Please listen to it." The social worker said, "Alright, leave the tape here. I'll listen to it later. Come back at four o'clock this afternoon."

On the way home, Sue asked, "Trent, why didn't you tell the lady?" He replied, "If I tell, Daddy be all gone." This was Trent's three-year-old way of saying that if he told the social worker, his father would be gone. Sue found out later that Roger had threatened Trent to keep him quiet.

At the appointed hour, Sue returned to child protective services only to find the social worker gone for the day. Another social worker handed Sue the tape and a note that read, "I didn't have time to listen to the tape. You will have to send the children on the visit." No one else in the office would help her. Sue called her attorney, but the attorney could see no way out of the visit. Sue hid her tears as she drove the children to the man she knew was a child molester.

After Sue dropped the children off at Roger's house, she had two hours to think as she drove home. By the time she pulled into her driveway, her mind was made up. Child protective services wouldn't help, so she was going to court to protect her children. A divorce was already under way, and she could ask the family court judge for help. The next morning, Sue called her lawyer, who suggested that they seek a judge's order that Roger's visits with the children be supervised by a responsible adult. Sue said, "That's a wonderful idea." She felt relieved and hopeful.

The children had been seeing a counselor since Sue and Roger separated, and the children told the counselor some of what Roger did. In particular, Trent told the counselor how Roger pushed his penis in his mouth and how "white stuff came out." Sue told the counselor she was going to court to get supervised visits, and the counselor said he would testify for her.

The court day arrived. Sue and Roger were there with their attorneys. Sue's lawyer told the judge, "Your honor, we are asking for supervised visits because there is evidence the father sexually abused the children." Roger's lawyer said, "Your honor, Roger absolutely denies these charges. He's a doctor, your honor. He's not the kind of man who would do such a horrible thing. I don't know where this idea of sexual abuse comes from, but it's ridiculous. There is no need for supervised visits." The judge said, "Alright, let's hear from the mother. What do you have to say?" Sue started to tell her story, but the judge cut her off, saying, "I don't have time for all the details. Just tell me the latest thing you say happened." Sue described what Trent said about his daddy going pee-pee in his mouth. After Sue finished, Trent's counselor testified that he was convinced Trent was sexually abused and that supervised visits were essential. Roger looked pale and worried, but he denied any abuse.

The judge ruled that visits would be supervised until a psychological evaluation was completed. Now the question was, who should supervise the visits? Sue's lawyer suggested someone from the child protection agency in Roger's city. Roger's attorney suggested Roger's housekeeper. To Sue's amazement, the judge chose the housekeeper despite the fact that the woman was financially dependent on Roger and, in the housekeeper's own words, "loved Roger like a son."

At the end of the day, Sue felt partially vindicated. It was true the housekeeper wasn't the best choice, but some supervision was better than none. The most important thing was that somebody finally seemed to believe what her children had been saying for so long. Sue was happy, but not for long.

The court hearing frightened Roger. He realized that if Sue could prove sexual abuse, he'd be ruined. Roger decided to go on the attack. In addition to his regular lawyer, Roger hired a $250-an-hour attorney who specialized in defending fathers accused of sexual abuse. This lawyer knew every angle, and the first thing he did was file a document in court seeking full custody of the children. Up to that point, Sue and Roger had agreed that Sue should have custody. But the new attorney charged that Sue was unfit, that she made false charges of sexual abuse, and that she had "parental alienation syndrome." (See Chapter 11 for a discussion of parental alienation syndrome.) Sue couldn't believe it. "Oh my God, he's trying to take the children!"

Sue was in for the fight of her life. The final court hearing on custody was six months away. Roger's new attorney was extremely aggressive, and he set out to prove that Sue was a vindictive, unstable woman who coached her children into false stories. One tactic was to keep Sue and her attorney off balance and distract them from the important job of getting ready for court. Roger's attorney buried Sue and her attorney in paperwork, demanding answers to hundreds of questions about every detail of Sue's life, all the way back to her childhood. It seemed new questions arrived every day. Sue's lawyer devoted more and more time to answering the questions, and before long Sue was paying her attorney nearly $4,000 a month! Roger had plenty of money for his team of lawyers, but Sue was quickly running out of funds. Roger was getting the upper hand.

The judge appointed a psychologist to evaluate the allegations of sexual abuse. The psychologist's report would be the most important evidence in the case. Yet, the psychologist knew very little about sexual abuse. The psychologist interviewed Sue, Roger, and the children and gave them some psychological tests. A week before the critical hearing, Sue looked in her mailbox, and there was the psychologist's report. Sue tore open the envelope. Her eyes raced over the pages, looking for the psychologist's opinion. Finally, at the bottom of the third page, she read, "No credible evidence of child sexual abuse." Her heart sank. No evidence of sexual abuse? What about the things the children said! Didn't anybody listen to the children? Didn't anybody care about them? Sue let the report flutter to the floor. She turned to the window and watched her children playing happily outside. The true meaning of what was happening pierced her like a knife. In a week's time, the children could be gone.

It was time for the final custody hearing in court. Sue and her lawyer sat at one table; Roger and his two lawyers occupied the other table. The judge entered and the hearing began. Sue was the first witness and things started out alright. Sue's lawyer asked her what she had seen and what her children had told her. For a while, the judge allowed her to repeat her children's words, but then Roger's attorney interrupted, saying, "Your honor, she should not repeat what the children may have said. It's hearsay and clearly inadmissible." The judge agreed, and Sue was not permitted to repeat any more of what her children had told her about abuse.

When Sue had told as much of the story as the judge would allow, Roger's lawyer started grilling her. He said, "What kind of a mother are you? What kind of a mother would invent such a preposterous story? You are just trying to hurt Roger, aren't you? You're just trying to get revenge. You're trying to get revenge with this little lie about sexual abuse. But it won't work. We know what you're up to. We know you planted those false ideas in your children's minds to alienate the children from the father who loves them so much. What kind of a mother are you? What kind of a mother?" The attack went on for hours.

The children's counselor testified that he believed the children were abused, but Roger's attorney made short work of the counselor.

The psychologist who conducted the evaluation for the judge testified. She said, "I could find no credible evidence of sexual abuse. The children said some things to me, but I couldn't make much out of it. The father does not have the personality to abuse children. The mother, on the other hand, is emotionally high-strung and borders on unstable."

Sue's attorney asked the psychologist, "If Sue is emotional, couldn't that be because she's worried about her children—worried that they are being sexually abused? Wouldn't such fear make any normal, loving mother emotional?" The psychologist said, "I suppose anything is possible."

Finally, Roger testified. He was calm and collected. He denied doing anything inappropriate to the children and said, "The only thing I care about is my children. I'm convinced I can provide a more stable home than their mother. They will be better off with me." Sue watched the judge's face. As Roger testified, the judge shook his head approvingly. The few times when the judge looked at Sue, he frowned.

At the end of the day, the judge said, "I will take the case under consideration and issue my decision within a week. In the meantime, the children will live with their father. Court is adjourned." Sue and her attorney walked slowly out of court. Roger was standing in the hall smiling and shaking hands with his attorneys and with the court-appointed psychologist. As Sue walked by, Roger said coldly, "Have the children at my house by five, and don't forget their clothes."

The days of waiting for the judge's decision dragged by. Sue wandered aimlessly through the now-empty house. The sounds of children's laughter were gone—there was nothing but silence. Sue walked in and out of her children's rooms, holding their toys. She pressed Trent's teddy bear against her cheek and put it down, damp with tears.

Late one morning, the phone rang. Sue picked it up. It was her lawyer. There was a long pause as the attorney struggled to find words. Finally, he said, "Sue, I'm so sorry, so very sorry. The judge ruled against you. Roger will have full custody. The judge thinks you shouldn't even have much visitation. All you will have is one day of visitation a month. And your visitation has to be supervised. I'm so sorry." Sue cried and her lawyer cried with her. Somewhere else, three little children cried too.

Sue's story is fact, not fiction, and she is not alone. Across the United States, many parents, primarily mothers, have tried and failed to protect their children from sexual abuse. Yet, if you are in Sue's position you should not lose heart. For every case like Sue's, there are ten where children are protected. The purpose of this book is not to discourage you or to persuade you to avoid the legal system. Rather, the purpose is to alert you to the very real dangers that await anyone who accuses a spouse of child sexual abuse. I hope this book will help you and other parents reduce the likelihood that the legal system will backfire.

Part I

Essential Information About Child Sexual Abuse

When parents suspect that a child of theirs has been sexually abused, a thousand questions race through their minds, including: What is child sexual abuse? How common is it? How can I tell whether my child was abused? What will happen to the child if he or she was abused? Who can I turn to for help? Should I call the police? Do I need a lawyer? The questions go on and on, but one question stands out above the rest, *How do I protect my child?*

This book was written to answer as many of these questions as possible, especially the last one. Of course, it's not feasible to answer all questions. My goal is to provide as much information as possible about child sexual abuse and about the legal institutions in our society that are designed to protect children from such abuse. Much of the book focuses on the law and its important role in protecting children. When you finish this book you will possess the information you need to work toward the all-important goal of protecting your child.

Part I of this book contains three chapters packed with critical information about child sexual abuse. Part I begins with Chapter 2, in which I define child sexual abuse as well as other types of child abuse. Chapter 2 also contains essential information on how common child sexual abuse is in our society.

Chapter 3 answers some of the questions that worry every parent, including, "Will my child ever be normal again?" "What are the short- and long-term harmful effects of sexual abuse?" "Will my child grow up to be a molester?" "Should I get mental health counseling for my child?"

Chapter 4 is focused on the men who sexually abuse children and answers questions such as, "How much sexual abuse is committed by fathers, stepfathers, other relatives, and strangers?" "Are there psychological tests that can tell if a man is a child molester?" "Can men who sexually abuse children be cured?" Although some sexual abuse is committed by women, the large majority of perpetrators are men.

When you finish the chapters in Part I, you will know a great deal about child sexual abuse. Equipped with this information, you will be ready for Part II, which introduces you to the enormously complex legal system.

2

Defining Child Sexual Abuse and Other
Forms of Child Maltreatment

In this chapter, I define child sexual abuse and other kinds of child maltreatment. Many children who are sexually abused are also subjected to other forms of maltreatment, and parents who are working to protect their children from sexual abuse need to understand these other kinds of abuse.

The following questions are addressed in this chapter:

□ What is child sexual abuse? (p. 14)
□ How common is child sexual abuse? (p. 15)
□ How old are the victims of child sexual abuse? (p. 16)
□ How does the law define child sexual abuse? (p. 16)
□ Can a child consent to sexual contact with an adult? (p. 17)
□ What is statutory rape? (p. 17)
□ What is incest? (p. 18)
□ Does penetration have special significance in the law? (p. 18)
□ If my child was sexually abused, why do I need to know about other kinds of child abuse? (p. 19)
□ What is physical child abuse? (p. 19)
□ What is psychological child abuse? (p. 20)
□ What is neglect? (p. 24)

What Is Child Sexual Abuse?

It's important to begin by saying that there is no single, universally agreed upon definition of child sexual abuse. Sexual abuse includes a broad range of conduct. Lucy Berliner and Diana Elliott give us insight into the expansive meaning of sexual abuse when they write,

> Sexual abuse involves any sexual activity with a child where consent is not or cannot be given. This includes sexual contact that is accomplished by force or threat of force, regardless of the age of the participants, and all sexual contact between an adult and a child, regardless of whether there is deception or the child understands the sexual nature of the activity. (1996, p. 51)

Basically, sexual abuse includes *any* touching by an adult of a child's body when the adult's purpose or motive for the touching is to arouse or gratify the adult's sexual desire. To put it in other words, sexual abuse is touching for sexual purposes. Obvious examples of sexual abuse include sexual intercourse, kissing a little girl's genitals, sucking a boy's penis, and forcing a child to touch or suck a man's penis.

Not all sexual abuse involves a child's genitals, buttocks, or breasts. Kissing on the mouth or other body part is abusive if the adult's purpose is sexual. Moreover, touching through a child's clothing can be as abusive as touching bare skin. Thus, it can be sexual abuse to touch a little girl's breasts through her blouse or a little boy's genitals through his pants.

In summary, any touching, anywhere on a child's body, is abuse when the adult's motive is sexual. Additionally, abuse occurs when a child touches an adult's body in response to the adult's request if the adult's motive is sexual gratification.

Obviously, not all touching of a child's body is abuse. Parents hug and kiss their children, and such touching is just the opposite of abuse. Moreover, parents often have good reasons to touch their young children's genitals or bottom. In caring for their children, parents clean, change diapers, check for injury or infection, and apply medications. It's important to ask, then, what is the difference between innocent touching and sexual abuse? For example, what distinguishes an appropriate act of putting salve on a little boy's penis from an act of sexual abuse? The answer lies in the mind of the adult. What is the *motive* for the touching? If the parent touched the boy to gratify the parent's sexual desires, the touching was abuse. On the other hand, if the parent touched the child's penis to apply needed medication, there was no abuse.

When we recognize that in many cases the difference between abuse and good parenting lies in the hidden recesses of the mind, we begin to appreciate why it's so often difficult to prove child sexual abuse. Because it's sometimes difficult to tell whether touching was abusive or benign, it's important to avoid jumping too quickly to conclusions about touching. Interpreting an innocent touch as sexual abuse is unfair to the adult and the child. In addition, misinterpreting innocent touching as abuse can have extremely serious consequences for the adult who misinterprets the touching. Much more is said in Chapter 12 about the danger of misinterpreting innocent behavior as evidence of sexual abuse.

Sexual touching is not the only kind of child sexual abuse. It's abuse to intentionally expose a child to pornography or to use a child in the production of pornography. Thus, it's child abuse to take indecent photographs or videos of children. An adult commits abuse when he persuades two children to engage in sex with each other. Abuse occurs when an adult masturbates knowing a child is watching. The exhibitionist lurking next to the school yard and the Peeping Tom at the bedroom window are child abusers.

How Common Is Child Sexual Abuse?

Unfortunately, child sexual abuse is common in the United States and other countries. The true prevalence of child sexual abuse is unknown because this crime occurs in secret, and most sexual abuse is not reported to the authorities. David Finkelhor, who is a leading authority on child abuse, reviewed the literature on prevalence and observed, "Because sexual abuse is usually a hidden offense, there are no statistics on how many cases actually occur each year" (1994, p. 32). Based on the best available research, Finkelhor estimates there are about 500,000 new cases of child sexual abuse every year in the United States.

Research discloses that approximately 20% of girls experience some form of sexual abuse during childhood. Abuse ranges from single episodes of relatively minor touching to brutal rape and incest that goes on for months or years. In the final analysis, Finkelhor concludes, "At least one in five adult women in North America experienced sexual abuse (either contact or noncontact) during childhood" (1994, p. 37).

Boys appear to be sexually abused at a lower rate than girls. Research discloses that approximately 5% to 10% of boys are sexually abused.

How Old Are the Victims of Child Sexual Abuse?

No child is safe from sexual abuse. Children between seven and thirteen years of age appear to be at the highest risk of abuse. Younger children are victimized too, however, and even babies have been molested.

How Does the Law Define Sexual Abuse?

Every state has laws that define child sexual abuse and make it illegal. As you saw earlier in this chapter, child sexual abuse includes a wide range of activity, and the laws against sexual abuse are written to be as wide ranging as the activity they seek to prohibit. For this reason, state laws defining child sexual abuse tend to be lengthy and complicated. Moreover, the laws of different states differ slightly. Although all states prohibit the same conduct, they do so with different words.

The terms *sodomy* and *oral copulation* figure prominently in legal definitions of sexual abuse. Sodomy is often defined as contact between the penis of one person and the anus of another person. Thus, a man commits sodomy by placing his penis inside a boy or girl's rectum. Even the slightest penetration is sufficient to constitute the crime.

Oral copulation refers to several forms of child sexual abuse, including putting a penis inside a child's mouth, licking or kissing genitals, and licking or kissing the anus. Oral copulation can be committed with a girl or a boy. For example, a man commits oral copulation when he forces a girl or boy to suck his penis. Similarly, oral copulation occurs when an adult sucks a boy's penis or kisses a girl's genitals.

Finally, it should be noted that in some states, oral copulation is included in the definition of sodomy.

It would serve no useful purpose in this book to provide the full legal definitions of child sexual abuse from all fifty states. Such a compilation would take up many pages of largely repetitive and extremely tedious text. Moreover, the laws are changed slightly from time to time, and by the time you combed through a table or chart of laws to find your state's legal definition, the law could be different. You can be sure that all the obvious forms of child sexual abuse are illegal in your state. If you find yourself involved in the legal system, your lawyer can provide you with the details of your state's current law.

Can a Child Consent to Sexual Contact With an Adult?

Men who sexually abuse children sometimes try to avoid responsibility by saying that the child "wanted" the sexual contact or that the victim "consented." This claim raises the issue of whether children have the legal capacity to consent to sexual activity with adults. The short answer is no. By law, children lack the capacity to consent to sexual conduct with adults. Many states define the age of consent as eighteen. In some states, the age is lowered to fourteen or sixteen. There is no state in the United States where young children have the legal capacity to consent to sexual activity with an adult. Thus, the perpetrator's plea that the child "wanted sex" or "consented" falls on deaf ears.

What Is Statutory Rape?

A man commits the crime of statutory rape when he has sexual intercourse with a female under the legal age of consent. The fact that the girl "consents" to the intercourse is not a defense for a man accused of statutory rape because the girl, by definition, is incapable of consent. Laws against statutory rape are designed to discourage men from taking advantage of young, immature females, and to protect such females from sexual exploitation.

If the victim in a statutory rape case was a teenager, the man may claim that he thought she was old enough to consent. In most states, however, the man's mistaken belief regarding the female's age—even if his mistake was reasonable—is not a defense to a charge of statutory rape.

What Is Incest?

In the law, incest is a crime that is defined as "sexual intercourse or cohabitation between a man and a woman who are related to each other within the degrees [of family relation] wherein marriage is prohibited" (*Black's Law Dictionary*, 1979, p. 685). A leading authority on sex offenders defines incest as "sexual acts, which may or may not include intercourse, between members of a family other than a husband and wife" (Becker, 1994, p. 176).

Does Penetration Have Special Significance in the Law?

Chapter 3 covers the point that sexual abuse involving penetration of a child's vagina, anus, or mouth is more likely than nonpenetrating abuse to have harmful psychological consequences for the child. Thus, penetration is important for psychological reasons. Penetration is also important for legal reasons. Some crimes, notably rape, are defined in terms of penetration. The California definition of rape, similar to the law in most states, provides, "Rape is an act of sexual intercourse [which includes penetration] accomplished with a person not the spouse of the perpetrator, where it is accomplished against a person's will by means of force, violence, duress, menace, or fear of immediate and unlawful bodily injury on the person or another" (*California Penal Code*, 1996, §261). The victim of rape may be an adult or a child of any age. Many states impose harsher criminal penalties for sex crimes involving penetration.

When people think of penetration, they usually imagine a penis going all the way into a vagina. In the law of rape and other sex offenses, however, penetration has a special meaning. In law, penetration is defined as *any* entry into a body cavity—vagina, anus, or mouth—*no matter how slight*. Penetration a fraction of an inch is enough. Thus, for rape, full penetration of the vagina is not required. Penetration is complete if the penis passes into the outer genital lips. The penis need not enter the vagina at all.

Penetration in the legal sense does not require that a female's hymen be ruptured. Penetration occurs whether or not the penis reaches the hymen, passes through it, or damages it in any way. Ejaculation is not required to meet the legal definition of penetration.

If My Child Was Sexually Abused, Why Do I Need to Know About Other Kinds of Child Abuse?

This book is primarily about child sexual abuse. It's important, however, for parents concerned with sexually abused children to understand other kinds of child abuse. Many sexually abused children are also physically abused, and virtually all sexually abused children are psychologically abused. Indeed, child sexual abuse is basically a form of severe psychological abuse.

Why is it important to understand nonsexual forms of child abuse? One important reason is that in many cases where children *are* sexually abused, it's *not* possible to prove the sexual abuse in court. That's right. Even though your child was sexually abused, you may not be able to prove it! But if you can't prove the sexual abuse, how can you protect your child?

The answer is that you may be able to protect your child by proving in court that the perpetrator committed some *other* kind of child abuse. For example, a man who sexually abuses his six-year-old daughter may also physically abuse her with a belt, leaving bruises all over her bottom and legs. The child's mother may not be able to prove the sexual abuse, but she should be able to convince a judge of the physical abuse. In case after case, protective parents find that it's easier to prove physical abuse than sexual abuse. Thus, protective parents have good reason to learn about nonsexual kinds of child abuse.

What Is Physical Child Abuse?

Physical child abuse is defined as nonaccidental physical injury. Every year, hundreds of thousands of children are punched, kicked, strangled, burned, and battered. Tragically, as many as 5,000 children die each year from severe physical abuse or neglect. Fatal child abuse and neglect are particularly common among very young children. Nearly

90% of abuse fatalities are younger than five, and more than 50% of fatalities are babies less than a year old.

Physical abuse should be distinguished from spanking for disciplinary purposes. Research shows that most U.S. parents use corporal punishment. Although parents and professionals debate the wisdom of spanking, the law generally tolerates "reasonable" corporal punishment for disciplinary purposes. For example, a California law states that physical abuse "does not include reasonable and age appropriate spanking to the buttocks where there is no evidence of serious physical injury" (*California Welfare and Institutions Code*, 1996, § 300).

When does corporal punishment exceed reasonable limits and cross the line into physical abuse? There is no simple answer to this question, and a judge who is trying to decide this issue considers the child's age, the type of discipline inflicted, the means used to punish the child (e.g., open hand vs. belt), and the degree of bodily injury and pain.

What Is Psychological Child Abuse?

Psychological child abuse has proven very difficult to define (See Brassard, Germain, & Hart, 1987). Although it's difficult to define psychological abuse, it's not difficult to see the damage caused by this form of maltreatment (Garbarino, Guttman, & Seeley, 1986). Indeed, experts increasingly agree that psychological abuse is the core issue in all forms of child maltreatment. For most physically abused children, the broken bones and bruises heal with time. For sexually abused children, physical injury is seldom the problem. The body of the physically or sexually abused child usually survives intact. But the child's essential sense of self-worth, his or her inner soul, may be damaged for life by the psychological abuse that lies at the heart of physical and sexual abuse.

Unfortunately, there are no national statistics on how many children are psychologically abused each year. It appears, however, that this form of child abuse is widespread. Of course, there are few perfect parents, and even the most loving parents occasionally say cruel things to their children. Such lapses are not psychological abuse. Despite regrettable words, children know their parents love them. Psychological abuse exists when there is a long-term pattern of negative messages that undermine a child's essential sense of self-worth.

The American Professional Society on the Abuse of Children (AP-SAC) has useful guidelines on psychological abuse. These guidelines, which are reproduced in Appendix D, define psychological abuse and describe the process used by mental health professionals to evaluate children who may be suffering from psychological maltreatment. The APSAC guidelines describe and provide examples of six forms of psychological maltreatment: (a) spurning; (b) terrorizing; (c) exploiting or corrupting; (d) denying emotional responsiveness; (e) isolating; and (f) mental, health, medical, and educational neglect:

SPURNING (Hostile/Degrading). Includes verbal and nonverbal caregiver acts that reject and degrade a child. Spurning includes:

☐ Belittling, degrading, and other nonphysical forms of overtly hostile or rejecting treatment
☐ Shaming or ridiculing the child for showing normal emotions such as affection, grief, or sorrow
☐ Consistently singling out one child to criticize and punish, to perform most of the household chores, or to receive fewer rewards
☐ Public humiliation

TERRORIZING. Includes caregiver behavior that threatens or is likely to physically hurt, kill, abandon, or place the child or the child's loved ones or objects in recognizably dangerous situations. Terrorizing includes:

☐ Placing a child in unpredictable or chaotic circumstances
☐ Placing a child in recognizably dangerous situations
☐ Setting rigid or unrealistic expectations with threat of loss, harm, or danger if they are not met
☐ Threatening or perpetrating violence against the child
☐ Threatening or perpetrating violence against a child's loved ones or objects

EXPLOITING or CORRUPTING. Includes caregiver acts that encourage the child to develop inappropriate behaviors (self-destructive, antisocial, criminal, deviant, or other maladaptive behaviors). Exploiting or corrupting includes:

☐ Modeling, permitting, or encouraging antisocial behavior (e.g., prostitution, performance in pornographic media, initiation of criminal activities, substance abuse, violence to or corruption of others)

☐ Modeling, permitting, or encouraging developmentally inappropriate behavior (e.g., parentification, infantilization, living the parent's unfilled dreams)

☐ Encouraging or coercing abandonment of developmentally appropriate autonomy through extreme overinvolvement, intrusiveness, or dominance (e.g., allowing little or no opportunity or support for the child's views, feelings, and wishes; micromanaging the child's life)

☐ Restricting or interfering with cognitive development

DENYING EMOTIONAL RESPONSIVENESS (Ignoring). Includes caregiver acts that ignore the child's attempts and need to interact (failing to express affection, caring, and love for the child) and showing no emotion in interactions with the child. Denying emotional responsiveness includes:

☐ Being detached and uninvolved through either incapacity or lack of motivation

☐ Interacting only when absolutely necessary

☐ Failing to express affection, caring, and love for the child

ISOLATING. Includes caregiver acts that consistently deny the child opportunities to meet needs for interacting or communicating with peers or adults inside or outside the home. Isolating includes:

☐ Confining the child or placing unreasonable limitations on the child's freedom of movement within his or her environment

☐ Placing unreasonable limitations or restrictions on the child's social interactions with peers or adults in the community

MENTAL, HEALTH, MEDICAL, AND EDUCATIONAL NEGLECT. Includes unwarranted caregiver acts that ignore, refuse to allow, or fail to provide the necessary treatment for the mental, health, medical, and educational problems or needs of the child. Mental, health, medical, and educational neglect include:

☐ Ignoring the need for or failing or refusing to allow or provide treatment for serious emotional or behavioral problems or needs of the child

☐ Ignoring the need for or failing or refusing to allow or provide treatment for serious physical health problems or needs of the child

☐ Ignoring the need for or failing or refusing to allow or provide treatment or services for serious educational problems or needs of the child

In addition to determining whether a child suffers one or more of the forms of psychological abuse described above, it's important to evaluate the level of severity of the abuse. On this point, the APSAC guidelines state:

In determining the level of severity of psychological maltreatment, consideration should be given to: (a) Intensity/ extremeness, frequency, chronicity; (b) The degree to which psychological maltreatment pervades the caregiver-child relationship; (c) Number of forms of psychological maltreatment which have been or are being perpetrated; (d) Influences in the child's life that may buffer the child from psychological maltreatment. For example, does the maltreating caregiver also provide nurturance for the child? Does the child have regular access to a nurturing, nonmaltreating adult?; (e) Salience of the maltreatment given the developmental period(s) in which it occurs and the developmental periods that will follow; and (f) Extent to which negative child development outcomes exist, are developing, or are predicted.

In legal proceedings, judges consider psychological abuse. This form of child abuse is particularly relevant when a judge decides which parent should have custody of a child. As the Colorado Supreme Court observed in a case called *People v. D.A.K.*, "The welfare of the child cannot be protected if courts must ignore the very real emotional abuses that a child may suffer. Emotional abuse may leave scars more permanent and damaging to a child's personality than bodily bruises from a physical beating" (1979, p. 750).

What Is Neglect?

Neglect is a broad concept that covers many types of child maltreatment. Neglect often overlaps psychological maltreatment. Unfortunately, because neglect covers so many harmful situations, the term does not lend itself to precise definition. The Utah Supreme Court provides helpful insight into the meaning of neglect in its decision in *In re K.S.*, where the court wrote,

> Children are entitled to the care of an adult who cares enough to provide the child with the opportunity to form psychological bonds, in addition to the physical necessities of life. An unfit or incompetent parent is one who "substantially and repeatedly refuses or fails to render proper parental care and protection." (1987, pp. 172-173)

Parents have a legal as well as a moral duty to provide their children with food, clothing, medical care, and a place to live. Unexcused failure to provide these basic necessities is neglect. Drug and alcohol abuse often contribute to neglect and other forms of child abuse. When substance abuse reaches the level of addiction, neglect is almost sure to follow. Addicted parents simply do not provide adequately for their children's needs.

3

What Does the Future Hold for a Child
Who Has Been Sexually Abused?

Parents of sexually abused children worry about what will happen to their child. This chapter should calm your worst fears while, at the same time, giving you an honest appraisal of the harm that sometimes follows sexual abuse. In this chapter, I discuss the following commonly asked questions:

- ☐ Will my child ever be normal again? (p. 26)
- ☐ What aspects of sexual abuse are associated with psychological harm? (p. 26)
- ☐ What are the short- and long-term harmful effects of sexual abuse? (p. 28)
- ☐ What is normal sexual behavior in children? (p. 34)
- ☐ Will my child grow up to be a child molester? (p. 35)
- ☐ Will my child blame me for the abuse? (p. 36)
- ☐ Will sexual abuse make my child gay? (p. 36)
- ☐ Could my child get AIDS or another sexually transmitted disease? (p. 38)
- ☐ Is my child still a virgin? (p. 38)
- ☐ Should I get mental health treatment for my child? (p. 39)
- ☐ Why does my child want to see the man who molested him or her? (p. 40)
- ☐ Should I tell my child's teacher or school principal? (p. 41)

Will My Child Ever Be Normal Again?

There is no denying that sexual abuse can harm children. Yet, parents of sexually abused children should not be fatalistic. With love and support, sexually abused children can be happy, normal children who grow up to be well adjusted, productive adults. Sexual abuse does not have to mark your child for life. To answer this vitally important question, then: Yes, your child can be normal again. Healing is easier for some children than others, but there is hope for *all* children.

Of course, when a child is sexually abused, life is never quite the same. We can't simply erase the past and pretend it didn't happen. The therapist Anna Salter observes poignantly that sexual abuse leaves footprints on the heart (1995). The psychiatrist Leonard Shengold refers to child abuse as "soul murder" (1979). Rather than dwell on the past, however, and what might have been, I urge you to look to the future and what might be. By focusing on the future, you avoid blaming yourself for something that is not your fault and you are in a better position to help your child move beyond the abuse.

**What Aspects of Sexual Abuse Are Associated
With Psychological Harm?**

There are many kinds of child sexual abuse, from the most horrendous to comparatively minor. Compare Tammy and Amy, for example, both age twelve. Tammy suffered years of sexual intercourse, oral copulation, threats, and physical and psychological abuse by her father. Amy, on the other hand, had one brief episode of inappropriate touching on the outside of her clothing by a school bus driver. Tammy received little support from her mother or anyone else. Amy, by contrast, got immediate support from her parents and school authorities. Both girls were sexually abused. It will not surprise you to know that Tammy is likely to suffer more serious harm than Amy, who may well escape entirely unscathed.

Thus, sexual abuse varies from child to child. Moreover, no two children are exactly alike and every child's reaction to abuse is unique. One child may fall apart at being fondled whereas another brushes it off as a mild irritant. Because abuse experiences vary and because each child's reaction is distinctive, it's not possible to predict exactly how your child will respond to abuse. It's possible, however, to describe some of the factors that research and experience tell us are likely to influence a child's reaction to sexual abuse. As you read this information, remember, your child may or may not react the same way as other children.

Seriousness of the Abuse—Does Penetration Occur. The more serious and invasive the sexual abuse, the more likely the child will suffer emotional harm. Use of force is associated with psychological damage. Penetration of the genitals, anus, or mouth is also associated with trauma. Penetration can be accomplished with a penis, tongue, finger, or object. Penetration is an extraordinary invasion of personal privacy and autonomy. Moreover, penetration is often accompanied by threats or force.

Duration of the Abuse. Some children are molested over a period of months or years; others are abused only once. Chronic abuse often causes more serious problems. Of course, onetime abuse, such as violent rape, can cause lasting psychological damage.

Relationship to the Abuser. In general, the closer the relationship between the child and the perpetrator, the greater the potential for lasting harm. It's not difficult to see why. Sexual assault by a complete stranger is horrible and can shatter a child's sense that the world is a safe place, but sexual abuse by a relative, especially a parent, is the ultimate betrayal of trust.

Maternal Support. Whenever children are traumatized, they turn to their parents, especially mother, for comfort. How many times have you heard, "I want my mommy!" When a child is sexually abused by his or her father or someone else, the mother's reaction is vitally important. If the mother is supportive when the child discloses the abuse and remains supportive thereafter—if she is "there for her child"—her love will go far toward easing the trauma and helping the child. The psychologist Kathleen Kendall-Tackett and her colleagues reviewed research on the importance of maternal support and found, "A key variable in recovery was family support. . . . Children who had maternal support recovered more quickly. Maternal support was demonstrated through believing the child and acting in a protective way toward the child" (Kendall-Tackett, Meyer Williams, & Finkelhor, 1993, p. 172).

The preceding paragraph emphasizes the importance of maternal support. I don't want to leave dads out of the picture, however. Like mothers, nonabusive fathers play a central role in helping their children recover from the trauma of sexual abuse.

The Child's Coping Style. As I said earlier, every child is unique. Some children—like some adults—are basically optimistic. These lucky ones seem to bounce back from adversity with relative ease. Other children have a more negative coping style, and for these children sexual abuse may be more damaging or, if not more damaging in the long run, more difficult to overcome.

What Are the Short- and Long-Term Harmful Effects of Sexual Abuse?

Sexual abuse has immediate short-term effects as well as long-term effects that may last into adulthood. Here, I describe the most common short- and long-term effects of sexual abuse.

At the outset, I should mention that not all sexually abused children show outward symptoms of harm or distress. The word *asymptomatic* is used to describe such children. In some research studies, up to 40% of sexually abused children are asymptomatic. Of course, the fact that a child does not demonstrate observable symptoms does not mean the child is not suffering. Some children cope with sexual abuse by doing their best not to think about the experience. Children who keep the abuse "bottled up inside" may become symptomatic in the future, perhaps months or years later.

Although some children are asymptomatic, the majority of sexually abused children manifest symptoms. But why? What is it about sexual abuse that hurts? There are several theories that account for the harm caused by sexual abuse. Among these theories, the conceptual framework articulated by David Finkelhor and Angela Browne (1985) is perhaps the most widely accepted. Finkelhor and Browne write:

> The model proposed here postulates that the experience of sexual abuse can be analyzed in terms of four trauma-causing factors, or what we will call traumagenic dynamics—traumatic sexualization, stigmatization, betrayal, and powerless-

ness. These traumagenic dynamics are generalized dynamics, not necessarily unique to sexual abuse; they occur in other kinds of trauma. But the conjunction of these four dynamics in one set of circumstances are what make the trauma of sexual abuse unique. . . .

These dynamics alter the child's cognitive and emotional orientation to the world, and create trauma by distorting a child's self-concept, worldview, and affective capacities. For example, the dynamic of stigmatization distorts children's sense of their own value and worth. The dynamic of powerlessness distorts children's sense of their ability to control their lives. . . .

Traumatic sexualization refers to a process in which a child's sexuality (including both sexual feelings and sexual attitudes) is shaped in a developmentally inappropriate and interpersonally dysfunctional fashion as a result of the sexual abuse. . . .

Betrayal refers to the dynamic in which children discover that someone on whom they are vitally dependent has caused them harm. . . .

Powerlessness—or what might also be called "disempowerment," the dynamic of rendering the victim powerless—refers to the process in which the child's will, desires, and sense of efficacy are continually contravened. . . .

Stigmatization, the final dynamic, refers to the negative connotations—e.g., badness, shame, and guilt—that are communicated to the child about the experiences and that then become incorporated into the child's self-image. These negative meanings are communicated in many ways. They can come directly from the abuser, who may blame the victim for the activity, demean the victim, or furtively convey a sense of shame about the behavior. Pressure for secrecy from the offender can also convey powerful messages of shame and guilt. But stigmatization is also reinforced by attitudes that the victim infers or hears from other persons in the family or community. (pp. 530-533)

Understanding these dynamics—traumatic sexualization, betrayal, powerlessness, and stigmatization—helps us understand why sexual abuse has such a powerful negative effect on many children.

▼   Short-Term Effects of Sexual Abuse

The immediate or short-term effects of sexual abuse vary from child to child, although certain symptoms are seen in many victims. Short-term symptoms of abuse are usually the result of the anxiety, stress, and fear caused by sexual abuse. Before describing specific symptoms, however, let me reiterate that children react in many ways to sexual abuse. Few children demonstrate all the symptoms discussed below. Indeed, with the exception of posttraumatic stress disorder (PTSD) (symptoms of PTSD are seen in approximately half of abused children), no symptom is seen in a majority of sexually abused children.

Anxiety. Anxiety is a state of heightened emotional arousal. The abused child may be preoccupied and worried about the abuse—unable to stop thinking about it. The child's anxiety leads to many of the symptoms described below.

Fear. Men who sexually abuse children often threaten them too. Every threat you can imagine has been made to keep children quiet, including, "If you tell, I'll go to jail and you'll never see me again." "If you tell your mother, I'll kill you both." "Don't bother telling anyone, because nobody would believe you anyway." The fear induced by threats is responsible for much of the child's anxiety.

Nightmares and Sleep Problems. Many sexually abused children have nightmares. Sometimes the nightmare is a terrifying reenactment of the abuse. More often, the child has dreams involving monsters or other frightening events.

Acting Out and General Misbehavior. All children misbehave, of course, but many sexually abused children are seriously distressed and their unhappiness can lead to acting out and misbehavior at home and school. The academic performance of abuse victims may suffer. Older children and adolescents may run away, abuse drugs or alcohol, become promiscuous, or engage in illegal conduct.

Withdrawal. Whereas some children act out, others withdraw into a shell. A seven-year-old who is normally happy-go-lucky and outgoing may become withdrawn and sullen.

Regression. It's called *regression* when a child reverts to an earlier stage of development. For example, a child who is toilet trained may start wetting the bed. The trauma of sexual abuse sometimes causes regression, and among young children, toileting accidents are a rather common manifestation of regression.

Poor Self-Concept. The stigmatization described by Finkelhor and Browne (1985) accounts for sexually abused children's poor self-concept. Many abused children think the abuse was their fault and that they are bad, dirty, worthless, or "damaged goods."

Depression. Needless to say, sexual abuse makes children sad. Clinical depression, however, goes beyond transitory sadness and is a serious psychiatric problem. Some people think young children don't get depressed in the psychiatric sense of the word, but this is untrue. Even very young children can become depressed, and sexual abuse can cause serious depression. Among older children and adolescents, depression is common, and quite a few victims think about suicide.

Inappropriate Sexual Behavior. Certain kinds of sexual behavior are normal during childhood (e.g., masturbation), and normal sexual conduct is described later in this chapter and in Chapter 14. Sexually abused children, however, have experienced inappropriate sexual acts—"traumatic sexualization." It's not surprising that some sexually abused children demonstrate developmentally *in*appropriate sexual behavior with other children or adults.

Posttraumatic Stress Disorder. Roughly half of sexually abused children develop some or all of the symptoms of posttraumatic stress disorder (PTSD). The *Diagnostic and Statistical Manual of Mental Disorders* of the American Psychiatric Association (1994) lists PTSD as an anxiety disorder. According to the *Manual:*

> The essential feature of Posttraumatic stress disorder is the development of characteristic symptoms following exposure to an extreme stressor involving direct personal experience of an event that involves actual or threatened death or serious injury, or other threat to one's physical integrity. . . . The person's response to the event must involve intense fear, help-

lessness, or horror (or in children, the response must involve disorganized or agitated behavior). The characteristic symptoms resulting from the exposure to the extreme trauma include persistent reexperiencing of the traumatic event, persistent avoidance of stimuli associated with the trauma and numbing of general responsiveness, and persistent symptoms of increased arousal. (p. 424)

Young sexually abused children with symptoms of PTSD may repetitively act out the abuse in their play. Many PTSD sufferers have difficulty sleeping and experience nightmares. Children may have stomachaches and headaches. Some children have an intense emotional reaction when they are reminded of the traumatic experience. It's not surprising that children with PTSD try to avoid people and things that remind them of the abuse. For example, a child who was raped in a field might not want to go near fields and might be intensely frightened of unfamiliar men. Because of the desire to avoid thinking about what happened, some children with PTSD are reluctant to talk about their abuse. Such reluctance makes it difficult to interview these children.

Summary. Child sexual abuse causes short-term psychological symptoms in many children. Symptoms vary from child to child, depending on the kind of abuse, the child's coping style, and the presence or absence of maternal support. Symptoms may last days, months, or years. Moreover, symptoms may abate temporarily only to reappear later on. Whatever the child's reaction, and even if the child seems fine, I recommend that parents obtain professional mental health services for their child. Therapy is discussed later in this chapter.

▼ Long-Term Effects of Child Sexual Abuse

This book is about children who are sexually abused, not adult survivors of childhood sexual abuse. Nevertheless, parents of abused children want to know what difficulties may lie ahead for their children. There is an extensive literature on the long-term effects of child sexual abuse. Although the literature shows that sexual abuse can have serious long-term effects, it's important to remember that not all victims suffer into adulthood. Moreover, even when the harm of child sexual abuse persists, most adult survivors lead happy and productive lives. Probably, their lives are not as happy as they would have been without abuse, but happy, constructive, valuable, and important lives nonetheless.

Research confirms that many adult survivors of child sexual abuse experience abuse-related problems. The psychologist John Briere is a leading authority on the long-term impact of child sexual abuse. He describes seven psychological disturbances found in adolescent and adult survivors: posttraumatic stress disorder, cognitive distortions, altered emotionality, dissociation, impaired self-reference, disturbed relatedness, and avoidance (1992, p. 18).

Among the *cognitive distortions* experienced by adult survivors, Briere describes feelings of helplessness, chronic danger, self-deprecation, and pessimism about the future. Turning to *altered emotional states*, Briere mentions depression, fear, and anxiety. Briere defines *dissociation* "as a defensive disruption in the normally occurring connections among feelings, thoughts, behavior, and memories, consciously or unconsciously invoked in order to reduce psychological distress" (1992, p. 36). Multiple personality disorder is a rare and extreme form of dissociation. Concerning *impaired self-reference*, Briere writes, "It is the impression of many clinicians who work with survivors of early and/or severe child abuse that such individuals often suffer from difficulties in how they relate to self" (p. 42). In the category of *disturbed relatedness*, Briere discusses problems with interpersonal relationships, especially intimate and sexual relationships. He writes, "Many adults molested as children report fear or anxiety-related difficulties during sexual contact, including reduced sexual arousal, erectile dysfunction or lubrication problems, extreme muscle tension, frightening flashbacks, vaginismus, and pain upon intercourse" (p. 34). Finally, Briere describes psychological *avoidance*. He observes that many adult survivors try to avoid the pain of sexual abuse by engaging in behaviors that consciously or unconsciously lessen their distress. Among the avoidance strategies are alcohol and drug abuse, self-mutilation, compulsive sexual behavior, and eating disorders.

This brief review of the long-term effects of child sexual abuse is a stark reminder of the terrible toll exacted by this betrayal of trust. Yet, you should not get the impression that the situation is hopeless. In every community, there are dedicated mental health professionals who are skilled at easing the suffering and guiding adult survivors along the sometimes rocky road to peace of mind.

What Is Normal Sexual Behavior in Children?

One effect of sexual abuse is that children gain knowledge of adult sex acts that young children should not possess. Young children can't make up detailed descriptions of adult sex acts unless they have been abused or exposed to pornography. The psychologist Jill Waterman makes the point this way:

> Children cannot manufacture stories based on information that they have not learned or experienced. For example, children will not make up a story about the comings and goings of Eskimos if they have never been exposed to any learning about Eskimos, and will not say someone attempted oral copulation with them if they have not had either direct or vicarious experience with that act. (1986, p. 27)

Because sexual abuse "teaches" children sexual information they should not know, parents who suspect abuse should know what kinds of sexual behaviors are considered normal and abnormal. The psychologist William Friedrich and his colleagues studied sexual behavior in *non*abused children. They write, "2- through 12-year-old children exhibit a wide variety of sexual behaviors at relatively high frequencies" (Friedrich, Grambsch, Broughton, Kupier, & Beilke, 1991, p. 462). For example, occasional masturbation begins early in life and is common, if not universal, among boys and girls. The pediatricians Martin Finkel and Allan DeJong write that by the time children are two or three years old they

> often enjoy displaying their nude bodies. . . . Young children like to touch not only their own bodies but also the genitals and breasts of their parents, siblings, and peers. Sex play with peers is common, which typically involves some degree of undressing and mutual touching. . . . By age 6 or 7 years, children are still interested in sexuality, but overt sexual behaviors diminish with age. (1994, p. 186)

The psychologist Susan Phipps-Yonas and her colleagues add, "Among preschoolers there is often considerable freedom regarding their bodies as well as touching of themselves, their peers, and family members. Children at this stage engage in games such as playing doctor or house which involve explorations through touch and sight of each others' so-called private parts" (Phipps-Yonas, Yonas, Turner, & Kauper, 1993, p. 1).

Thus, children are sexual beings, and they engage in sexual behavior. Having said that, however, I must add that certain sexual behaviors are seldom seen in nonabused children, and these "tend to be those behaviors that are either more aggressive or more imitative of adult sexual behavior" (Friedrich et al., 1991, p. 462). For example, it's extremely unusual for a nonabused girl or boy to put her or his mouth on someone else's genitals, to imitate sexual intercourse, to masturbate with an object, or to insert objects into the anus or vagina. Concern about sexual abuse increases when a young child demonstrates such unusual sexual behavior.

If your child engages in sexual behavior that concerns you, talk to the child's pediatrician. In addition, take notes describing the child's behavior, when it happened, and how often. If it becomes necessary to prove in court that your child was sexually abused, your notes describing unusual sexual behavior may prove valuable. More is said in Chapter 14 about the importance of developmentally unusual sexual behavior in proving sexual abuse.

Will My Child Grow Up to Be a Child Molester?

Parents of sexually abused children, particularly little boys, worry that their child may grow up to be a child molester. The research literature does not support this fear. The psychologists William Murphy and Timothy Smith write, "The vast majority of victims of sexual abuse do not become offenders" (1996, p. 181). In studies of child molesters, about 30% report that they were molested as children. Overall, however, Murphy and Smith state, "The empirical literature does not support a strong link between victimization and offending" (p. 181).

I do not mean to imply that parents of sexually abused children should have no concern that their child may offend. Some abused children do offend. According to the psychologist Anna Salter, "A sizable proportion of sex offenders, including incest offenders, develop their interest in deviant sexuality in adolescence, and even begin their offending careers while still in their teens" (1995, p. 26) (see p. 45). Issues of sexuality are a proper subject for discussion with your child's therapist. The important point is that parents of sexually abused children should reject the idea that their child's sexual fate is sealed by abuse.

Will My Child Blame Me for the Abuse?

Many parents of sexually abused children are racked with guilt. Parents berate themselves with questions like, "What could I have done differently?" "Why didn't I see the signs that something was wrong?" "How could I let this happen to the child I love so much?" If you find yourself asking such questions, remember: You did *not* abuse your child. You are *not* the child molester. You *are* the one who is trying to protect your child. Of course, in retrospect—with the perfect 20-20 vision of hindsight—it's nearly always possible to see how things might have been different. Nevertheless, the vast majority of protective parents did nothing wrong. When they learned that abuse was a possibility, they took action. That's all you can ask of yourself.

As if self-blame weren't enough, many parents worry that their child will blame them for the abuse. Some children do wonder why their nonabusive parent did not prevent the abuse or step in to stop it once it started. The best advice is to discuss your concerns with your child's therapist and, if you are seeing a professional for yourself, with your own therapist. Mental health professionals can help you and your child understand that the fault for sexual abuse lies *entirely* with the molester, not with the victim and not with the protective parent.

Will Sexual Abuse Make My Child Gay?

Parents of sexually abused children, particularly boys, sometimes ask whether the abuse will cause their child to become homosexual. The short answer is no. The research literature does not support the conclusion that sexual abuse dictates or guides sexual orientation.

Mental health professionals who treat abused children are sensitive to the concern parents and older children have about the impact of abuse on gender identity and sexuality. In discussing treatment of adolescent and adult survivors of sexual abuse, the psychologist John Briere writes:

> Treatment should also address sex differences in how child abuse is cognitively processed. Because boys and men are expected to be strong and aggressive, victimization may be more of a sex role violation for them than it is for girls and women. This additional trauma can result in somewhat different cognitive responses to abuse for male and female survivors. Physically abused males, for example, often present with feelings of inadequacy and desire for retribution, as though a boy's inability to fight off maltreatment reflects lesser masculinity in adolescence or adulthood. Many sexually abused males have sexual concerns related to their molestation. Heterosexual boys and men may believe that childhood sexual abuse by another male has caused them to be latently homosexual—a fear that, in a culture as homophobic as ours, may result in compensatory hypermasculinity or overinvolvement in heterosexual activity. Conversely, homosexual men who were sexually abused by males may be concerned that their sexual orientation somehow caused them to be abused by men, or that their abuse caused them to be homosexual—conclusions that can lead to feelings of guilt, shame, and self-betrayal.
>
> Female abuse survivors may also fear that they in some way enticed their abusers into molesting them—a concern that appears to reflect the stereotype of females as sex objects and as almost inherently seductive. This fear may be exacerbated when the sexually abused girl had learned before the abuse to behave in a "cute" or "flirtatious" manner in order to gain male attention. As a result, she may falsely interpret her pseudosexual behavior as having caused or provoked her molestation.

Because of these different cognitive sequelae, clinicians may find it advantageous to approach male and female abuse survivors in slightly different ways during treatment. (1992, p. 157)

Could My Child Get AIDS or Another Sexually Transmitted Disease?

If your child is sexually abused, he or she probably will not get a sexually transmitted disease (STD). With some kinds of abuse—for example, fondling—STD is simply not a concern. The possibility of STD increases when there is penetration. The pediatrician Carole Jenny observes, "All the sexually transmitted diseases that affect adults also can be transmitted to children" (1996, p. 196). Two other pediatricians, Martin Finkel and Allan DeJong, state "Sexually transmitted diseases have been detected in approximately 2 to 28% of children examined for sexual abuse" (1994, p. 224).

One horrifying possibility is that sexual abuse could cause HIV infection and AIDS. "Cases have been reported of children contracting acquired immunodeficiency syndrome (AIDS) from sexual abuse" (Jenny, 1996, p. 201). Nevertheless, the chances of getting AIDS are very, very small. According to Finkel and DeJong,

It would be extremely unlikely for HIV infection to follow a single episode of sexual abuse. . . . Screening of victims for HIV infection seems most reasonable if the child gives a history of repeated abuse, with vaginal or rectal penetration, by multiple perpetrators, if the child is symptomatic, or if the perpetrator is known to have HIV infection, is a known homosexual or bisexual, or is a known intravenous drug abuser. (1994, p. 230)

Is My Child Still a Virgin?

Some parents ask whether a girl is still a virgin following sexual abuse that includes vaginal penetration. Usually, the answer is yes, the child is still a virgin. The fact that an adult penis enters a child's vagina does not necessarily mean the hymen will be injured. Even if there is injury, the genitalia heal quickly. It's likely that within a few months, nobody will be able to tell that the child was sexually abused.

Should I Get Mental Health Treatment for My Child?

Parents want to know whether their child should see a mental health professional. Most experts agree that a child who has been sexually abused should receive help from a qualified professional. Earlier sections of this chapter make clear that the potential for short- and long-term harm from sexual abuse is sufficiently high to justify therapy. Two leading U.S. experts on child abuse, the sociologist David Finkelhor and the social worker Lucy Berliner, reviewed the literature on mental health treatment and concluded, "Taken as a whole, the studies of sexually abused children in treatment show improvements that are consistent with the belief that therapeutic intervention facilitates children's recovery" (1995, p. 1414). Treatment is effective for children as young as eighteen months old.

Therapists differ in their approach to treatment, and there is no one single "correct" method to treat sexually abused children. Many therapists use some version of what is commonly called abuse-specific treatment. Finkelhor and Berliner write that the common elements of abuse-specific treatment

> include (1) encouraging expression of abuse-related feelings (e.g., anger, ambivalence, fear), (2) clarifying erroneous beliefs that might lead to negative attributions about self or others (e.g., self-blame), (3) teaching abuse prevention skills, and (4) diminishing the sense of stigma and isolation through reassurance or exposure to other victims (e.g., group therapy). (1995, pp. 1418-1419)

With young children, play therapy is often used.

Many sexually abused children do not require long-term treatment. The goal of short-term treatment is to get the trauma under control and to help the child understand that the abuse was not his or her fault.

Some children need to return to therapy later during childhood or adolescence. When children go through major developmental changes, such as puberty, issues relating to the abuse may resurface and require further treatment. Parents should not feel that treatment was unsuccessful or that they somehow failed their child if more treatment is needed later on.

Deciding to obtain mental health treatment is one thing, finding a qualified therapist and paying for treatment is another and often more difficult matter. By no means all mental health professionals have the training and experience required to treat sexually abused children. Working with such children requires highly specialized knowledge of the effects of trauma, child sexual abuse, and developmental psychology. Your child's pediatrician may know qualified professionals. If your community has a specialized treatment center for sexually abused children, give the center a call. Finally, you might consider calling a university medical school or affiliated hospital. Frequently, university hospitals employ professionals who are specialists in treatment of child abuse. If your community has a public mental health center, give the center a call to see if its staff treats sexually abused children and, if so, what fees they charge. If you are lucky, you live in a community that has a specialized center devoted entirely to treatment of abused children.

Mental health care, like other professional services, is expensive. If you have medical insurance, check with your carrier to see if insurance will help pay for treatment. All states have victims' compensation funds that pay for treatment of crime victims. Richard Saldana has written a book describing crime victims' compensation funds (1994). Most state compensation programs include treatment for abused children. Appendix B reproduces Saldana's list of addresses and phone numbers for crime victim compensation programs throughout the United States.

Why Does My Child Want to See the Man
Who Molested Him or Her?

Children who are sexually abused by someone they love don't stop loving that person. For many children, the hurt of sexual abuse coexists with happy memories. Sexually abused children want the abuse to stop, but they seldom want the relationship to end. Thus, it's entirely normal for sexually abused children to enjoy being with their abuser, especially when the abuser is a parent, grandparent, or other important adult in the child's life.

Should I Tell My Child's Teacher or School Principal?

Parents wonder whether they should tell someone at the child's school or day care about the abuse. This is a delicate matter, and the answer depends on what is best for each child. It's worth remembering, however, that some abused children act out in sexually inappropriate ways. If this is the case with your child, it may be wise to sit down with the teacher, the principal, and perhaps the school psychologist. You may want your child's therapist to attend the meeting or to communicate by phone with the teacher. It's often better for the teacher to know in advance that your child has special needs. Plans can be made to reduce the opportunity for sexual acting out. For example, it may be appropriate to supervise bathroom visits so your child is not alone in the bathroom with other children. Finally, you and the education professionals can work out age-appropriate rules for your child: do's and don't's your child can understand and follow.

4

Who Are the Men Who Sexually Abuse Children? Why Do They Do It? Can Molesters Be Cured?

When we think of child molesters, we imagine a "dirty old man" lurking in the park, waiting to lure children into the bushes. Such men exist, of course, and they are a very real threat to children. But this stereotype of the "typical" child molester is not accurate. Men who sexually abuse children come from every walk of life, every ethnic background, and every economic status—doctors, lawyers, teachers, plumbers, truck drivers, clergy, butchers, bakers, and candlestick makers. There is no "typical" child molester.

Parents who are worried about sexual abuse often ask the following questions:

- How often is sexual abuse committed by strangers, and how often by people the child knows? (p. 44)
- How much sexual abuse is committed by fathers and stepfathers? (p. 44)
- How much sexual abuse is committed by teenagers? (p. 45)
- Do women sexually abuse children? (p. 46)
- Are there psychological tests that can tell whether a man is a child molester? (p. 46)
- Why do men sexually abuse children? (p. 49)
- What is pedophilia? Do pedophiles have other types of sexual deviance? (p. 50)

☐ Do child molesters often molest more than one child? (p. 51)
☐ How do child molesters gain children's confidence? (p. 51)
☐ Is treatment available for child molesters? (p. 52)
☐ Are fathers who molest their own children good candidates for treatment? (p. 54)
☐ Does treatment work? (p. 55)

How Often Is Sexual Abuse Committed by Strangers and How Often by People the Child Knows?

Contrary to popular belief, most child sexual abuse is not committed by strangers. Sexual abuse is usually perpetrated by a man the child knows, including fathers, stepfathers, other relatives, teachers, coaches, and neighbors. According to the sociologist David Finkelhor, "No more than 10% to 30% of offenders were strangers, with the remainder being either family members or acquaintances" (1994, p. 45).

Girls are molested by a member of their family more often than boys. With girls, from one third to one half of offenders are members of the child's family, including fathers and other relatives. By contrast, with boys, only one tenth to one fifth of offenders are related to their victims. Finkelhor writes, "A major difference between boy victims and girl victims is that boys are less likely to be abused within the family" (1994, p. 47).

Thus, when sexual abuse occurs, the child is likely to know the perpetrator. Although fathers and stepfathers do not commit the majority of sexual abuse, they are certainly responsible for the suffering of many children. Moreover, the closer the relationship between the child and the molester, the more likely the child will suffer psychologically (see p. 27).

How Much Sexual Abuse Is Committed by Fathers and Stepfathers?

Researchers differ regarding how much sexual abuse is committed by fathers and stepfathers. Some researchers study this issue by questioning adult women in the general population. For example, the researcher might send a questionnaire to a random sample of adult women in a particular city asking whether the woman was sexually abused during childhood. In studies like this, approximately 6% to 16% of women who report being sexually abused as children were molested by their father or stepfather (Berliner & Elliott, 1996).

Other research is conducted with adult survivors of childhood sexual abuse who are receiving therapy for the long-term effects of abuse. In this clinical population, the percentage of abuse committed by fathers and stepfathers is higher, with approximately one third of women reporting abuse by male parent figures.

As I mentioned earlier, although most abused children are not abused by fathers or stepfathers, the majority are molested by someone they know. When abuse is discovered and suspicion points to the child's father, it's always a good idea to ask, "Could the abuse have been committed by someone else?" This question should be answered before accusing the father.

How Much Sexual Abuse Is Committed by Teenagers?

Older children and teenagers sometimes sexually abuse younger children. Youthful offenders range in age from five on up. Research discloses that a high percentage of adult sex offenders began their deviance during adolescence. In a study of 411 adult sex offenders, 58% became sexually interested in children during adolescence (Abel, Mittelman, & Becker, 1985). In another study, 60% to 80% of adult offenders confessed that they began their deviant sexual careers as teenagers (Groth, Longo, & McFadin, 1982).

Adults sometimes shrug off sexual contact between a teenager and a young child as "innocent sex play" or a "normal" part of growing up. This is a serious mistake. Such deviant behavior must be taken very seriously. Sexual activity between teenagers and younger children is often clearly abusive. Moreover, such conduct is a warning sign that the teenager may be developing a deviant sexual interest in children that can last a lifetime. Although teenage sex offenders are often resistant to treatment, there is better hope for success when the offender is young than when he is an adult entrenched in a chronic pattern of sexual deviance.

Do Women Sexually Abuse Children?

The vast majority of sexual abuse is perpetrated by men. There is no doubt, however, that some women sexually abuse children. Although there exists relatively little research on female perpetrators, David Finkelhor reports, "About 5% of prepubescent girls' sexual contacts with older partners involve female partners" (1994, p. 46). He continues,

> Studies of female perpetrators of child sexual abuse in recent years have documented certain distinct types, including (1) many women who act in concert with or in the service of abusive boyfriends or husbands, (2) adolescent girls participating in baby-sitting situations, (3) lonely and isolated single-parent mothers with small children, and (4) some women who develop romantic relationships with adolescent boys. (p. 46)

Are There Psychological Tests That Can Tell Whether a Man Is a Child Molester?

Parents often want to know whether there is some psychological test that can tell whether a man is a child molester, whether he has the psychological profile of a "typical" child molester, or whether he molested a particular child. Some psychologists and psychiatrists believe there is a psychological profile of a "typical" child molester, and a few of these mental health professionals claim that by administering psychological tests and interviewing a man they can tell whether he molested a child. Most experts on sex offenders strongly disagree with such claims, however. From a scientific point of view it's quite clear that there is *no* psychological test or combination of tests that can tell whether a man is a child molester or whether he sexually abused a child.

The psychologists Judith Becker and Vernon Quinsey are two leading authorities on sex offenders. They write, "The question of determining whether or not a person has committed a sexual offence is not one that clinical assessment can address. There are no psychological tests or techniques that indicate whether someone has engaged in sexual behaviors with children" (1993, p. 169). Nicholas and Molinder add, "No test, no device, has the power to pick out a sexually deviant person from any other person in a crowd" (1984, p. 3). In 1989, my colleagues and I wrote, "Sex offenders are a heterogeneous group with few shared characteristics apart from a predilection for deviant sexual behavior. Furthermore, there is no psychological test or device that reliably detects persons who have or will sexually abuse children. . . . There is no profile of a 'typical' child molester" (Myers et al., 1989, p. 142). The psychiatrist Judith Herman adds, "The most striking characteristic of sex offenders, from a diagnostic standpoint, is their apparent normality" (1990, p. 180). Finally, the psychologist Anna Salter observes, "Research confirms the fact that many sex offenders have no pathology discernible by generic psychological tests or clinical interview" (1995, p. 30).

Although the experts are nearly unanimous that psychological tests can't tell whether a man is a child molester and that there is no psychological profile of a "typical" child abuser, the most convincing proof of the "apparent normality" of child molesters comes from molesters themselves. Consider the words of this man:

> I want to describe a child molester I know very well. This man was raised by devout Christian parents. As a child he rarely missed church. Even after he became an adult he was faithful as a church member. He was a straight-A student in high school and college. He has been married and has a child of his own. He coached little league baseball. He was Choir Director at his church. He never used any illegal drugs. He never had a drink of alcohol. He was considered a clean-cut all-American-boy. Everyone seemed to like him. He was a volunteer in numerous community civic functions. He had a well-paying career job. He was considered "well-to-do" in society. But from the age of thirteen-years-old he sexually molested little boys. He never victimized a stranger. All of his victims were friends. He is now serving a five-year term in prison for sexual abuse. I know this child molester very well because he is me!!! (child molester of up to 100 male children quoted in Salter, 1995, p. 30)

Minnesota Multiphasic Personality Inventory (MMPI.) The MMPI is one of the most widely used and well accepted psychological tests of personality. Although a man's scores on the MMPI may tell a good deal about his mental health status, the MMPI provides no insight into whether a man is sexually interested in children or whether he abused a child. William Murphy reviewed the psychological literature on use of the MMPI with sex offenders and wrote, "What the MMPI literature actually suggests is that individual offenders against children vary tremendously in their psychological functioning, as measured by the MMPI. No particular profile predicts a propensity for sexual offend-ing. A significant proportion of offenders may exhibit no measurable psychopathology" (1994, p. 4).

Penile Plethysmography. The penile plethysmograph is a device that is placed around the base of a man's flaccid penis. With the device in place, the man looks at pictures or reads text that may give him an erec-tion. The plethysmograph measures changes in the size of his penis. Basically, the plethysmograph provides a measure of sexual arousal.

The penile plethysmograph is useful in treatment of sex offenders. The therapist can use the device to help a man understand his pattern of deviant sexual arousal. But can the plethysmograph tell if a man is a child molester? No. To one degree or another, men can control whether they get an erection, so a man can fake the results of the plethysmograph. William Murphy reviewed the literature on the plethysmograph and wrote,

> There is very limited evidence for the use of sexual arousal data to profile an offender. . . . In incest cases or in cases of the denying offender, the most frequently observed profiles are probably a nondeviant arousal pattern or a pattern of low arousal to all of the stimuli. (1994, p. 28)

Walter Simon and Peter Schouten add, "With an 80-year history, plethysmography is not a new or innovative assessment technique. However, critical aspects of the procedure have not been resolved. Its scientific status remains that of an experimental technique" (1993, p. 511). Finally, Judith Becker and Vernon Quinsey write that phal-lometric assessment can't "detect whether someone has committed a specific sexual offense" (1993, p. 172).

The "Lie Detector." The lie detector, or polygraph, can't determine whether a man is a child molester or whether he sexually abused a child.

The Clinical Interview. A clinical interview by a mental health professional is one method used to evaluate men who may be child molesters. Unfortunately, the clinical interview is not particularly reliable for this purpose. Judith Becker and Vernon Quinsey write, "Interviews of the offender are similar to other clinical interviews except the validity of the information provided by the offender is more likely to be suspect. Frequently, alleged child molesters distort information, falsely deny that the alleged offence occurred, and report difficulty in recalling events surrounding the offence" (1993, p. 170).

Why Do Men Sexually Abuse Children?

Mental health professionals do not know why some men develop a deviant sexual interest in children. The psychologist Judith Becker writes, "In all likelihood, there is not one causative factor, but rather multiple pathways by which a person develops a sexual attraction to minors" (1994, p. 181).

Research on sex offenders discloses that for many men, deviant behavior is highly compulsive and repetitive. The psychologist Anna Salter describes "the deviant cycle" of many offenders: "Sexual abuse is frequently thought to be an accident or happenstance. It is more accurate to think of it as a deviant cycle, an interlocking series of thoughts, feelings, and behaviors that culminate in sexual assault" (1995, p. 36).

Sex offenders often try to avoid responsibility for their behavior by blaming sexual abuse on stress, alcohol, or other factors. None of these excuses hold up. Neither alcohol nor drugs cause men to be sexually interested in children. True, some men work up the courage to molest by getting drunk, but the deviant thought patterns were there long before the alcohol. The man, not the booze, is to blame. No amount of stress causes men to fantasize about sex with children. The claim that sexual abuse results from stress is, to be blunt, ridiculous.

What Is Pedophilia? Do Pedophiles Have Other Types of Sexual Deviance?

Pedophilia is sexual deviance in which a man is sexually interested in children. A pedophile is a man who is sexually attracted to children.

Pedophilia is one of eight types of sexual deviance—called paraphilia—listed in the fourth edition of the *Diagnostic and Statistical Manual of Mental Disorders* of the American Psychiatric Association (1994). The eight paraphilia are:

☐ Exhibitionism: Exposing one's genitals to strangers
☐ Frotteurism: Sexual stimulation obtained by touching or rubbing against people without their consent
☐ Fetishism: Sexual arousal to nonliving objects such as underwear or shoes
☐ Pedophilia: Sexual conduct with children
☐ Sexual Masochism: Sexual arousal to being humiliated or hurt
☐ Sexual Sadism: Sexual arousal derived from inflicting suffering or pain
☐ Transvestic Fetishism: Cross-dressing
☐ Voyeurism: Surreptitiously watching someone getting undressed or engaged in sexual activity

Men who are sexually interested in children—pedophiles—often have other paraphilias as well. According to Anna Salter, "There is considerable research evidence at present that multiple paraphilias should be considered in every case of sexual offense" (1995, p. 14). The likelihood of multiple paraphilias extends to incest offenders. Many men who sexually abuse their own children also have other types of sexual deviance. Moreover, many incest offenders also molest other children. Research suggests that from one third to one half of men who molest their own children molest other children. Judith Becker writes, "Child molesters may engage in incestuous, as well as nonincentuous, abuse and may target children of both genders" (1994, p. 178). In a large-scale study of 561 child molesters conducted by Gene Abel and his colleagues, 67% of the offenders molested only girls, 12% molested only boys, and 21% molested both (Abel, Becker, Cunningham-Rathner, Mittelman, & Rouleau, 1988). In the same study, 56% of offenders engaged only in nonincestuous abuse, 12% engaged only in incest, and 23% of offenders molested both their own and other children.

Some people believe that a man who molests his daughter or son is unlikely to abuse other children. The research summarized above shows that this is wrong. Many incest offenders also prey on children to whom they are not related.

Do Child Molesters Often Molest More Than One Child?

Pedophiles may have one or many victims. Gene Abel and his colleagues found in their research on sex offenders that the 561 men they studied victimized a total of 195,407 children! (Abel et al., 1988). No, you did not misread the last sentence. The 561 sex offenders in this study victimized nearly 200,000 children. Men who molested only girls had an average of 19.8 victims. Men who targeted boys averaged 150.2 victims. The study included 203 incest offenders. The incest offenders committed 15,668 deviant acts against 361 different children. The researchers calculated that the chance of getting caught for a sex offense is about 3%!

You may wonder whether these researchers' findings of extraordinarily high rates of victimization are accurate. The psychologist Anna Salter studied the research on sex offending and concluded that the findings of Abel and his colleagues paint an accurate picture of the staggering number of victims (1995).

How Do Child Molesters Gain Children's Confidence?

Despite the claims of many sex offenders that abuse "just happened on the spur of the moment," most offenders plan their abuse by grooming their victims. Anna Salter writes:

> Grooming appears nearly universal, either in place of or in addition to coercion as a technique for gaining sexual access to children. The establishment (and eventual betrayal) of affection and trust occupies a central role in the child molester's interactions with children. . . .
> Warner-Kearney (1987) found that 90% of incestuous fathers admitted that they deliberately tried to build trust with

their intended victims. Seventy-three percent of the offenders felt that the trust was "important" in that it decreased the chance of exposure.

To further reduce the risk of exposure, many offenders follow a slow progression in which most of the time is spent gaining the child's and the family's trust. (1995, pp. 74, 77)

Is Treatment Available for Child Molesters?

When a man is sexually attracted to children, an important issue is whether mental health professionals can treat him to eliminate his deviant sexual interest. All experts agree that men can't be treated unless they want to be. Even when an offender desires treatment, most experts believe treatment can't "cure" a man's sexual interest in children. Some men learn to control their deviant impulses, but we do not know how to cure, that is, eliminate, sexual deviance.

Some sex offenders are dangerous predators who molest many children over a lifetime of deviance. Treatment seldom works for such criminals. Moreover, most of them don't want treatment. As far as they are concerned, their only problem is that they got caught.

Approximately 2% to 5% of men who sexually abuse children and adults are sadists who derive pleasure from inflicting pain. For sadists, the primary goal is causing suffering. Sexual gratification is secondary. It's hardly surprising that genuine sadists are very poor candidates for treatment. Fortunately, the vast majority of child molesters are not sadists. Nonsadistic child molesters do what they do because it gives them sexual pleasure, not primarily because they enjoy making children suffer. Nonsadistic offenders use mind games to fool themselves into thinking their conduct is not harmful. Indeed, child molesters are masters at rationalizing their conduct. Anna Salter describes the thinking errors offenders use to excuse and justify their deviant behavior: "Sex offenders routinely blame the sexual offenses on stress, impulse, happenstance, marital problems, alcohol, or even the victim herself" (1995, p. 37). In other words, offenders blame everybody but themselves. Offenders sometimes assert that the child was the seducer. Someone once told me of an offender describing his five-year-old victim this way: "She was coming on to me in a really sexy, seductive way." Many offenders distort reality by thinking that sexual abuse does not harm children and that children "want" or "need" sex with adults.

Because child molesters engage in thinking errors that allow them to ignore the suffering they cause, successful treatment is often very difficult. Traditional psychotherapy or "talk therapy" does not appear to be useful with men who sexually abuse children. Most experts on offender treatment agree that for treatment to be successful, the therapist must confront the man's deviance head on. The offender's thinking errors have to be revealed and challenged. The focus of effective treatment is on techniques designed to help offenders control their lifelong tendency toward deviance.

The most promising sex offender treatment relies on a cognitive-behavioral approach to therapy (Myers, Berliner, Murphy, Pithers, & Prentky, 1991). The focus of treatment is on preventing relapse rather than "cure." Cognitive-behavioral therapy concentrates on the thinking errors, feelings, and behaviors linked to offending. Efforts are made to help offenders recognize the psychological processes that allow them to maintain their deviant behavior. Cognitive-behavioral treatment usually involves some combination of the following elements:

1. Confronting Denial. Denial is extremely common among sex offenders. Overcoming denial and encouraging honesty are necessary first steps in treatment. Of course, some offenders continue to deny the abuse despite the best efforts of professionals. When an offender persists in denial, successful treatment is impossible.

2. Correcting Thinking Errors. An important component of offender treatment consists of confronting and correcting the man's thinking errors, or as they are often called, cognitive distortions. Treatment can't progress until the offender acknowledges the role of thinking errors and willingly discusses the use of cognitive distortion in offending.

3. Increasing the Molester's Ability to Empathize With the Victim. Lack of empathy for the victim is common among child molesters. As with thinking errors, lack of empathy facilitates sexual abuse by insulating the offender from the consequences of his behavior. Thus, insisting that offenders to come to terms with the harm they cause—to have empathy with the victim—is a crucial step in treatment. The capacity to empathize with the victim increases the offender's ability to control the urge to engage in deviant sexual behavior.

4. Risk Factors and Antecedents to Sexual Abuse. Most sex offenses are not spur of the moment events. On the contrary, most offenses are planned, and it's possible—*if* the man cooperates—to identify the sequence of events that triggers the cycle of offending. Once the man's "risk factors" are identified, the therapist can teach the molester to detect early warning signs leading to deviance and to interrupt the deviant cycle before a new offense occurs. This aspect of treatment is sometimes called relapse prevention.

5. Increasing Social Competence. Sex offenders often have deficits in basic social skills. Many offenders are poor problem solvers, have poor anger and stress management skills, and lack skills in developing healthy adult relationships. One goal of treatment is to improve the man's ability to deal effectively with adult social situations.

6. Sexual Arousal. A primary goal of offender treatment is to alter patterns of deviant sexual arousal or, at a minimum, teach offenders to recognize and control their deviant arousal patterns.

7. The Role of the Law in Offender Treatment. Professionals who treat sex offenders recognize that the courts—particularly criminal courts—play an important role in getting offenders into treatment and keeping them there. The threat of going to jail provides the incentive that many offenders need to remain in therapy.

Are Fathers Who Molest Their Own Children Good Candidates for Treatment?

There is no simple answer to this important question. Some incest offenders are good candidates for treatment, particularly if they abused only one child—usually a daughter—and if they are *highly motivated* to change. The offender treatment expert Judith Becker reminds us "A sex offender can be considered amenable to treatment only if he acknowledges that he has committed a sexual offense, he considers his sexual offending a problem behavior that he wants to stop, and he is willing to participate fully in treatment" (1994, p. 187).

Motivation to change is the key to successful treatment. Unless a man has a genuine commitment to change, treatment will fail.

Does Treatment Work?

Are sex offenders who have been treated less likely to reoffend than untreated offenders? Research on the effectiveness of treatment yields mixed results, with some researchers reporting good results and others expressing doubt. Judith Becker is among the optimists regarding treatment, and she writes, "While no treatment has been shown to be 100% effective, this author believes the research literature provides definite grounds for optimism about the responsiveness of some segments of the offender population to existing treatment modalities" (1994, p. 188). As I mentioned earlier, incest offenders with one victim often have the greatest motivation to change and the best chance of success. Remember, however, that there is no "cure" for sexual deviance. Even with successful treatment, men who sexually abuse children are always at some risk of slipping back into their old ways.

Part II

A Mother's Allies

The Legal System, a Good Lawyer,
Mental Health Professionals

If you suspect that your child has been sexually abused, you need help from professionals. From mental health professionals, you need advice and treatment for your child. If legal action is necessary, you need a lawyer. Part II of this book starts you on the road to finding the professional help you need during this time of crisis.

Chapter 5 introduces the enormously complicated legal system. The chapter describes the three components of the legal system that are critical to abused children: the criminal justice system, family court, and the juvenile court. With this introduction to the legal system under your belt, you will be ready for Chapters 8, 9, and 10, which go into more detail about the legal system.

Chapter 6 answers the question, "Do I need a lawyer if my child was sexually abused?" It's not easy finding a lawyer who knows about child abuse, and in Chapter 6 I give you tips on what to look for in an attorney.

Chapter 7 discusses the importance of obtaining a thorough psychosocial assessment of your child from a mental health professional who is an expert on child sexual abuse. In Chapter 7, I explain the difference between therapy for your child and a psychosocial assessment designed to help determine whether abuse happened.

5

Introduction to the U.S. Legal System

Criminal Court,
Family Court, Juvenile Court

When parents learn their child may have been sexually abused, they turn to friends, doctors, counselors, religious leaders, and others for guidance and support. In addition, many parents find themselves deeply involved—usually for the first time—in the legal system. The world of lawyers, judges, police, and courts is unfamiliar and forbidding to most people. Despite the unfamiliarity of the legal system, however, parents of abused children need to understand the legal system.

Before I begin this brief introduction to the legal system, it's important to make two points. First, a good deal of the information in this chapter is quite basic, and you may already know much of what follows. If you are familiar with the workings of the legal system, you may decide to skip this chapter. I include the chapter because I've observed in twenty years as a lawyer that many people have gaps in their understanding of the legal system. Such gaps are hardly surprising in light of the enormous complexity of the law. Even first-year law students, all of whom are college graduates with a keen interest in law, sometimes amaze me with how little they know about many aspects of the law. Indeed, portions of the first year of law school are devoted to teaching the basics. So, although this chapter is focused on fundamentals, it serves the important function of informing readers who are unfamiliar with the legal system. And I hope that readers who are already knowledgeable about the law will pick up a few bits of useful new information.

The second point that needs to be made before I discuss the legal system is a point I emphasized at the beginning of this book: The legal system usually works well to protect children. The law puts a high priority on protecting children and punishing those who abuse them. Thousands of dedicated judges, social workers, lawyers, and police officers work diligently to protect children. All the same, however, there are times when the system backfires and turns its back on parents who are trying desperately to protect their children. Such cases occur most often in family court, where parents are battling over custody or visitation. One of these tragic cases is described in detail in Chapter 1, and this book is largely concerned with the potential of the legal system to backfire. Because so much of the book is focused on what can go wrong in the legal system, some readers may become disillusioned with the law. That is not my goal. As you read this book, please don't lose sight of the fact that backfire cases are the exception, not the rule. Most of the time, children are protected. My goal in these pages is to increase your chances of protecting your child and decrease the odds that the system will backfire against you.

With these preliminaries out of the way, in this chapter I address the following questions:

☐ What are the three main components of the legal system? (p. 60)
☐ How do the three components of the legal system work together to protect children from abuse? (p. 63)
☐ Why is the legal system so adversarial? (p. 66)

What Are the Three Main Components of the Legal System?

The U.S. legal system has three major components: (a) the criminal justice system, (b) the civil justice system, including family court, and (c) the juvenile court system, which is a specialized branch of the civil justice system. These components of the legal system are described in detail in subsequent chapters. This introductory chapter gets you started with a brief overview of the legal system.

First, it's important to clarify that these are not three completely separate systems housed, for example, in separate buildings. On the contrary, in nearly all communities the criminal and civil courts are housed in the same building—the county courthouse. In a rural community, one judge may be in charge of everything—civil, criminal, and juvenile. In cities, there may be a handful or a hundred judges, some handling criminal cases and others civil matters. In many communities, the juvenile court is located in a separate building.

▼   The Criminal Justice System

Child sexual abuse is a crime in every state (see Chapter 2 for the definition of child sexual abuse). When allegations of sexual abuse are made by a parent, a child, or someone else, the police investigate and, if there is enough evidence to prove abuse, formal criminal charges may be filed against the person suspected of abuse.

A criminal case is called a prosecution, and prosecutions are started by public attorneys called district attorneys or county attorneys. In most large communities, specialized prosecutors work on child abuse cases. These dedicated professionals possess extensive knowledge about child abuse and the legal system. In small communities and rural areas, prosecution staffs are small, and prosecutors are generalists, handling a wide range of criminal and civil matters, including child abuse.

In criminal cases, the parties to the litigation are the individual accused of crime, called the *defendant,* on the one hand, and the people of the state, on the other. The victim is *not* a party to a criminal case. Because the victim is not a party, the victim has fewer rights than the defendant. Although this *im*balance of rights often rankles victims and their families, there are good reasons to protect the rights of persons accused of crime. We should not lose sight of the fact that the police sometimes arrest the "wrong man." Innocent people are occasionally prosecuted, convicted, and sent to prison. The criminal justice system is set up to guard against such miscarriages of justice by giving special rights to persons accused of crime. Although more should be done to protect the rights of victims, we should try to remember the importance of protecting the rights of the accused. Everyone recognizes the importance of avoiding unjust arrests and convictions, and it's to those ends that the law gives special rights to defendants.

▼   The Civil Justice System, Including Divorce,
     Child Custody, and Visitation Cases

The civil justice system is basically everything that is not part of
the criminal justice system. The civil system handles an enormous
variety of cases—everything from medical malpractice to auto accidents, from disputes between landlords and tenants to claims for un-
employment compensation, from contract cases to litigation regarding divorce and child custody.

The Parties to a Civil Case. In a typical civil case, the person who is
suing is the *plaintiff* or *petitioner.* The person being sued is the *defendant*
or *respondent.* The plaintiff and defendant are the parties to the lawsuit.
Although the parties to a civil suit do not have precisely the same
rights, the balance of rights between civil litigants is much closer than
the rather unequal balance of rights between victims and people
charged with crime.

Some civil cases are resolved quickly, whereas others languish in
the courts for years. Most civil cases are settled, that is, the parties and
their attorneys eventually work out an agreement to resolve the dispute without the necessity of a trial.

In many civil cases, the amount of paperwork is staggering. Documents fly back and forth between the lawyers carrying such arcane
labels as *complaint, answer, interrogatories, affidavit, motion, declaration,
subpoena duces tecum, request for production of documents,* and on and on.

Discovery. In most civil cases, the attorneys engage in what is typically called *pretrial discovery.* Boiled down to its essentials, discovery
is the process each attorney uses to find out as much as possible about
the other side's case. If you become embroiled in a civil suit (e.g., a
contested divorce), you can expect to spend a lot of time and money
helping your attorney with discovery. Because discovery is so important in child custody and visitation litigation, more is said about the
discovery process in Chapter 9.

Family Law Matters. For many readers of this book, the most important part of the civil legal system is the part that is responsible for
divorce, child custody, and visitation. In many communities this component of the legal system is called *family court* or *domestic relations*

court. The family court handles (a) divorce; (b) division of property at the time of divorce (e.g., who gets the family home, bank accounts, cars, etc.); (c) child custody; (d) disputes over visitation with children; (e) child support; and (f) spousal support, or as it used to be called, alimony.

In most cities, family law matters are routed to a group of judges who are assigned to hear such cases. For example, in your city there may be a "Domestic Relations Division" at the county courthouse. If you live in a small community, there may be one judge for the entire county, and he or she decides all criminal and civil cases, including divorce, custody, and visitation.

Litigation regarding child custody and visitation is not only extremely important, it's often exceedingly complex. In Chapter 9, I describe the intricacies of such litigation and give you practical information on how to increase your chances of success in family court.

▼   The Juvenile Court

Every state has laws that deal specifically with two groups of children: (a) juvenile delinquents, that is, children and teenagers who commit crimes; and (b) children who are abused or neglected at home by parents or caretakers. Both categories of children come under the authority of the juvenile court. In large communities, the juvenile court usually has its own building, judges, and staff. In rural communities, the county judge handles juvenile matters along with everything else. The juvenile court system is described is more detail in Chapter 10.

How Do the Three Components of the Legal System Work Together to Protect Children From Abuse?

When child abuse is suspected, the law plays a decisive role in protecting the child. In some cases, all three components of the legal system come into play. Consider, for example, the sad case of the Flowers family:

> Linda and Mike Flowers had a three-year-old son. Unfortunately, Linda and Mike were both addicted to crack cocaine.

Mike made his living as a drug dealer. Linda hated the fact that she was hooked on cocaine, but her addiction was so powerful that she couldn't stop.

Three or four times a week, Mike beat Linda. When Mike lost his temper, which was often, he also hit the three-year-old, sometimes with a belt, sometimes with his fist. The little boy was covered with bruises. Linda tried to protect her son, but when she attempted to stop Mike from beating their son, Mike just hit her.

After the latest beating, Linda took the little boy to the hospital, where a doctor quickly diagnosed child abuse, and called child protective services (CPS). CPS is the government agency responsible for protecting children who are abused or neglected at home by their parents. CPS works closely with the juvenile court. (CPS is discussed in more detail in Chapter 10.) A CPS social worker went to the hospital and took the little boy into emergency protective custody. The social worker also notified the police.

The next day, the social worker started legal proceedings in the juvenile court, and the judge of the juvenile court made an order temporarily removing the child from the home.

Linda loves her child, and the shock of the juvenile court judge's order taking her baby away was the reality check Linda needed to begin getting her life under control. Linda escaped to a battered woman's shelter and got herself into a drug treatment program. A few weeks later, Linda started a divorce case in family court, where she sought custody of the child.

The police investigated, and a prosecutor filed criminal child abuse charges against Mike. Mike was convicted and sent to prison.

In the Flowers case, all three components of the legal system were in operation at the same time. Mike was prosecuted and punished in the criminal court. The family court granted Linda a divorce, but did not give her custody of the child until the juvenile court judge determined that she was off drugs and that she could provide a good home for her son. After six months of hard work with her social worker and her therapist, Linda was ready to start a new life with her son. The judge of the juvenile court closed the case in juvenile court, and the judge of the family court awarded full custody to Linda.

This case had a happy ending. Linda escaped an abusive relationship and a terrible addiction. Once she kicked her drug habit, she was able to be the kind of parent she wanted to be and that her son needed. In Linda's case, all three components of the system worked in harmony to protect the child and put Mike behind bars. Of course, the legal system doesn't always operate so smoothly. Children sometimes fall between the cracks, and judges of different courts occasionally work at cross-purposes. In many cases, however, the legal system works the way it's supposed to, and when that happens good things happen for kids and protective parents.

Now consider the Smiths, a family with different problems:

Mary and Bill Smith have two young children: Larry, age five, and Ellen, age eight. One day, Ellen disclosed to her mother that Bill was touching her "in my privates and making me touch his penis." Shocked, Mary confronted Bill, who strongly denied that he did any such thing. Mary took her daughter to a therapist, and Ellen repeated the story of abuse in more detail. The therapist reported the sexual abuse to CPS, as she was required to do by the child abuse reporting law (see Chapter 10 for discussion of the child abuse reporting law).

The discovery that her husband was sexually abusing their eight-year-old daughter sent Mary into a tailspin of confusion, rage, despair, and fear. Shortly after Mary and Ellen arrived home from the counselor's office, a CPS social worker visited. The social worker chatted with Mary and Ellen for about an hour. The worker told Mary that as long as Ellen was safe, the worker did not think it necessary to involve the juvenile court. The worker told Mary that the case would be referred to the police.

After consulting with friends, Mary got a lawyer and started a divorce in the family court. In the divorce, Mary seeks custody of the children. The divorce is still pending. In the meantime, Bill moved into an apartment, and Mary has temporary custody of the kids.

The police are investigating the case, and we still don't know whether Bill will face criminal charges.

How will the Smith case ultimately turn out? We don't know. One thing to note, however, is that the juvenile court is not involved. In the Smith case, and cases like it, juvenile court involvement is frequently unnecessary because only one parent is abusive and the *non*abusive parent is able to protect the child. Thus, in the Smith case, only two components of the legal system—criminal court and family court— are involved.

Why Is the Legal System So Adversarial?

In the United States, the legal system is based on the adversarial model developed long ago in England and transplanted across the Atlantic during colonial times. In the adversary system, the two sides of a lawsuit—plaintiff and defendant—are legal adversaries who "fight it out" in court. The theory of the adversary system is that the best way to arrive at the truth is to provide each party an opportunity to give its version of the facts—its side of the story—to an impartial judge or jury. The judge or jury evaluates the evidence and decides where the truth lies.

When Americans think of a court trial, they usually picture a jury. Juries are not used in all trials, however, and when there is no jury, the judge does the job normally carried out by the jury. Juries are used most often in criminal cases and in some types of civil cases. Juries are rare in divorce, child custody, and visitation cases. In fact, in most states, juries are not used at all in divorce, child custody, and visitation proceedings. Thus, in most family court proceedings, the judge is the ultimate decision maker. In juvenile courts, there typically is no jury.

Many parents, psychologists, social workers, and doctors are a bit put off by the adversary system. For those who are not trained in law, it's reasonable to ask, "Is it really necessary for litigation to be so adversarial, contentious, and unpleasant?" "Aren't there less hostile and adversarial ways to resolve disagreements, particularly disagree-ments involving children?" These are fair questions, and some com-munities take steps, particularly in child custody cases, to make liti-gation less adversarial. For example, in some communities, divorcing parents who can't agree about child custody or visitation are required to consult a professional mediator who is trained to help parents find common ground. With the assistance of a mediator, many divorcing parents come to terms on custody and visitation, thus avoiding the psychological and financial cost of "fighting it out in court." In many juvenile courts, judges make the process less adversarial and formal. In criminal cases, however, the process is and will remain highly adversarial.

Like it or not, our legal system is adversarial. If the divorcing couple can agree on how custody or visitation should be handled, the legal wrangling can be reduced to a minimum. When one parent accuses the other of child abuse, however, the chances of agreement are slight, and parents should prepare themselves for the legal system at its *most* adversarial.

6

Finding a Lawyer

This chapter covers two important issues. First, I briefly describe the roles, responsibilities, and loyalties of lawyers. Before you get involved in the legal system, you need to know what to expect from your attorney and, just as important, what to expect from the other attorney. Second, this chapter gives you basic information on how to find an attorney. Parents often ask:

- ☐ If I suspect my child has been sexually abused, do I really need a lawyer? (p. 69)
- ☐ What can I expect from the lawyer for the other side? (p. 71)
- ☐ Do lawyers specialize in particular fields of law such as child custody or divorce? (p. 72)
- ☐ How do I find a competent lawyer? (p. 72)

If I Suspect My Child Has Been Sexually Abused, Do I Really Need a Lawyer?

Parents who suspect their child has been sexually abused may wonder whether they need a lawyer. The answer often depends on the type of legal proceeding, if any, that is under way or planned. Consider, for example, a case in which a child is molested by a stranger. The police apprehend the perpetrator and the prosecutor charges him with child molestation. The child will be interviewed by police officers and the prosecutor. If there is a trial, the child will probably testify. In this criminal case, the child's parents probably do not need an attorney. The parents will undoubtedly have questions, but the police and the prosecutor will answer most of them. Of course, there is nothing to prevent the child's parents from consulting an attorney, perhaps to consider filing a civil lawsuit against the perpetrator or to answer questions about the legal system.

Although an attorney is usually unnecessary in criminal cases, there are other circumstances where legal representation is, in my opinion, *indispensable*. In particular, an attorney is critical if you suspect your child has been sexually abused by the child's father. In this terrible situation, you will almost certainly consider divorce and possibly other legal action as well. Long before you set foot in a courtroom, you need a lawyer.

The immediate problem for many protective parents, however, is that lawyers are expensive—very expensive! Parents who suspect abuse sometimes say, "I can't afford an attorney. Besides, I don't know if I really need one. I can go to family court myself. I'll explain everything to the judge. Can't I protect my child myself?"

This is a fair question. Why can't a parent protect her child herself? After all, the law does not require parents who are appearing in family court to have a lawyer. Before I answer this question, I want to be honest with you. I have a very strong opinion on this issue. My mind is already made up. Perhaps others will disagree, but I believe a parent *must* have an attorney—and a good one—before she alleges any kind of child abuse, especially child sexual abuse. There is an old saying that a person who represents herself in court has a fool for a client, and this adage is nowhere more true than in contested child custody cases where abuse is suspected.

To reinforce my point about the importance of an attorney, let me change the context and ask you to assume for a moment that your child has a very serious illness, such as cancer or a brain tumor. Will you treat her yourself? Will you say, "Doctors are expensive. I can't afford one. Can't I heal my daughter myself?" Of course not. If you are lucky enough to have medical insurance, you say a prayer of thanks and search for the best doctor you can find. But even if you don't have medical insurance, you find a good doctor, regardless of the expense. Why? Because there is nothing more precious than your child, and you know he or she *has* to have a doctor. Well, when a mother suspects that her child has been sexually abused by the child's father, the mother needs a lawyer *just as much* as the sick child needs a doctor. When sexual abuse is suspected, the mother may have to go to court, and going to court without a lawyer can be extremely dangerous. Of course, I can't deny that you might win without a lawyer, but why would you risk it?

What Can I Expect From the Lawyer for the Other Side?

It's important for parents to understand the lawyer's role in the adversary system of justice. Lawyers must adhere to a code of professional ethics that requires them to be zealous advocates for their clients. Thus, in the adversary system, a lawyer's responsibility is to his or her client. The lawyer has a solemn obligation of loyalty to clients.

In litigation, the lawyer's responsibility can be summed up in one word: *Win*. The lawyer presents the client's case in the best possible light and, when necessary, attacks, challenges, and undermines the other side. Although a lawyer should be courteous to the other side, a lawyer has no obligation to help or be sympathetic to the adversary. Moreover, the lawyer for one side may not give legal advice to the adversary. Indeed, a lawyer who gives advice, aid, or succor to the adversary probably violates the ethical duty of loyalty and zealous advocacy owed the client.

In litigation, you should expect loyalty from your lawyer; you should expect *nothing* from the other lawyer. Keep in mind that in a lawsuit, the other lawyer is not overly concerned with whether you are right. In a hotly contested child custody case, for example, the other lawyer's job is not to concern himself or herself with the fact that you are the better parent. The other lawyer owes loyalty to his or her client, *not* to you. Moreover, your husband's lawyer does *not* represent the child or the child's interests. In the adversary system, the fact of the matter is that the other lawyer's job is to defeat you.

On reading the last paragraph, you may ask, "How do lawyers sleep at night?" "How can anyone with a heart or a conscience be an attorney?" You may conclude that lawyers are pugnacious by nature. Finally, you may ask, "Do lawyers care about the truth?" It probably comes as no surprise to you that there are some lawyers who like nothing better than a good fight, and there are a few who enjoy making people squirm. But most lawyers don't fit this description. Lawyers are ordinary people—moms and dads, coaches and couch potatoes—

who just happen to be highly trained and committed to the adversary system of justice. When they are at home, they are just like everyone else. When a lawyer is on the job, however, it's a different story. In the adversary system, the lawyer's *loyalty* is to the client. Do lawyers care about the truth? Yes, lawyers care deeply about the truth and about justice. Lawyers understand that the adversary system is not perfect. Yet, lawyers believe the system leads to the truth most of the time and that despite its faults the adversary system is the best method we have to resolve difficult legal problems.

Do Lawyers Specialize in Particular Fields of Law Such as Child Custody or Divorce?

The law is enormously complex and becoming more so every day. It's impossible for a single attorney to be an expert on everything, and lawyers today tend to specialize, just as physicians specialize in surgery, pediatrics, or OB-GYN. Thus, attorney Jones may specialize in criminal defense work, whereas attorney Smith specializes in divorce and child custody cases. Of course, most lawyers practice in more than one narrow area, and the average attorney is experienced in two or three fields.

You should know that most lawyers know little or nothing about child abuse. In particular, most lawyers know very little about how to prove abuse—especially sexual abuse—in court. This lack of knowledge extends to many lawyers to specialize in divorce, child custody, and visitation cases. The legal issues involved in proving child sexual abuse are enormously complex, and a lawyer who lacks knowledge of these issues can do more harm than good. I need to add, however, that simply because an attorney has not handled child sexual abuse cases does not necessarily mean the lawyer can't help you. If the attorney has expertise in family law and is willing to learn about sexual abuse, the attorney may provide excellent representation.

How Do I Find a Competent Lawyer?

Finding a lawyer who is competent in family law and knowledgeable about child abuse is no simple matter. Starting with the phone book is not illogical, although it's difficult to tell very much from the yellow

…ooks list lawyers by specialty, such
…d if nothing else, specialty listings

…wide bar association. Most lawyers
…in many states lawyers are required
t … r information on finding an attorney.
… can't provide legal advice, a call is
s … ht direction.
…nties have a county bar association.
M … e a lawyer referral service that pro-
v … s and telephone numbers of attor-
n … as of law. To find the lawyer referral
se … or look under "lawyer referral ser-
vi … e yellow pages of your phone book.
In … vyer referral service." Although the
co … erral service does not guarantee the
qu … es it provides, at a minimum the
la … ding of the bar association.
… ations concerned with child abuse
th … National Association of Counsel for
Ch … ocated in Denver, Colorado, has 2,000 members across the United States. Although the association itself does not represent clients in court or provide legal advice on individual cases, it maintains a list of attorneys who are knowledgeable about child abuse. Many association members specialize in family law, child custody, and child abuse. The association's address is 1825 Marion St., Denver, Colorado 80218. The phone number is (303) 322-2260. The fax number is (303) 329-3523.

The second national organization is the American Professional Society on the Abuse of Children (APSAC). Most APSAC members are mental health professionals, social workers, and doctors, although APSAC has a growing number of attorneys. APSAC is located in Chicago and has members in all fifty states. APSAC's address is 407 South Dearborn Street, Suite 1300, Chicago, IL 60605. The phone number is (312) 554-0166. The fax number is (312) 554-0919. Like the National Association of Counsel for Children, APSAC itself does not represent clients in court. Nevertheless, APSAC has a wealth of information about child abuse in general and child sexual abuse in particular. The APSAC staff may be able to provide leads on locating qualified attorneys or mental health professionals.

In addition to the National Association of Counsel for Children and APSAC, you may want to contact the National Center for Protective Parents in Civil Child Sexual Abuse Cases. The center is a very small organization dedicated to helping parents of sexually abused children. It provides information on attorneys who handle child sexual abuse cases. The center's address is 1908 Riverside Drive, Trenton, NJ 08618. The phone number is (609) 394-1506. The fax number is (609) 394-2574.

You may call the National Center on Children and the Law in Washington, D.C. This center is part of the American Bar Association. Although the center does not represent individuals in court, the attorneys at the center know a great deal about family law and child abuse. The address is 740 15th Street, NW, 9th Floor, Washington, D.C. The telephone number is (202) 662-1720. The fax number is (202) 662-1755.

Many cities and towns have a legal services or legal aid office that provides free or low-cost legal services to low income individuals. Some legal aid offices take family law cases, others do not. Although legal aid or legal services may not be able to represent a particular individual, the office may have a list of attorneys to contact.

A battered women's shelter may be a useful source of information on attorneys who are dedicated to helping women.

In some states, lawyers can take an examination to be certified as a specialist in a particular field of practice. In California, for example, attorneys can be certified as family law specialists. Although certification is not a guarantee of competence, most attorneys who pass the specialty examination are experienced and knowledgeable, although not necessarily about child abuse.

In many cases, finding a lawyer is a great deal like finding a doctor or a dentist. Word of mouth is often the best method. Friends, relatives, and coworkers can provide a candid appraisal of the skills and compassion, or lack thereof, of attorneys they know.

With a list of potential attorneys in hand, it's useful to make some telephone calls. Some attorneys say, "I don't do custody cases" or "I stay away from allegations of abuse" or "I'm not taking any new cases at the moment." If attorneys fail to return your calls, cross them off the list.

Find out whether an attorney charges a fee for an initial office consultation. At the initial consultation, the client and the attorney discuss the case and decide whether they want to work with each other. Needless to say, the attorney should provide detailed information about the fees and costs involved.

7

Help From Mental Health Professionals

The Critically Important Psychosocial Assessment

Mental health professionals, including social workers, counselors, psychologists, and psychiatrists, play three important roles regarding child sexual abuse. First, mental health professionals provide treatment to reduce the short- and long-term harmful effects of child sexual abuse (see Chapter 3 for discussion of the harmful effects of sexual abuse). Second, when sexual abuse is suspected, mental health professionals perform psychosocial assessments to help determine whether abuse occurred (see discussion in this chapter). Finally, mental health professionals testify in court to provide expert evidence on sexual abuse (see Chapter 14 for discussion of expert testimony in court).

In this chapter, I address the following important questions:

☐ Who is qualified to provide mental health treatment for my child? (p. 76)

☐ What is a psychosocial assessment for child sexual abuse? (p. 76)

☐ What credentials and experience are needed to perform a psychosocial assessment for child sexual abuse? (p. 77)

☐ Are mental health professionals who do custody evaluations in divorce cases qualified to do psychosocial assessments for sexual abuse? (p. 79)

☐ Should my child's therapist perform the psychosocial assessment? (p. 79)

☐ What should I do to prepare my child for the psychosocial assessment? (p. 80)

☐ Can I be criticized for getting more than one assessment? (p. 80)

Who Is Qualified to Provide Mental Health Treatment for My Child?

Your child's mental health is extremely important. Unfortunately, most mental health professionals do not have the training and experience needed to provide treatment for sexually abused children. Your child's pediatrician is likely to know qualified professionals in your community.

What Is a Psychosocial Assessment for Child Sexual Abuse?

When child sexual abuse is suspected, it's very often important to obtain a thorough psychosocial assessment of the child by a mental health professional who is an *expert* on child sexual abuse. The American Professional Society on the Abuse of Children (APSAC) has excellent guidelines on psychosocial assessment of sexual abuse (these guidelines are reproduced in full as Appendix A). Reading the guidelines will give you a good idea of what you and your lawyer can expect from a psychosocial assessment of your child.

Psychosocial assessment regarding child sexual abuse is a systematic process of gathering as much information as possible to determine the likelihood of abuse. Sometimes, a single mental health professional conducts the entire assessment. In other cases, a small group of experts team up to perform the assessment.

Professionals differ in the way they conduct psychosocial assessments, although most experts agree that interviewing the child is indispensable. In addition to interviewing the child one or more times, the professional may interview the protective parent and the parent who is suspected of committing the abuse. Of course, some suspected parents won't cooperate.

Some, but by no means all, professionals ask the child and parents to take a battery of psychological tests. You will recall from Chapter 4 that there is no psychological test that can tell whether a man sexually abused a child. By the same token, there is no psychological test that can tell whether a child was sexually abused. Thus, the role of psychological testing is not to determine whether abuse occurred but to provide the professional with basic information about the personality style and functioning of the adults and the child.

The professional conducting a psychosocial assessment may contact other professionals who know the child, such as the child's pediatrician, therapist, or teacher. The professional obtains and reviews all pertinent records on the child, including medical records, records from child protective services, and police reports. With as much information in hand as possible, the professional uses his or her knowledge of child development, trauma, and child sexual abuse to work toward a conclusion about the probability of abuse.

I must note here that a psychosocial assessment performed by a mental health professional is not the same as a police investigation. If the police are involved, they conduct their own investigation, using standard police practices. The police often find the results of the psychosocial assessment helpful, but the police investigation and the psychosocial assessment are not the same.

A psychosocial assessment performed by an expert mental health professional is often extremely helpful in proving or disproving abuse. Don't pin all your hopes on the assessment, however. It's almost never possible to be 100% certain one way or the other about child sexual abuse. In the best-case scenario, the assessment will turn up evidence that points strongly toward or away from abuse. In many cases, however, despite days or even months of hard work, the results of the assessment are inconclusive. An inconclusive assessment does not mean there was anything wrong with the assessment. The sad truth is that in many cases there just isn't enough evidence to tell whether abuse happened, and this is true even in cases where the child *was* abused.

What Credentials and Experience Are Needed to Perform a Psychosocial Assessment for Child Sexual Abuse?

What should you look for in a mental health professional to conduct a psychosocial assessment regarding sexual abuse? Not just any mental health professional will do. It comes as a surprise to some parents that most mental health professionals know very little about child sexual abuse. Only a small fraction of social workers, psychiatrists, psychologists, and counselors possess the knowledge and experience required to conduct a competent psychosocial assessment of sexual abuse. You should also note that many mental health professionals who *are* competent to treat sexually abused children are *not* competent to conduct a thorough psychosocial assessment for sexual abuse. Thus, your child's therapist may be a wonderful clinician but may lack the training and experience needed to perform psychosocial assessments.

The APSAC guidelines on psychosocial assessment, referred to above and reproduced as Appendix A, recommend the following credentials and experience for mental health professionals conducting psychosocial assessments of child sexual abuse:

1. The evaluator should possess an advanced mental health degree in a recognized discipline (e.g., M.D., or Master's or Ph.D. in psychology, social work, counseling, or psychiatric nursing).
2. The evaluator should have experience evaluating and treating children and families. A minimum of two years of professional experience with children is expected, three to five years is preferred. The evaluator should also possess at least two years of professional experience with sexually abused children. If the evaluator does not possess such experience, supervision is essential.
3. It is essential that the evaluator have specialized training in child development and child sexual abuse. This should be documented in terms of formal course work, supervision, or attendance at conferences, seminars, and workshops.
4. The evaluator should be familiar with current professional literature on sexual abuse and be knowledgeable about the dynamics and the emotional and behavioral consequences of abuse experiences.
5. The evaluator should have experience in conducting forensic evaluations and providing court testimony. If the evaluator does not possess such experience, supervision is essential.
6. The evaluator should approach the evaluation with an open mind to all possible responses from the child and all possible explanations for the concern about possible sexual abuse.

Finding a professional with these credentials is not easy. The child's pediatrician may know a professional with the necessary qualifications. Some larger hospitals have child abuse specialists in the pediatrics department. A call to a university hospital pediatric center may lead in the right direction. If the child is in therapy, the therapist may know competent evaluators.

Are Mental Health Professionals Who Do Custody Evaluations in Divorce Cases Qualified to Do Psychosocial Assessments for Sexual Abuse?

Some mental health professionals routinely perform evaluations of parents involved in child custody and visitation litigation in family court. In some communities, these professionals work directly for the family court judge. In other communities, professionals who do custody evaluations are mental health professionals in private practice. The important point for you is this: The fact that a mental health professional has experience conducting custody evaluations does *not* mean the professional knows the first thing about sexual abuse. In fact, the majority of mental health professionals who conduct custody evaluations are *not* competent to perform psychosocial assessments for child sexual abuse. There is an old saying that a little knowledge is a dangerous thing, and many custody evaluators know just enough about sexual abuse to be dangerous. If you suspect your children have been sexually abused by their father and you are involved in custody or visitation litigation in family court, do *not* automatically agree to an assessment by a mental health professional who conducts custody evaluations. A custody evaluator may be quite capable of addressing issues that have little or nothing to do with abuse, but when it comes to the possibility of sexual abuse, you need an expert on child sexual abuse, not a custody evaluator.

Should My Child's Therapist Perform the Psychosocial Assessment?

If your child is in therapy, should the therapist perform the psychosocial assessment? Many mental health professionals believe it's generally inappropriate for a child's therapist to conduct a psychosocial assessment that may be used in legal proceedings. Moreover, as I mentioned earlier, many excellent therapists lack the experience and special training needed to conduct psychosocial assessments. Even so, in some cases the child's therapist is the best person to conduct the assessment. When that is the case, the therapist may do so.

What Should I Do to Prepare My Child for the Psychosocial Assessment?

How should you prepare your child for the assessment? What should you tell your child? My advice is to talk about this issue with the professional who is going to conduct the assessment. Many experts believe it's wise for the parent to say relatively little to the child about the assessment. Under no circumstances should you tell your child what to say during the assessment. Of course, if your child asks what he or she should say, you can respond with something like, "Just tell the truth" or "Answer the questions the best you can."

Can I Be Criticized for Getting More Than One Assessment?

As I mentioned earlier, in some cases the professional conducting a psychosocial assessment is not able to tell whether sexual abuse occurred. If this happens to you, you may decide to get a second assessment. This decision seems entirely reasonable. To see why getting an additional assessment is reasonable, all we have to do is think of parents who suspect that their child may have cancer. What will a parent do if the first doctor who examines the child is uncertain about the diagnosis? Obviously, the parent will seek a second opinion. Thus, getting a second opinion is medically appropriate and precisely what concerned parents are expected to do.

Like cancer, child sexual abuse can be very serious. It's completely understandable that a parent who is deeply concerned about sexual abuse would seek a second assessment when the results of the first assessment are uncertain. Before you get a second assessment, however, you should know the potential for danger that lurks in multiple assessments. If you are locked in a custody battle, you may be criticized for getting "too many assessments." The other lawyer may argue to the judge:

Your honor, there was no sexual abuse here. The only reason the mother took the child from one professional to another was because she couldn't prove these trumped-up charges of abuse, and she knew that. She was just shopping around until she found some so-called expert who would agree with her crazy suspicions. In fact, these repeated assessments are proof that there was no abuse by my client. The only abuse in this case was by the mother. By subjecting the poor child to repeated mental health assessments the *mother* is guilty of neglect.

You may not believe a lawyer would say such things. Well, believe it. Lawyers say it, and judges sometimes buy it. How can you avoid the criticism that you got "too many" assessments? Of course, the first step is to be aware of the problem: Forewarned is forearmed. Second, you should consult your attorney and mental health professional about the need for and the timing of additional assessments.

Part III

Detailed Discussion of the Criminal Justice
System, Family Court, Child Protective
Services, and Juvenile Court

Part II introduced you to the criminal justice system, family court, and the juvenile court. Now it's time to get better acquainted. You may wonder if it's worth the effort to become familiar with details of the legal system. After all, I've urged you to get a lawyer (see p. 69), and you might well say, "If I'm going to get a lawyer, why should *I* become an expert on the law? I'll pay the lawyer to be the expert!" The goal of Part III is not to turn you into an instant attorney. In fact, as I point out later (p. 161), you should not try to become an expert on the law. Nevertheless, if your child was sexually abused, you have a much greater need than the average parent to know about the legal system. Understanding the law lets you know what to expect and increases your odds of making the system work for you rather than against you and your child. Moreover, a basic understanding of the legal system places you in a better position to help your lawyer.

8

The Criminal Justice System

The criminal justice system plays an important role in protecting children from sexual abuse. When allegations of abuse arise, the police are notified, and in most cases an investigation ensues. If the investigation turns up sufficient evidence, the police contact a prosecuting attorney, who decides whether to file criminal charges against the person suspected of abuse. When charges are filed, most suspects either confess or are found guilty following a trial. When the perpetrator is convicted or confesses, the judge imposes punishment to fit the crime.

Most people who read this book have had very little contact with police, prosecutors, and criminal court. Nevertheless, if your child has been sexually abused, there is a reasonably good possibility that you, your child, and the abuser will encounter the criminal justice system. Thus, it's important for you to know something about this complicated system. Increasing your level of knowledge helps you understand what questions to ask the professionals in the system. Moreover, when you know how the criminal justice system works, you are in a better position to help your child through the system.

Most of the other chapters in this book begin with a list of questions that parents often ask about child sexual abuse and the legal system. As a change of pace, I've adopted a different format for this chapter. Rather than questions and answers, I'd like to tell you the story of one family, the Reddings, and what they experienced in the criminal justice system. What happened to the Reddings is typical of the procedures in the criminal justice system and should give you a good idea of what to expect when the wheels of the criminal justice system start to roll.

The Reddings' Story

Diane Redding is the ten-year-old daughter of Beth and Roger Redding. The Reddings live in a comfortable middle-class neighborhood. Both parents work full-time. Roger is a computer engineer and travels a lot. Beth is a kindergarten teacher.

▼   The Secret Is Disclosed

Not long ago, Diane was staying the night at her best friend's house. It was then that Diane whispered to her friend: "My dad is molesting me. It's got to be a secret, so promise not to tell anybody." Although Diane's friend promised not to tell, she couldn't keep the promise and soon told her own mother, who telephoned Beth Redding.

Beth was shocked and confused. She scooped Diane up and drove to the pediatrician's office. The doctor examined Diane and found medical evidence of sexual abuse. Once the doctor assured Diane that it was "okay to talk about it," Diane tearfully described a yearlong history of molestation by her father. He began with touching her and slowly progressed to full sexual intercourse. This progression—from inappropriate but relatively minor touching to more serious abuse—is typical, and is called *grooming*. Grooming is discussed in Chapter 4. Diane told the doctor that her father said, "If you ever tell, I'll go to jail. The family will break up, and you will be taken away from your mother and me forever."

The doctor telephoned child protective services (CPS) as she was required to do by the state child abuse reporting law. The reporting law is described in Chapter 10. The doctor told Beth to plan on visits from a CPS social worker and the police. Beth told the doctor that she and Diane would stay with Beth's brother until she could figure out what to do. That night, Roger returned home from a business trip to an empty house and no note from his wife.

▼ The Visit From Child Protective Services

The same evening, a CPS social worker interviewed Diane and her mother at the brother's home. The social worker believed Diane's story. Beth told the social worker that she would keep Diane away from Roger. The social worker decided Diane was safe with her mother and that there was no need for CPS or the juvenile court to get involved. The social worker told Beth the police would contact her soon.

▼ The Police Investigation

The next morning, there was a knock on the brother's door. Beth opened the door to find a uniformed police officer. Beth invited her in, and the officer told Beth that CPS had called the police. The officer interviewed Diane, who repeated what her father had done. Beth said, "I can't understand how my husband could do such a thing, but I believe my daughter." The officer called the pediatrician, and the doctor told the officer about the medical evidence of sexual abuse.

▼ Roger Redding Is Arrested

The investigating officer returned to the police station and discussed the case with a detective from the police department child abuse unit. The detective and the officer decided they had enough evidence to arrest Roger. The next step was to get a warrant for his arrest. The detective went to the courthouse and asked a judge called a magistrate to issue an arrest warrant. Armed with an arrest warrant, the detective and the investigating officer arrived at the Redding home, where Roger was frantically trying to find his family. The detective said, "Are you Roger Redding?" Roger replied, "Yes. What do you know?" The detective handed Roger the arrest warrant and said, "Mr. Redding, you are under arrest for sexual abuse of your daughter. You will need to come with us to the police station." Roger slumped into a chair, dropped his head into his hands, and said, "Oh no. How did you find out?" The detective replied, "Find out what?" Roger said, "You know, about my daughter? I'm just sick about this." The detective carefully wrote down what Roger said while the uniformed officer told Roger that he had a right to remain silent, that he had a right to an attorney, and that anything he said could be used against him.

Roger was handcuffed, searched, and taken to the police station. At the station, Roger was fingerprinted, photographed, and put in a jail cell.

▼   The Prosecutor's Decision to File Charges

The next step in the criminal process was the prosecutor's decision to file formal criminal charges. Many people believe criminal charges can't be filed unless the victim agrees, presses charges, or signs a complaint. Generally, this is not true. With serious crimes like child sexual abuse, the prosecutor has the authority to file charges whether the victim agrees or not. Of course, if the victim or his or her protective parent is uncooperative, the prosecutor may decline to file. In the final analysis, however, the decision to file charges is made by the prosecutor, not the victim or the victim's family.

Prosecutors have the authority—called prosecutorial discretion—to decide whether or not to file criminal charges. In child sexual abuse cases, prosecutors consider several factors in deciding whether to file charges. The prosecutor first wants to know how serious is the abuse and how strong is the evidence against the suspect? When the evidence is strong, the prosecutor is more likely to file charges than when the evidence is weak. The prosecutor makes a judgment about whether the child will be a good witness if there is a trial. In most child sexual abuse cases, the child is the most important witness, and if the child is quite young, the prosecutor may decide the child will not be a good witness. In addition to considering whether the child will be a good witness in court, the prosecutor evaluates what the child said about the abuse to parents, teachers, doctors, friends, and others. If the child's story remained basically consistent over time, the prosecutor is more likely to file charges. If the child's story changed with each telling, however, the prosecutor may hesitate because inconsistencies can be used to undermine the child's credibility as a witness. In addition to what the child said, the prosecutor considers whether there is evidence to corroborate the child's story. For example, if there is medical evidence of sexual abuse, the prosecutor is more likely to file charges. It should be mentioned, however, that medical evidence exists in only a small percent of cases.

If the prosecutor decides *not* to file criminal charges against the man you think molested your child, you may feel frustrated and angry. On learning that charges will not be filed, it's common for protective parents ask, "How can you make a decision not to prosecute? My child said he did it! Isn't that enough? Are you going to let that child molester get away with it?" Unfortunately, there are quite a few cases where prosecutors do believe children, and where prosecutors are convinced that abuse happened, but they decline to file charges because they know there just isn't enough evidence to prove the abuse in court. In criminal cases, a prosecutor has to produce enough evidence to meet a very high burden of proof to win a conviction. If there isn't enough evidence to prove the abuse beyond a reasonable doubt, there is little point filing charges in the first place. Thus, it's not uncommon for prosecutors to tell protective parents, "I'm sorry, I can't file charges. I believe your child was molested, but there isn't enough evidence to prove it in court." Prosecutors don't enjoy disappointing protective parents, and they don't like it when an offender escapes justice. Nevertheless, prosecutors have an ethical as well as a legal duty to file charges only when evidence of guilt is strong.

Returning to the Redding case, several hours after Roger's arrest the detective dropped by the office of the deputy district attorney responsible for child abuse cases. The prosecutor reviewed the papers in the case and chatted with the detective. The prosecutor agreed with the detective that the evidence against Roger was strong, and the prosecutor decided to file charges. The prosecutor prepared a document called a complaint and filed it with the court. The complaint started the formal criminal court process.

▼   Roger Redding's Initial Appearance in
    Court and His Release on Bail

A person who is arrested and charged with a crime has a right to be taken before an impartial magistrate (judge) as soon as possible. Roger Redding's first appearance in court was on the morning following his arrest. Roger was in court along with his lawyer. The prosecutor who filed the charges was there too. Diane and Beth were not in court. Roger's first court appearance was brief. The magistrate informed Roger of the charges against him and told him his preliminary hearing would be in two weeks. After some discussion between the magistrate and the attorneys, the magistrate set bail at $50,000 and told Roger that if he was released from jail on bail, he was not to live at home or have any contact with his daughter until the criminal charges were resolved. In less than fifteen minutes, the hearing was over and Roger was escorted back to jail by a sheriff's deputy. Later that day, Roger's attorney arranged bail and Roger was released from jail.

▼ Roger's Preliminary Hearing

In many states, a person charged with crime has a right to a court proceeding called a *preliminary hearing*. The purpose of a preliminary hearing is to enable a judge decide whether there is enough evidence of guilt to require the accused person, now called the defendant, to stand trial. Although a preliminary hearing is less formal than a trial, the hearing is adversarial. The defendant is present with his attorney. The prosecutor must introduce enough evidence of guilt to convince the judge that a trial should be held. In some cases, the child testifies at the preliminary hearing, and this is usually the child's first experience in court. If the judge decides there is enough evidence for a trial, the child will probably have to testify again at the trial, if there is one. There is no jury at a preliminary hearing.

In some states, a person suspected of crime has a right to *grand jury indictment*. A grand jury is a group of citizens from the community who are responsible for deciding whether formal criminal charges should be filed against individuals suspected of crime. The prosecutor meets with the grand jury behind closed doors and presents evidence of the suspect's guilt. If the grand jury decides the prosecutor's evidence is sufficient, the grand jury issues a document known as an indictment. The indictment charges the defendant with specific crimes.

A grand jury does not decide guilt or innocence in individual trials. Rather, the grand jury serves as a screening device early in the process to ensure that innocent people are not charged with violating the law. The jury that decides an individual case is called a *petit jury*, and it's the petit jury that we are used to seeing on television.

Returning to the Redding case, Roger's preliminary hearing was held two weeks after his initial appearance in court. The prosecutor decided not to ask Diane to testify at the preliminary hearing because the prosecutor believed there was enough evidence to convince the judge that Roger should stand trial without putting Diane through the ordeal of appearing in court. The doctor testified for the prosecution and told the judge about the medical evidence of sexual abuse. The investigating police officer testified and told the judge what Diane had said. Although Roger's attorney had the right to call witnesses— including Diane and her mother—at the preliminary hearing, the defense attorney decided against calling witnesses. The judge ruled that the testimony of the doctor and the police officer was sufficient to require Roger to stand trial.

▼ Roger's Attorney Tries to Negotiate a
   Plea With the Prosecutor

With Roger on his way to trial on serious charges, his attorney telephoned the prosecutor to begin plea negotiation, or as it's usually called, plea bargaining. Plea bargaining is a process of back-and-forth negotiation between a prosecutor and a defense attorney. Reduced to its essentials, the defense attorney's goal in plea bargaining is to get the best possible "deal" for the defendant. In exchange for the deal, the defendant promises to plead guilty. In some cases, the defendant pleads guilty to reduced charges. In other cases, the defendant pleads guilty to the original charges and the prosecutor agrees to ask the judge to be lenient when the judge decides what punishment the defendant should receive.

There is nothing unethical or improper about plea bargaining. Indeed, plea bargaining is common in nearly all kinds of criminal cases, including child abuse. As a result of plea bargaining, the vast majority of criminal cases do not go all the way to a full-blown trial in court. In fact, between 70% and 90% of all criminal cases end in guilty pleas prior to trial. Thus, trials are the somewhat rare exception rather than the rule.

In the Redding case, Roger's attorney and the prosecutor discussed the possibility of Roger pleading guilty to a less serious crime, but Roger insisted he wasn't guilty of *anything*, and the lawyers could not strike a bargain that Roger would accept.

▼ Roger's Trial in Criminal Court

A defendant charged with a serious crime like child sexual abuse has the right to a jury trial. If the defendant does not want a jury, the judge performs the job normally carried out by the jury. In jury trials, the first step is for the lawyers to pick a jury from a pool of potential jurors. In picking a jury, each lawyer selects jurors whom the lawyer thinks will be sympathetic to his or her side of the case.

Once a jury is selected, the lawyers make their opening statements. The prosecutor goes first and explains to the jury what the prosecutor believes the evidence will prove. The opening statement gives the prosecutor an opportunity to paint a verbal picture of what is to come. Following the prosecutor's opening statement, the defense attorney makes an opening statement. Needless to say, the defense attorney paints a different picture from that of the prosecutor.

With opening statements complete, the prosecutor begins presenting evidence of the defendant's guilt. The prosecutor's most important evidence is usually testimony from the child. Indeed, in the great majority of cases, the child is the prosecution's "star" witness. In addition to the child, the prosecutor may ask the protective parent to testify. Finally, the prosecutor may offer testimony from medical or mental health professionals. The one person the prosecutor can't call as a witness is the defendant. The defendant in a criminal trial has a constitutional right not to testify.

When a person testifies, he or she takes an oath to tell the truth. Following the oath, the attorney who requested the person to testify asks questions. This part of the testimony is called *direct examination.* The purpose of direct examination is provide the witness an opportunity to tell the jury what the witness knows about the case. For example, when a child testifies on direct examination, the child tells the jury about the abuse. Obviously, describing sexual abuse to a group of unfamiliar adults sitting in a large and forbidding courtroom is difficult for children, especially when the defendant is sitting there too. Nevertheless, you would be amazed—and encouraged—by how well most kids do on the witness stand.

Testifying is seldom easy for children. Yet, when children are prepared for what to expect in court and have the support of a loving parent, they cope well with testifying. Moreover, psychological research indicates that when children receive support from parents, testifying is very unlikely to cause any serious or lasting harm. Children don't enjoy testifying, but once it's over they bounce back to their old selves. In fact, after they testify, many children report that although it was a "scary" experience, they are glad to have had an opportunity to "tell the jury what happened."

If your child is going to be a witness, I urge you to talk to the prosecutor about steps you can take to prepare your child. Some prosecutors have a staff of professionals called victim or witness advocates whose job is helping crime victims, including children, navigate the criminal justice system.

There are two things you definitely should *not* do. First, don't rehearse your child about what to say in court. No matter how benign your intentions, if the defense attorney finds out you rehearsed your child, the attorney will accuse you of coaching. As a result, your child's credibility could be seriously damaged or destroyed. The second thing to avoid is, I'm sure, obvious to you. Don't talk about testifying in a way that scares the daylights out of your child. Depending on their age, children can be told something like this: "When you go to court, you will tell what happened. In court, you tell only the truth, and you don't make up anything. The grown-ups listen, and two of the grown-ups will ask you questions." Of course, your child may have specific questions. Again, if you are uncertain how to answer, give the prosecutor a call or, if your child has a victim or witness advocate, contact the advocate.

After direct examination, the other attorney has the right to cross-examine. When a child testifies, the defense attorney usually cross-examines the child. The defense attorney may try to make the child look like an unreliable witness or even a liar. For example, if the child did not say anything about the abuse for a long time, the defense attorney may ask the child questions about the delay. The defense attorney may focus on delay in an effort to convince the jury that the abuse never happened and that the child is lying. Another way to cross-examine a child is to catch the child saying inconsistent things about the abuse.

For many protective parents, cross-examination by the defense attorney seems unfair. After all, how is a six- or ten-year-old child supposed to cope with the tricks of an experienced attorney? But don't be too hard on defense attorneys. The cross-examining defense attorney is just doing his or her job. In our adversary system of justice, the defense attorney owes loyalty only to his or her client. If the case goes to trial, the defense attorney is duty bound to attack the prosecution's witnesses, including the child. After all, the child is usually the prosecution's most important witness. (The adversary system is described in Chapter 5.)

If your child has to testify, you may wonder if it's possible for him or her to testify via videotape so as not to have to appear in court, face to face with the defendant. Although most states have laws that allow selected children to testify in this way, these laws are seldom used. The vast majority of children who testify do so in the traditional manner.

When the prosecution has presented all its witnesses and other evidence, the prosecution rests its case. Next, the defense calls its witnesses in an effort to poke holes in the prosecutor's case. The defendant may testify during this part of the trial. If the defendant testifies, the prosecutor is allowed to cross-examine. Finally, the defense rests.

When both sides have rested, the prosecutor and defense attorney make their closing arguments to the jury. Each lawyer uses closing argument to summarize the evidence and persuade the jury to vote for the attorney's side. After closing arguments, the judge instructs the jurors on the law they must follow to decide whether the defendant is guilty. The jury then retires to decide the defendant's fate. If the jury decides the defendant is not guilty, the case is over. The prosecution is not allowed to appeal an acquittal to a higher court. If the jury decides that the defendant is guilty, however, the defendant *is* allowed to appeal to a higher court. The responsibility of the higher court— called an appellate court—is to decide whether serious mistakes were made at the trial. If serious mistakes occurred, the appellate court may order a new trial.

What if the jury can't make up its mind? Suppose, for example, that some of the jurors believe the defendant is guilty but others think he's innocent. This is called a *hung jury*, and, when this happens, the judge declares a mistrial. The prosecutor then has the option to ask for another trial.

Let's get back to the Reddings. At Roger's trial, Diane testified against her father. As you can imagine, testifying was very difficult. Like so many incest victims, Diane was torn between love for her father and her desire to stop the abuse. The detective testified and told the jury the incriminating things Roger said the day he was arrested. The pediatrician testified and described the medical evidence of sexual abuse.

Roger's attorney vigorously cross-examined Diane to attack her credibility. The defense attorney asked Diane, "Why did you wait so long to tell?" and "You could have told your mother, couldn't you?" and "Did your mother put you up to this testimony here in court?" The defense attorney tried to convince the jury that Diane was lying and that she had been coached by Beth.

...ed in his own behalf and denied that he touched Di-
...ay. Roger testified that Diane was coached into a false
...her.

...erated for two days, and still could not reach a ver-
... deliberation is not unusual. The hours dragged like
... waited on pins and needles. Finally, on the third
... note to the judge: It had reached a verdict. Everyone
...rt. Roger sat stony faced and pale next to his attor-
... public area of the courtroom wringing her hands.
...andmother's home in another city, anxiously wait-
ing. The judge turned to the jury and said, "Ladies and gentlemen of
the jury, have you reached a verdict?" The forewoman of the jury stood
and said, "Yes, your honor, we have a verdict." The judge said, "What
is your verdict?" The forewoman nervously fingered the slip of paper
clenched in her hand. Slowly, she opened the paper and read, "We the
jury find Roger Redding guilty as charged." Roger put his head on the
table. Beth sobbed quietly. When Beth telephoned the news to Diane,
the child nestled in her grandmother's arms and cried tears of grief
and relief.

▼   Roger Redding Receives His Punishment

When a defendant pleads guilty or is found guilty after a trial, the
judge decides what punishment the person deserves. Depending on
the seriousness of the crime and the defendant's prior criminal record,
the judge may sentence the defendant to prison. In some cases, the
judge suspends the prison sentence and places the person on probation. With probation, the defendant lives in the community under the
supervision of a probation officer. In some child sexual abuse cases,
the defendant is placed on probation and ordered to get psychological
treatment.

In Roger Redding's case, the judge sentenced Roger to five years
in state prison. All but six months of the prison sentence was sus-
pended. Roger served six months in the county jail and was released
on probation. Roger was required to move out of the family home.
He was ordered to have no contact with his family until he completed a treatment program for child molesters. At last report, Roger
was working hard in therapy. Diane was in therapy too. Somehow,
Beth found the courage to bring her daughter through this difficult

experience. Beth has not decided what the future holds. For now she is content to help her daughter heal.

Conclusion

Roger Redding's conviction was bittersweet for Diane and her mother, and the same is true for thousands of other families afflicted by incest. On the one hand, involvement in the criminal justice system is difficult for everyone. Careers and reputations are ruined, and families fly apart at the seams. On the other hand, conviction sends a clear message: Child sexual abuse is wrong; it's an extraordinary betrayal of trust that will not be tolerated. Moreover, for many offenders, the brutal reality of a criminal conviction supplies the motivation that is needed to make meaningful progress toward controlling their deviant behavior.

9

Family Court

Divorce, Child Custody, and Child Visitation

In this chapter, I discuss family court, or as it's called some places, domestic relations court. Nearly half of U.S. marriages end in divorce, and millions of us find our way at one time or another into family court. A divorce is started when the attorney for one spouse files a document in court called a complaint or petition. The complaint or petition is the first of many documents that are filed in a typical divorce. The last document, and the one that officially ends the marriage, is the judge's decree or judgment of divorce. This chapter answers the following frequently asked questions:

- ☐ Do I need an attorney to get a divorce or custody? (p. 98)
- ☐ What happens in a divorce? (p. 99)
- ☐ What is the technical meaning of child custody? (p. 100)
- ☐ What is visitation, and is it a right or a privilege? (p. 101)
- ☐ When it comes to custody, do the mother and father have equal rights, or does Mom have an advantage? (p. 101)
- ☐ If parents can't agree on custody, who decides? What is the "best interest of the child" standard? (p. 102)

Do I Need an Attorney to Get a Divorce or Custody?

The law does not require divorcing spouses to be represented by attorneys, and some couples obtain a divorce without the assistance of lawyers. Usually, however, going ahead without a lawyer is wise only in very limited circumstances in which the legal issues are simple and clear-cut. For example, Mary and Tom have been married one year. Both want a divorce, and they agree on how to divide what little property they have. There are no children, Mary and Tom are young, and each is capable of self-support. For this divorcing couple, lawyers may be unnecessary.

If you don't fit Mary and Tom's simple situation, you probably need a lawyer. Clearly, if you have children, and there is any dispute at all about custody or visitation, legal assistance is critical. Moreover, if you suspect your child was sexually abused by your spouse, legal help is *indispensable.*

Because lawyers are expensive, parents sometimes ask whether both spouses need a lawyer. I've been asked, "My husband already has a lawyer. I don't have the money to pay for one, so can't I let my husband's lawyer draw up the legal papers?" Again, if you have children, if abuse is suspected, if custody or visitation is up in the air, the answer is clear: You should not rely on your spouse's attorney *for anything.* In fact, if your spouse's lawyer is on the ball, the only advice he or she will give you is to get your own attorney.

What Happens in a Divorce?

A divorce accomplishes five things.

Ending the Marriage. First, of course, the divorce ends the marriage. The judge's decree or judgment of divorce returns you to the legal status of an unmarried person. You are free to remarry.

Property Division. The second important issue resolved in a divorce is the division of property, including the family home, furniture, cars, investments, and so on. In most cases, the couple—with the assistance of their lawyers—work out an agreement regarding the property division. Following negotiations, the lawyers prepare a formal document called a *stipulation* or *marriage settlement agreement* describing the property division. The wife and husband sign the final agreement. Finally, the property agreement is generally incorporated into the divorce decree or judgment, thus making the agreement enforceable as a court order.

If the spouses can't agree on some aspect of dividing their property, then a trial on that issue may be necessary. Every state has a complex set of laws governing property division on divorce. If a trial is necessary, the judge applies these rules and decides who gets what. I mention only the judge here because in most states there is no jury in divorce litigation.

Spousal Support. The third aspect of divorce concerns spousal support, or as it used to be called, alimony. Spousal support is not provided in all divorces. For example, if the marriage is relatively short and both spouses are employable, the judge is unlikely to order spousal support. When spousal support is ordered, it may be for a limited time. Although the law concerning spousal support is complex, it will suffice for our purposes to say that spousal support is most likely to be ordered when one spouse has financial need (e.g., lacks employment skills) and the other spouse has the ability to pay.

Child Support. The fourth component of divorce concerns child support. When a marriage ends, both parents remain financially responsible for the children. If one parent receives primary or sole custody of the children, the noncustodial parent is typically ordered to make monthly child support payments to the custodial parent.

In blended marriages, there is a biological parent and a stepparent. During the marriage, both "parents" pool their resources to support the family. When blended marriages end, however, the stepparent has no further financial obligation to the stepchild unless the stepparent adopted the child or agreed to provide continuing support. For financial purposes, an adopted child is treated the same as a biological child.

Custody and Visitation. The fifth aspect of divorce is the most important to readers of this book: child custody and visitation. I address custody and visitation in the following sections.

What Is the Technical Meaning of Child Custody?

In child custody law the word *custody* is used several ways to describe postdivorce child rearing:

- ☐ *Sole legal custody* means that one parent has the primary right to make important decisions for the child. For example, the parent with legal custody has authority to decide where the child will go to school and whether the child should receive medical care.
- ☐ *Sole or primary physical custody* means that one parent has the primary right to physical control of the child. The parent with sole physical custody—the custodial parent—is the parent with whom the child lives most of the time. The custodial parent does most of the day-to-day parenting, including getting the kids up and ready for school, taking them to the doctor, driving them to lessons, tucking them in at night, and so on. The parent with sole physical custody often, although not invariably, has legal custody as well. In some cases, one parent has sole physical custody and both parents share joint legal custody.
- ☐ *Joint legal custody* means that the parents share the right and the responsibility to make the decisions relating to the health, education, and welfare of their child.
- ☐ *Joint physical custody* means that each parent has significant periods of physical custody.

□ *Joint legal and physical custody* means that the parents share physical custody and legal custody.

Some form of joint custody is a good solution for divorced parents who are able to work cooperatively. When there is friction and animosity between parents, however, joint custody seldom works. When one parent accuses the other of child abuse, the chances of a successful joint custody arrangement are, in my experience, practically nil.

What Is Visitation, and Is It a Right or a Privilege?

In the typical divorce, one parent gets primary custody and the other gets visitation. Visitation is a legally enforceable *right*, not a mere privilege. Visitation is granted automatically unless the noncustodial parent has engaged in serious misbehavior such as child abuse or criminal activity.

The divorce decree usually describes the visitation schedule of the noncustodial parent, and the custodial parent has no right to unilaterally change that schedule. If for some reason the custodial parent believes visitation should be stopped, he or she must return to court and ask a judge to modify the visitation schedule. A custodial parent can't simply cut off visitation.

When It Comes to Custody, Do the Mother and Father Have Equal Rights, or Does Mom Have an Advantage?

Until fifteen or twenty years ago, many states had custody laws that favored mothers of young children. This maternal preference was the so-called *tender years presumption*. The belief was that young children—children of tender years—are usually better off with their mother. Today, however, the law has changed. Today, the fundamental rule of child custody is that a child's mother and father have *equal* rights to custody of their children. Thus, in a dispute over custody, the parents begin on equal legal footing. Neither parent has an advantage over the other. Despite the parents' equal legal footing, we will see below that even today many mothers start with an advantage because they are the child's primary caretaker. But more about the primary caretaker in a minute. As a final note, I should add that the equal right to custody applies whether or not the parents were ever married.

If Parents Can't Agree on Custody, Who Decides?
What Is the "Best Interest of the Child" Standard?

Most divorcing parents work out a custody and visitation arrangement that suits their needs and the needs of their children. The lawyers write up the parents' agreement and present it to the judge. So long as the agreement is in the best interest of the children, the judge approves it. When parents can't agree on custody or visitation, however, a trial may be necessary, and the judge determines who should have custody and what visitation is appropriate.

Contested custody litigation is extremely difficult for parents and children alike. Most divorcing couples are not on the best terms anyway, and when child custody becomes an issue things can turn very ugly. The degree of hostility in some custody battles is difficult to describe. Although bitterness, anger, frustration, and hurt feelings are not an inevitable byproduct of custody litigation, they are the norm rather than the exception.

As I mentioned above, when divorcing parents can't agree on custody, the judge decides. To determine custody, the judge applies a legal rule called the *best interest of the child* standard. Under this standard, the judge evaluates all available evidence about the parents and the child and makes the custody decision that serves the child's best interests. In many cases, the best interest question boils down to this: Which parent is better equipped and more likely to meet the child's needs?

The best interest of the child standard sounds simple, and sometimes it is. For example, suppose mother is a doting parent who struggles with a limited budget to meet her child's emotional, educational, and other needs. Father, by contrast, is an alcoholic who regularly drinks his paycheck, beats his wife, and yells at the child. The custody decision is easy. Mother gets sole custody and father will be lucky to get visitation. As you can imagine, most custody cases are not so simple. More often than not, both parents are decent people and loving parents. Many times, there is no clear right answer, and judges agonize over these decisions.

In some communities, parents battling over custody are urged or required to consult a professional mediator who is trained to help divorcing parents work out their differences and reach a friendly—or at least not openly hostile—custody and visitation arrangement. When mediation succeeds, there is no need for an adversarial custody battle in court.

When parents can't agree on custody and a judge must decide, the judge needs as much information as possible about each parent's strengths and weaknesses. In the adversary system of justice, the judge does not conduct an independent investigation of the parents. Rather, the judge holds a trial at which the lawyers present evidence and do what lawyers are trained to do: Win. Thus, the mother's attorney presents evidence designed to convince the judge that mother is the better parent. The mother's attorney also points out the father's weaknesses. The father's attorney returns the favor by presenting evidence that puts the father in a good light and casts a shadow over the mother. If you have skeletons in your closet—and who among us doesn't—expect the other side to make the most of them. After listening to all the evidence, the judge decides the child's best interest.

What Is a Custody Evaluation?

In custody litigation, the judge may order the parents to submit to a custody evaluation by a mental health professional. I discussed custody evaluations in Chapter 7; what follows builds on the earlier discussion.

In some custody cases, one mental health professional evaluates both parents as well as the children. In other cases, each parent obtains a separate evaluator. In some communities, custody evaluations are performed by a staff of professionals who work directly for the court or some other county agency. In other communities, parents select a custody evaluator from among mental health professionals in private practice. Not all mental health professionals do custody evaluations. If your attorney practices family law on a regular basis, he or she will know competent evaluators in your community.

A mental health professional conducting a custody evaluation typically meets with one or both parents and the children. The evaluator may administer psychological tests such as the Minnesota Multiphasic Personality Inventory (MMPI). Such tests give the evaluator insight into the personality and mental health status of the parents and children. The evaluator prepares a report that is submitted to the judge. In addition, if there is a trial regarding custody, the evaluator testifies. Judges responsible for child custody put great stock in the reports and opinions of mental health professionals who perform custody evaluations. I can't emphasize too strongly the importance of the custody evaluation. Having said that, however, I want to repeat a point I made in Chapter 7. Most custody evaluators know very little about child sexual abuse. One can be a superb custody evaluator and know virtually nothing about child abuse. I venture a guess that of all the custody evaluators in the United States, no more than 10% are truly knowledgeable about child sexual abuse. This dearth of knowledge has important implications if you suspect your child was abused. First and foremost, a custody evaluator who lacks expertise on sexual abuse is not competent to perform a psychosocial assessment regarding such abuse. (The extensive experience and credentials needed to perform such assessments are described in Chapter 7.) Nevertheless, despite a rather obvious lack of expertise, in case after case I have seen custody evaluators who know very little about sexual abuse barge right ahead anyway, with the result that they fail to substantiate abuse where it exists or, at the other extreme, find abuse where there is none. Either way, the result can be disaster. The upshot is that you can't automatically assume that a custody evaluator—even a highly regarded evaluator—is competent when it comes to child sexual abuse.

What Is Most Important to a Judge Deciding Custody?

To determine the custody arrangement that is in the child's best interest, the judge considers a wide range of evidence. The following factors play a key role in the judge's decision.

The Primary Caretaker Presumption. In many families, one parent does most of the day-to-day parenting. For example, the mother may be a full-time homemaker while the father holds down a forty-hour-a-week job. When young children are involved and the mother and the father are both good parents, judges often decide that custody should be awarded to the primary caretaker.

In many states, there is a presumption that the primary caretaker should have custody. Thus, if you are your child's primary caretaker, you begin with an advantage in court. To overcome or rebut the presumption favoring the primary caretaker, the other parent usually tries to prove that the primary caretaker has some rather serious faults that render him or her a less-than-ideal parent. If the judge is convinced that the child's best interest will be fostered by awarding custody to the nonprimary caretaker, the judge may do so.

If both parents are primary caretakers, and such cases exist, then neither parent has the advantage of the presumption favoring the primary caretaker.

Which Is the Better Parent? Most contested custody cases boil down to this: Who is the better parent? Which parent is more likely to provide the love, guidance, discipline, support, and nurturance children need to develop into happy and well-adjusted adults? Custody is awarded accordingly.

After the Divorce, Which Parent Is Most Likely to Encourage the Child's Relationship With the Other Parent? When parents divorce, it's usually in the children's best interest to have regular contact with the parent who does not receive custody. Of course, this is not the case when child abuse is involved. Contact with the abuser may be unwise. Apart from abuse cases, however, judges deciding custody consider which parent is more likely to encourage the child's postdivorce relationship with the other parent. The parent who is most likely to foster continued contact with the other parent has an advantage in court.

Mental Illness. The fact that a person has mental health problems does not make him or her a bad parent. Many people struggling with mental illness are wonderful parents. It's also true, however, that some parents with serious mental illness are not up to the demands of day-to-day parenting. Judges consider the mental health and stability of both parents, and if one parent has a mental illness that could seriously interfere with the ability to care for children, the judge may decide that the other parent should have custody.

Alcohol and Drugs. Drinking in moderation is generally not important in custody cases. Problem drinking and alcoholism, on the other hand, are definite black marks. If a judge has to choose between an alcoholic parent and a parent who does not drink or who drinks responsibly, the choice is not difficult.

Drug abuse is illegal, and judges unquestionably frown on such behavior. For many judges so-called recreational drug use is a clear indication of irresponsibility that is inconsistent with good parenting. Parents who are addicted to drugs like cocaine or heroin can't take proper care of children and should not have custody.

Suppose a Parent Has an Extramarital Affair? Many divorces start because one spouse is unfaithful. An extramarital affair does not necessarily make someone a bad parent. Thus, the affair itself is usually not very important, especially if it's over.

Although marital infidelity is usually not decisive, the way the unfaithful partner handles the situation can influence the judge's thinking. Suppose, for example, that the father had an affair with a woman at the office. The children knew nothing about it and as far as they were concerned everything was normal. The affair ended six months ago. In this situation, the father's affair probably will not count against him in the custody case. Suppose, however, that the father handled things differently. While he was still married, he spent weekend nights at his lover's apartment. Moreover, he insisted that the children sleep there too. In this case, the judge is likely to conclude that the father's behavior sets a bad example for the children.

Spousal Abuse. A man who beats or sexually assaults his wife does not deserve custody of children, and judges take spousal abuse very seriously. If you have suffered the indignity and injury of spousal abuse, the only "good" to come out of it may be that your husband's inexcusable conduct will help you win custody.

A Parent's Religious Beliefs. A parent's religious belief or lack of belief usually does not play a major role in custody decision making.

The Child's Wishes. The law in most states requires judges to consider the child's wishes about custody, at least by the time children reach age eight or nine. Judges give very little weight to the wishes of young children. Indeed, some judges do not consider young children's wishes at all. By the time children approach adolescence, most judges consider their preference. Although judges listen to older children, they are not required to go along with the child's wishes.

Child Physical Abuse. Physically abusing a child is grossly inappropriate, and a physically abusive parent has two strikes against him or her. Of course, a parent who hit a child may argue that he or she was disciplining, not abusing, the child. You will recall from Chapter 2 that the law allows parents to use reasonable corporal punishment. Thus, in a custody case the question is whether the parent crossed the line that separates reasonable corporal punishment from abuse.

Psychological Abuse. Psychological abuse is extremely destructive to children. For discussion of psychological abuse see Chapter 2. Although it's not always easy to prove psychological abuse, a judge will consider this form of maltreatment.

Child Sexual Abuse. Sexual abuse is a flagrant violation a parent's responsibility. If sexual abuse can be proven, the abusive parent should not have custody. I stress *if* the abuse can be proven, because sexual abuse is often extremely difficult to prove in court, and if the allegation is not proven, then, as far as the law is concerned, the abuse didn't happen. This bears repeating: It may be *true* as a matter of objective fact that a child was sexually abused, but if the accusing parent can't prove it in court, it's as though nothing happened. Sometimes, there is a world of difference between what is true and what can be proven in court.

If I Accuse My Husband of Sexually Abusing Our Child, Could the Legal System Backfire on Me?

Here, I make one of the most important points in this book. There are cases—many, I fear—where a father sexually abused his child but the child's mother and her lawyer can't prove it in court. If the mother can't prove the abuse, she can't persuade the judge to give her custody. In fact—and this is the important point—if the mother fails to prove the abuse, the law can backfire on her. Not only does she fail to prove the abuse, she is branded a false accuser and an hysterical woman. The judge awards custody to father! Why? Because the judge concludes, at the urging of the father's attorney, that the mother made a false charge of abuse and that she is crazy, hysterical, vindictive, unstable, unreliable, and utterly unfit for custody. This disaster—loss of the child you are trying desperately to protect—could happen to you.

Don't panic. I don't want to exaggerate the danger that allegations of sexual abuse will backfire. In many cases, the child's mother and her lawyer are able to prove the abuse, and when that happens, judges usually protect the child. Moreover, even if the evidence of abuse falls short, the judge may be sufficiently suspicious to give custody to the mother. It's important not to lose faith in the legal system. At the same time, however, it's important for me to be honest. There are times when the legal system fails miserably, and the probability of such failure goes up when a mother accuses her husband of sexually abusing their child.

Bearing in mind the frightening prospect of being labeled an hysterical false accuser and losing your child to the man you believe in your heart is molesting him or her, we arrive at this conclusion: You must approach allegations of sexual abuse with extraordinary caution. If you make the allegation, you have to be able to prove it in court. Part IV is devoted to the complex issue of proving child sexual abuse.

What Are the Steps in a Child Custody Case?

The process that leads to a court decision about child custody is complex, and it's neither possible nor desirable in this short book to describe the entire process in detail. It's important, however, for you to have some familiarity with six aspects of child custody litigation: (a) the burden of proof, (b) temporary custody, (c) discovery, (d) the finality of the judge's custody decision, (e) appeal to a higher court, and (f) future modification of child custody decisions. These vitally important aspects of the custody process are discussed below.

Who Has the Burden of Proof, and
What Difference Does It Make?

Burden of proof sounds like some technical legal principle that could hardly be very important to parents, but nothing could be further from the truth. The burden of proof often determines who wins or loses custody.

When one parent tries to gain custody by accusing the other parent of misbehavior (e.g., child molestation, alcohol abuse, violence), the accusing parent has the burden of proof, which means that the accuser has the burden of proving the misbehavior in court. Thus, if you accuse your spouse of abusing your child, you are the accuser, and you have the burden of proof. Of course, your attorney is the one who actually presents in court the evidence that is designed to prove the accusation, or as lawyers say, carry the burden of proof. Nevertheless, although your attorney presents the evidence, it's you—the accuser—who ultimately shoulders the burden of proof and, along with it, the fallout if you fail to carry the burden.

Here is an example of what can happen. Ruth sought custody of her four-year-old son, Tim. Ruth accused her husband, Bob, of sexually abusing Tim. Bob denied the accusation and charged that Ruth invented the accusation to get revenge for Bob's decision to end the marriage. Ruth was the accuser and thus she had the burden of proving the sexual abuse. Recall, however, sexual abuse is often extremely difficult to prove. Unfortunately for Ruth, she was unable to prove the abuse in court: She failed to carry her burden of proof. The judge became convinced that Ruth was a false accuser. Not only that, the judge firmly believes that any woman who would stoop to such a scurrilous accusation is unfit for custody. Thus, in the final analysis, the judge awarded custody of Tim to his father. Ruth lost because she failed to carry her burden of proof. Poor Ruth. Poor Timmy.

Should I Try for Temporary Custody?

When parents are battling over custody, a trial will be necessary unless the parents work out a custody arrangement on their own. As you probably know, however, it usually takes months to get a trial date on a judge's busy calendar. This raises the critical issue of who has custody in the interim. Of course, in some cases parents agree on temporary custody. When they can't agree, however, either parent can ask a judge for *temporary custody*. The judge's decision regarding temporary custody remains in effect until the same or a different judge changes temporary custody or until the matter is finally resolved in a trial or by agreement.

An example may be useful to illustrate temporary custody: Sarah's lawyer started a divorce by filing a petition in family court. Along with the petition, Sarah's attorney filed a motion for temporary child custody. A *motion* is simply a request—written or oral—that a judge make a particular decision. In addition to requesting temporary custody, Sarah's motion sought temporary child support. The motion provided a brief factual account of why Sarah was entitled to temporary custody and support.

Because Sarah's case was an emergency, the judge had authority to grant her motion on the spot, despite the fact that Sarah's husband was not notified of the motion or given an opportunity to tell his side of the story. When one party approaches a judge alone, without notifying the other side, it's called an *ex parte communication* with the judge. The law sets strict limits on ex parte communications.

When a judge grants or approves a motion for temporary child custody, especially an ex parte motion, the judge typically schedules a brief court hearing a few days later to give both sides an opportunity to have their say. That's what happened to Sarah. The judge granted her ex parte motion for temporary custody and support. Three days later, both Sarah and her husband were in court. After listening to Sarah and her husband, the judge continued Sarah's temporary custody and scheduled a custody trial in four months.

When one parent suspects the other of child abuse, the first thought is to rush to court for emergency temporary custody. The protective parent thinks, "Temporary custody is the way to go. The judge can give me immediate temporary custody and deny visitation to the abuser." But wait! Before you rush off to court, let's think this through. Although a motion for emergency temporary custody often is "the way to go," dashing to court is not always wise. Remember, if you seek temporary custody based on an allegation of child abuse, *you have the burden of proof:* You must prove the abuse. Although the judge won't require a high degree of proof for temporary custody, the judge will require some evidence, not just suspicion, speculation, or fear.

Whether you are just beginning your fight for custody or are nearing the end, it can be very dangerous to allege sexual abuse before you can prove it, and if you seek temporary custody before you can prove the abuse, you run the risk of being labeled a false accuser. Once that label attaches, it's extremely difficult to shake. If you are perceived as a false accuser, you have little chance of getting temporary custody, let alone permanent custody.

But you say, "Well, that's all very nice, but what am I supposed to do if I suspect abuse before I have the evidence to prove it? I can't just sit here twiddling my thumbs while the evidence slowly builds up.

My child needs protection today, not next week or next month!" You're right, of course. Nevertheless, I stand by my belief that rushing to court can be extremely dangerous for your and your child.

Consider Betty's case. Betty is separated from her husband, Jake. Betty and Jake have a three-year-old daughter, Sally. Based on something Sally said after a bath, Betty suspected for the first time that Jake was sexually abusing the little girl at his apartment on weekends. It's Friday afternoon and Jake will be there in two hours to pick up Sally for the weekend. What is Betty to do?

First, Betty should call her lawyer. If she doesn't have a lawyer, she needs one immediately. This is a genuine emergency, and mistakes at this stage can haunt Betty for the rest of her life. Deciding whether to seek temporary custody on the basis of child sexual abuse is a momentous decision that no parent should make alone. It's to be hoped that the lawyer is sufficiently knowledgeable about sexual abuse to provide an accurate assessment of the evidence. (See Chapter 6 on finding a lawyer.)

There are numerous options for Betty to consider. The lawyer may advise going to court immediately or waiting for further evidence. Perhaps, this is not the time to alert Jake to Betty's suspicions. Is there some legitimate reason to cancel the upcoming visit without mentioning abuse? The lawyer may advise a call to the child's pediatrician or child protective services.

If the decision is made to seek emergency temporary custody, the attorney may advise against mentioning sexual abuse. There may be other grounds for temporary custody that are easier to prove. For example, if Jake uses illegal drugs or drinks to excess, the substance abuse is likely to be easier to prove than sexual abuse. Whatever the decision, the lawyer's advice is critical.

Temporary custody is critical for protecting sexually abused children, but as in all aspects of this emotional and difficult issue, you've got to think before you act.

What Is Pretrial Discovery?

Pretrial discovery is an important aspect of civil lawsuits, including divorce and child custody cases. Discovery consists of several techniques that lawyers use long before trial to find out—discover—as much as possible about the other side's case.

As part of discovery, a lawyer typically takes *depositions* of witnesses for the other side. A deposition is much like testifying in court except that the deposition usually takes place in an attorney's office. Attending the deposition are the person being deposed (called the deponent), the lawyers, the parties, and a court reporter. The court reporter creates a verbatim record of everything that is said "on the record" at the deposition. The judge does not attend. Prior to questioning by the attorney who requested the deposition, the court reporter administers the oath to the deponent. The questioning lawyer is allowed to ask about anything that has a connection to the lawsuit. A deposition may last minutes; hours; or, in rare cases, days. If your deposition is coming up, don't go without a lawyer. Remember, the other lawyer is deposing you to uncover your weaknesses. You need your lawyer at your side.

In addition to depositions, lawyers prepare written questions called *interrogatories* and *requests for admissions* that are sent to the other side and must be answered in writing. Again, I advise you never to respond to a set of interrogatories or requests for admissions—or any other discovery document, for that matter—on your own.

Is the Judge's Custody Decision Final or Can the Decision Be Modified in the Future?

In the U.S. legal system—criminal and civil—a judge's a decision at the end of a case, called a *final judgment* or *final decree*, is just that, final. The case is over. The losing party can't begin the case anew. Lawyers use the Latin phrase *res judicata*, which means "a thing decided," to describe the finality of judgments and decrees.

An example may illustrate the effect of res judicata. Suppose Allen is driving down the street and hits Sarah, a pedestrian. Sarah sues Allen, claiming he was negligent. At trial, the jury evaluates the evidence and decides that is was actually Sarah who caused the accident. The jury concludes that Allen was traveling at the speed limit when Sarah stepped off the curb right into the path of Allan's car. After the jury renders its verdict, the judge signs a final judgment in Allen's favor. Obviously, Sarah is not happy with the result. Nevertheless, because the judgment is final—because it's res judicata—Sarah can't sue Allen again. Sarah may have the right to appeal to a higher court (see next section), but she can't start her lawsuit over again. To put it colloquially: Sarah gets only one bite at the apple.

The principle that judgments and decrees are final applies in divorce and child custody litigation, but with a twist. You will recall from earlier in this chapter that a judgment or decree of divorce affects five major aspects of a marriage: (a) the divorce itself, (b) division of property, (c) spousal support, (d) child support, and (e) child custody. When it comes to the principle of finality of judgments, these five aspects of divorce are divided into two categories:

▼ Category 1: The Judgment or Decree Is Final Regarding the Divorce and Division of Property

Normal principles of res judicata apply to the divorce itself and the division of property. Thus, once the judgment or decree of divorce is final, the parties are no longer married, and this fact can't be relitigated. The same is true regarding the division of property (e.g., house, bank accounts, etc.). The property division is res judicata, and the parties can't relitigate the division of property.

▼ Category 2: The Judgment or Decree Is Final Regarding Child Custody, Child Support, and Spousal Support, *but the Judgment or Decree Can Be Modified in the Future If Circumstances Change Substantially*

Turning to child custody, child support, and spousal support, the principle of finality of judgments applies here too, but in a special way. Let's begin with child custody. When it comes to custody, two aspects of res judicata require discussion. First, a judge's decision regarding *temporary* custody is not a final judgment. Therefore, res judicata does not apply to temporary custody, and a judge may change temporary custody without offending the principle of the finality of judgments.

The second way in which the principle of finality applies uniquely in child custody cases relates to the judge's *final* custody judgment or decree, that is, the judgment or decree that awards final custody to one parent and visitation to the other. The final custody judgment or decree *is* res judicata regarding all the evidence that was presented or that was available for presentation at the custody trial. The losing side can't have another trial on that evidence, and in this respect a final custody judgment or decree is no different from any other final judgment. When it comes to custody, however, there is an extremely important way in which a final judgment or decree is different from a normal judgment. Unlike nearly all other final judgments in the U.S. legal system, a final custody judgment or decree *can* be modified in the future *if* circumstances change significantly from the circumstances that existed at the time of the original custody judgment or decree.

This is all rather technical and dry, so allow me to illustrate what I'm talking about with three examples. The first example does not involve child abuse: Sue sought a divorce and sole custody of her two children. Sue charged her husband, Phil, with ignoring the children. Phil shot back that Sue drank too much, and he too sought sole custody. At the custody trial, Sue had the burden of proving that Phil ignored the children, and Phil had the burden of proving Sue's drinking. The judge considered the evidence as it existed *at the time of the trial*. Sue prevailed, and the judge signed a final judgment awarding sole custody to Sue. The judgment was res judicata. Phil could not ask for another trial on the evidence that existed at the time of the trial.

But what about the future? Can Phil go back to court at some future date to ask for a change of custody? The answer may be yes, but *not* on the basis of the evidence that existed *at the time* of the original custody trial. The judge's custody decision on the basis of that evidence is res judicata. But if circumstances change substantially *in the future*, Phil may return to court and ask a judge to reexamine the custody issue. If this happens, Phil will not ask the judge to revisit the evidence considered at the original trial. Rather, Phil will ask the judge to modify the original custody decision on the basis of substantial changes that have occurred *since* the original decision. Thus, suppose that a year after the custody trial, Sue is seriously injured and can no longer care for the children. Now the circumstances have changed substantially from the circumstances at the original custody trial. In light of these substantially changed circumstances, Phil may ask a judge to give custody to him. Phil's request does not violate the res judicata principle because Phil is not asking for another trial on the circumstances that existed at the time of the original custody trial.

Now let's take a look at a second example, this time involving child sexual abuse: Linda suspected that her husband, Mack, was sexually abusing their daughter. Linda started a divorce and sought sole custody. Mack denied the abuse and charged that Linda was a vindictive, hysterical woman who invented the abuse charges. Mack won the custody battle and the judge signed a final custody judgment giving custody to him. Linda can't have a second trial on the evidence of abuse that existed at the time of the trial. As to that evidence the judge's decision is res judicata. What can Linda do? She can appeal to a higher court, but as I explain in the next section, Linda's chances of success on appeal are slim.

Linda's only real hope is that circumstances will change substantially in the future. If that happens, Linda can go back to court and ask a judge to *modify* the original custody decree. As to the evidence that existed *at the time of the original trial*, however, the decision in Mack's favor is final. It's res judicata. And this is true even though Mack really was sexually abusing his daughter! Mack won in court, and that's what counts.

Our third example again involves child sexual abuse. Gail and Harry were married in 1990. In 1997, Gail started divorce and child custody proceedings when her five-year-old daughter, Hillary, revealed that Harry was molesting her. Harry denied Gail's accusations and decided to fight for custody himself. Gail was unable to prove the abuse, and she lost custody. Gail's is another in the depressing line of backfire cases. The judge's custody decision was final—res judicata. Gail appealed to a higher court, but the appellate judges approved the custody decision. Gail was limited to weekly visits with Hillary.

Two years after the original custody decision, Gail picked Hillary up for her weekly visit. On the way to the mall, Hillary disclosed further abuse by her father. The abuse had progressed to full sexual intercourse and Hillary complained of a vaginal discharge. Gail called her lawyer, who advised her to go the hospital emergency room. The doctor found physical evidence of recent sexual abuse. Hillary made a detailed disclosure to the doctor. A laboratory test disclosed gonorrhea, a sexually transmitted disease. Now Gail had compelling *new* evidence of sexual abuse. Armed with this new evidence, Gail went back to court and proved the substantially changed circumstances that are required to modify custody. This time, Gail won.

Now back to you, the reader. Suppose you accuse your husband of sexually abusing your child. You go to court seeking custody, but for some reason you lose. The judge gives custody to your husband. Disaster! The judge's final custody decree is res judicata as to the circumstances at the time of the custody trial. You can't change the original custody decree. Is there any hope? Yes, there's a glimmer of hope. The custody decree is subject to modification in the future if circumstances change. Don't get your hopes up too high, however. A parent who tries to modify a custody decree has a tough, uphill battle. Modification is allowed only when circumstances change *substantially* from the circumstances that existed at the time of the original custody decision. Children are usually better off in a long-term, stable custodial arrangement, and the parent who wants to upset that stability has to convince a judge that circumstances have changed so dramatically that the judge should take another look at the best interest of the children. In a case like Gail's, with powerful new evidence of sexual abuse, modification is likely. Most of the time, however, the evidence is not so strong and the chances of success are not high. Despite the fact that modification of custody is difficult, the possibility of returning to court in the future is, for many mothers, the thin ray of hope that keeps them going.

If I Lose in Court, Can I Appeal to a Higher Court?

The court system is divided into two levels: trial courts and appellate courts. All trials are held in trial courts. Appellate courts do not hold trials. Appellate courts review the decisions of trial judges to see if serious legal mistakes were made and, if so, to correct those mistakes. When an appellate court is persuaded that serious legal errors infected a trial, the appellate judges may order a new trial before the same or a different trial judge.

If you lose custody, you have a right to appeal the judge's decision to an appellate court. An appeal must be filed within a short period of time, typically thirty days, and if the deadline is missed no appeal is allowed.

I'm afraid that if you lose custody your chances of success on appeal are modest at best. Remember that appellate court judges don't hold another trial. Appellate judges generally don't consider new evidence, and appellate judges are very reluctant to second-guess a trial judge's decision about which witnesses to believe. Thus, if the judge in your case believes your husband and disbelieves you, the appellate judges are unlikely to part company with the trial judge. Appellate judges usually step in only when serious legal errors were committed by the trial judge.

Conclusion

When children are abused by a parent, the family court is available to protect the child. Great care must be exercised, however, before you go to court. Success is not preordained, and protective parents must proceed cautiously.

10

Child Protective Services and Juvenile Court

Every community has a government system to protect children from abuse and neglect. The system has three main components: (a) child protective services (CPS); (b) the courts, including the juvenile court; and (c) law enforcement. In this chapter, I focus briefly on CPS and the juvenile court. The criminal justice system is described in Chapter 8; the family court, in Chapter 9. Because this chapter is short, I depart from the usual format of setting out questions at the beginning.

Child Protective Services

The government agency with primary responsibility for protecting children from abuse and neglect is CPS. CPS is normally a branch of the county social services or welfare department. CPS is not a law enforcement agency, and the professionals employed by CPS are social workers, not police officers. CPS social workers investigate cases of physical abuse, sexual abuse, and neglect (see Chapter 2 for the meaning of these terms).

In a few communities, CPS investigates all allegations of child abuse, whether the offender is a parent, another family member, an acquaintance, or a stranger. More often, however, the mission of CPS is limited to protecting children from abuse within the family, particularly abuse by parents. In most communities, CPS does not become involved when abuse is committed by adults outside the family. When CPS social workers learn of extrafamilial abuse, they usually let the police handle the investigation.

CPS is staffed by social workers who work very hard to protect children. CPS has an extraordinarily difficult job, and in my many years in the field of child protection, I have been impressed at how often CPS does its job well. Of course, CPS is a bureaucracy, and like all bureaucracies it occasionally drops the ball. In Chapter 1, for example, you saw how the incompetence of CPS social workers contributed to Sue's tragic inability to protect her children from their abusive father. Despite some notable failures, CPS is normally a staunch supporter of children and an ally of protective parents.

Juvenile Court

Every county has a court that is responsible for two types of cases involving young people: juvenile delinquency cases and child abuse and neglect cases. Juvenile delinquency is criminal activity committed by minors, primarily teenagers. Although juvenile delinquency is an important social issue, delinquency is beyond the scope of this book and I won't discuss it further, except to say that when teenagers sexually abuse younger children, the offending youngster may be taken before the juvenile court on a charge of delinquency. The juvenile court judge may order the young offender into treatment, place him in an institution, or take other steps to protect the community and reform the boy's deviant sexual interest in children.

The second important responsibility of the juvenile court is protecting children from abuse and neglect. For the most part, the juvenile court's authority is limited to abuse that occurs within the family. The juvenile court does not typically exercise authority over abuse by strangers, teachers, coaches, or relatives who do not live with the child. Abuse by outsiders is handled in criminal court.

The juvenile court judge has broad authority over parents who abuse or neglect their children. For example, the judge can remove the child from the parents' custody and establish conditions the parents must fulfill to regain custody. The juvenile court judge can order maltreating parents to attend counseling or parenting classes or participate in other services. If efforts to reform an abusive parent fail, the juvenile court judge has the power to terminate the legal relationship between the abusive parent and the child, although this drastic measure is used only as a last resort.

In some cities, the juvenile court is housed in a separate courthouse with two or more judges and a staff of probation officers and social workers. In small communities and rural areas, one or two judges are responsible for all court work, including criminal, civil, and juvenile court cases.

The Child Abuse Reporting Law

Every state has a law that requires professionals who have contact with children to report suspected child abuse and neglect to CPS. Thus, teachers, doctors, nurses, police, and mental health professionals must notify CPS whenever they suspect a child has been abused or neglected.

In many cases, parents first begin to suspect sexual abuse when their child's behavior changes or when the child hints that something "bad" happened. The parent is likely to consult the child's pediatrician or a mental health professional. Under the child abuse reporting law, the professional *must* notify CPS. Indeed, professionals can get in serious trouble if they fail to report suspected abuse or neglect to CPS.

How a Typical Case Works Its Way
Through CPS and Juvenile Court

CPS receives reports of child abuse from parents, neighbors, doctors, teachers, and others. When a report is received, a CPS social worker, sometimes called an intake worker, decides whether an investigation is warranted. If so, a social worker is dispatched to interview the child, the parents, and others who may have relevant information. If the social worker believes a crime has been committed, the police are notified.

When a CPS investigation uncovers evidence of abuse or neglect, the social worker has several options. If only one parent is responsible for the abuse or neglect, and the maltreating parent is willing to move out or there is very little likelihood of further maltreatment, the social worker will probably leave the child at home under the protection of the nonabusive parent. If the abusive parent poses an immediate threat to the child and refuses to vacate the family home, the social worker or a police officer may take the child into emergency protective custody. When one parent is abusive and the other parent can't or won't protect the child, protective custody may be necessary.

When a child is taken into emergency protective custody by a social worker or the police, the child is placed with relatives or in a foster home or children's receiving home. As soon as the child is removed, CPS is required to commence proceedings in the juvenile court. Within a day or two, the juvenile court judge decides whether the child should remain in protective custody or return home.

Whether or not a child is taken into emergency protective custody, if CPS believes abuse or neglect occurred and the child needs protection, CPS requests the appropriate government attorney to commence legal proceedings in the juvenile court. The attorney, who is typically the local district attorney, files a document called a *petition* with the juvenile court. The parents may retain an attorney to contest the allegations of maltreatment. In many counties, if parents can't afford an attorney, the county will pay for the parents' attorney.

In most juvenile court cases, the parents, with the assistance of their lawyer, work out an agreement with the government attorney and CPS. For example, the parents may agree to seek counseling. Thus, most juvenile court cases do not proceed all the way to a trial on the allegations of abuse. Social workers employed by CPS or the juvenile court monitor the parents to ensure that progress is being made. The ultimate goal is usually to keep the family together and help the parents avoid further maltreatment.

In many communities, CPS is reluctant to become involved when parents are embroiled in child custody or visitation litigation in family court. CPS social workers may conclude that the family court judge will protect the child without assistance from CPS or the juvenile court. Of course, in many cases this conclusion is warranted. In other cases, however, it's appropriate for CPS to become involved despite the fact that the family court is also playing a role. Each case should be decided on its own merits, with the focus on the safety of the child.

Part IV

Proving Child Sexual Abuse in Court

*Overcoming Obstacles and
Protecting Your Child*

How do you prove child sexual abuse in court? Two essentials are required: Strong evidence and a good lawyer. Without strong evidence, the world's best lawyer can't prove abuse. On the other side of the coin, a poor lawyer can make a shambles of strong evidence. The chapters in Part IV focus attention on piecing together a strong legal case. Finding a competent lawyer is discussed in Chapter 6.

Before I discuss proof of sexual abuse, it's important to revisit a point I made earlier (pp. 107-108) about a vitally important but frequently overlooked reality of the adversary system of justice: Strange as it sounds, when one parent accuses the other of child sexual abuse, the issue in court is *not* whether the abuse happened. Rather, the issue is whether the accusing parent can *prove* that it happened. As far as the law is concerned, nothing happened—there was no abuse—unless the accuser convinces the judge that the accusation is true. Remember, if you are the accuser, you have the burden of proof (see p. 108). If you fail to carry your burden—if your evidence falls short—the judge may conclude that your accusation was, at worst, a deliberate lie or, at best, an innocent misunderstanding. If the judge concludes that your accusation was fabricated, you may be branded a "hysterical woman who'll do anything to hurt her man" and unfit to care for children. If you charge child sexual abuse but fail to prove it, you could *lose* custody of the child you want so desperately to protect. This tragedy has befallen many women.

With the harsh reality of the burden of proof in mind, let's begin Part IV. In Chapter 11, I discuss obstacles that await you in court if you accuse your child's father of sexual abuse. In Chapter 12, I shift gears to analyze the importance of sorting out your suspicions about abuse so that you avoid jumping too quickly to conclusions. Chapter 12 also provides a frank discussion of how women's emotions are sometimes used against them. In Chapter 13, I provide practical guidance on the legal implications of talking to your child about abuse. In particular, I emphasize the danger of asking your child what lawyers call leading questions. Chapter 13 also gives you advice on what to watch for and document when your child describes sexual abuse. Finally, in Chapter 14, I tackle the complex issue of how changes in your child's behavior may provide evidence of sexual abuse.

11

Obstacles to Proving Child
Sexual Abuse in Court

This chapter covers obstacles to proving child sexual abuse. If you allege abuse, you are likely to encounter one or more of these obstacles on your way to proving abuse and protecting your child:

- [ ] Why is it often so difficult to prove child sexual abuse in court? (p. 126)
- [ ] It seems that there is a tradition of not believing women and children who claim to be victims of sexual assault. Why is this? (p. 126)
- [ ] Are doubts about women and children's credibility especially strong in child custody cases? (p. 133)
- [ ] What does research on fabricated allegations of abuse show? (p. 133)
- [ ] Do mothers make all the allegations of sexual abuse in custody cases? (p. 135)
- [ ] What is parental alienation syndrome, and why is it so often used against mothers? (p. 135)
- [ ] How reliable are children as witnesses? (p. 138)

Why Is It Often So Difficult to Prove
Child Sexual Abuse in Court?

If you allege that your child was sexually abused, you come face to face with the fact that sexual abuse is often very difficult to prove in court. The U.S. Supreme Court has observed that "child abuse is one of the most difficult crimes to detect and prosecute" (*Pennsylvania v. Ritchie*, 1987, p. 60). Child sexual abuse is hard to prove because it occurs in secret and the child is usually the only witness. Although many children are good witnesses, others are too young, too shy, or too traumatized to testify. Medical and other corroborating evidence of abuse exists in only a small percent of cases. Unfortunately, there is no psychological test or device that determines whether a child was sexually abused. Nor is there a psychological test that determines whether a man abused a child (see p. 46). In the final analysis, therefore, the reason it's so hard to prove sexual abuse is that in many cases there is a dearth of evidence. Because sexual abuse is often so difficult to prove, you and your attorney must search out every clue, every scrap of evidence. But what are the clues? What are the scraps of evidence to watch for? We'll get to that in Chapters 13 and 14. Now, however, we need to turn our attention to the long legacy of skepticism about allegations of sexual abuse.

It Seems That There Is a Tradition of Not
Believing Women and Children Who Claim to
Be Victims of Sexual Assault. Why Is This?

In Western society, there is a long tradition of disbelieving women who claim they were raped or sexually assaulted. This tradition of disbelief extends equally if not more so to children. But why? The pioneering psychiatrist Roland Summit believes society has a kind of blind spot for child sexual abuse, a collective desire to avert our eyes from this ugly reality (1988). Out of sight, out of mind. Until recently, society was quite good at ignoring child sexual abuse. Yet, the problem just won't go away. The psychologist and historian Erna Olafson and her psychiatrist colleagues David Corwin and Roland Summit observe, "Sexual abuse of children has repeatedly surfaced into public and professional awareness in the past century and a half, only to be re-suppressed by the negative reaction it elicits" (Summit, Olafson, &

Corwin, 1993, p. 8). A useful way to understand the remarkable tenacity of skepticism regarding allegations of sexual abuse is to examine how the issue surfaced and submerged over time.

▼ Cycles of Recognition and Denial

In 1857, the influential French physician Ambrose Tardieu published a book titled *A Medico-Legal Study of Assaults on Decency* (1857/1873). In this unique book, Tardieu discussed many instances of child sexual abuse. Later, Tardieu reviewed cases of attempted and completed sexual assault in France between 1858 and 1869. Of the 11,576 cases studied, an astonishing 80% of the victims were children from four to twelve years of age. Tardieu's revelations sparked brief interest in the scientific study of child sexual abuse. According to Summit, "Tardieu generated an oasis of concern for children in a generally indifferent, adult-preoccupied society. Challenging the tradition that children typically lied about sexual assault, a few clinicians dared to argue for the truth and reality of those complaints" (1988, p. 46).

Tardieu's work was met with skepticism. Despite Tardieu's stature as a leader in French medicine, his successors rejected his discoveries about child sexual abuse. Barely a year after Tardieu's death, Alfred Fournier gave a speech at the French Academy of Medicine titled "Simulation of Sexual Attacks on Young Children" (see Summit, 1988, p. 46). Fournier warned that respectable men are targeted for blackmail by depraved children and their lower-class parents. Another successor to Tardieu stated, "Girls accuse their fathers of imaginary assaults on them or on other children in order to obtain their freedom to give themselves over to debauchery" (Brouardel, quoted in Masson, 1984, p. 44). This critic argued that 60% to 80% of children's complaints of sexual abuse are false. In the end, Tardieu's effort to open French eyes to the reality of child sexual abuse was suppressed and forgotten.

The second important recognition of child sexual abuse occurred in 1896, and none other than Sigmund Freud raised the issue. In April of that year, Freud presented a paper at the Vienna Society for Psychiatry and Neurology titled "The Aetiology of Hysteria" (see Summit, 1988). In this paper, Freud theorized that the neurotic symptoms he observed in his adult female patients were caused by sexual abuse during childhood. Freud described this as the "seduction theory." The seduction theory received a chilly reception from Freud's psychiatric colleagues, and not long after he presented the theory, Freud wrote to a friend, "I am as isolated as you could wish me to be: The word has been given out to abandon me, and a void is forming around me" (quoted in Masson, 1984, p. 10). Rather than defend the seduction theory, Freud abandoned the theory in favor of the Oedipus complex, which explains neurotic symptoms in terms of sexual *fantasy* during childhood rather than *actual* sexual abuse. Thus, Freud bowed to criticism of his initial beliefs. Of course, sexual abuse of children did not stop, but society once again closed its eyes.

The third notable recognition of child sexual abuse occurred in the early 1930s with the work of Sandor Ferenczi. Like Freud, Ferenczi was a member of the psychiatric inner circle. Unlike Freud, however, Ferenczi did not abandon his belief that child sexual abuse was responsible for adult neurosis. In 1932, Ferenczi presented a paper titled "The Sexual Passion of Adults and Their Influence on the Character Development and Sexual Development of Children." In the paper, Ferenczi explored the subject of deeply repressed memories of child sexual abuse. According to Roland Summit, "Like Freud 36 years before, Ferenczi hoped to change entrenched beliefs by presenting outrageous discoveries. And like his mentor before him, Ferenczi was banished from kinship. Unlike his teacher, Ferenczi did not recant his beliefs, so he remains an awkward footnote in the chronicle of scientific thought" (1988, p. 49).

Moving forward in time, we are now living in the fourth and most widespread period of recognition that child sexual abuse is a serious problem. I hope that the modern era of recognition is sufficiently well established that we will avoid the mistakes of the past. I am reasonably confident that society will not once more close its eyes to the pain of sexual abuse. Despite my confidence, however, I know the blind spot for sexual abuse still exists and some people prefer to deny the reality of abuse. People continue to make statements like, "Sexual abuse is rare," "You can't trust kids," and "All this fuss about sexual abuse is nothing but hysteria." Thoughts like these perpetuate the legacy of disbelief.

▼ The Contribution of the Professional Literature to the Tradition of Skepticism

Throughout the first six decades of the twentieth century, relatively little was written about child sexual abuse in psychiatric, psychological, medical, and sociological journals. As late as 1977, the famed pediatrician Henry Kempe, who was one of the founders of the modern era of child protection, said in a speech that child sexual abuse was a "hidden pediatric problem and a neglected area" (1978, p. 382). Prior to the mid-1970s, what little professional writing there was about sexual abuse was dominated by four themes: (a) children are responsible for their own molestation, (b) mothers are to blame, (c) child sexual abuse is rare, and (d) sexual abuse does no harm. A few examples from the professional journals of the time illustrate these themes.

Children Are Responsible for Their Own Molestation. In 1937, the psychiatrists Lauretta Bender and Abraham Blau wrote that young incest victims "may not resist and often play an active or even initiating role" (p. 513) in their abuse. Thus, according to Bender and Blau, children are often responsible for their own molestation. Indeed, "the idea that children are responsible for their own seduction has been at the center of almost all writing on sexual abuse since the topic was first broached" (Finkelhor, 1979, p. 11).

Mothers Are to Blame. In early journal articles, children were not the only ones responsible for sexual abuse. Mothers were to blame too. Theresa Reid, former executive director of the American Professional Society on the Abuse of Children, reviewed the early literature and concluded, "Mother-blaming is as common as victim-blaming in the psychological and sociological literature. Mothers of incest victims are routinely referred to as frigid, hostile, unloving women. As women who are so cold and rejecting that they cause their husbands to seek sexual satisfaction elsewhere" (1995).

Child Sexual Abuse Is Rare. Early writers not only blamed the victims and their mothers—they also claimed that child sexual abuse in general occurred so rarely that it was hardly worth getting worked up about. In 1955, a sociologist wrote that sexual abuse is so uncommon that it causes few social problems (Blumer, 1969). A textbook on psychiatry stated that father-daughter incest occurs at a rate of one girl in a million (Henderson, 1975). We know the rate has always been higher.

Sexual Abuse Does No Harm. In addition to claiming that sexual abuse was uncommon, numerous contributors to the early professional literature asserted that abuse does little harm. In 1952, Bender and Grugett wrote, "In contrast to the harsh social taboos surrounding such relationships, there exists no scientific proof that there are any resulting deleterious effects" (p. 827). The famous sex researcher Alfred Kinsey advanced the theory that incest is seldom harmful. In 1953, Kinsey wrote, "It is difficult to understand why a child, except for its cultural conditioning, should be disturbed at having its genitalia touched, or disturbed at seeing the genitalia of other persons, or disturbed at even more specific sexual contacts" (Kinsey, 1953, p. 121). In 1964, Brunold wrote, "Lasting psychological injury as a result of sexual assaults suffered in infancy is not very common" (p. 8). In 1976, one of Kinsey's colleagues, Wardell Pomeroy, wrote, "When we examine a cross-section of the population as we did in the Kinsey Report we find many beautiful and mutually satisfying relationships between fathers and daughters. These may be transient or ongoing, but they have no harmful effects" (p. 13). Finally, in 1979, a professor of social work stated that incest "may be either a positive, healthy experience or, at worst, neutral and dull" (DeMott, 1980). According to the psychologist Anna Salter, "Prior to 1980, it is fair to conclude that the harmfulness of child sexual abuse was not well-established" (1995, p. 165). As the discussion in Chapter 3 makes clear, we know today that child sexual abuse often has serious short- and long-term harmful effects.

Influence of the Psychiatric, Psychological, Medical, and Sociological Literatures. To summarize, prior to the mid-1970s, psychiatric, psychological, medical, and sociological writing on child sexual abuse was quite skeptical about allegations of sexual abuse in general and particularly within the family. The psychiatrist Judith Herman reviewed the early literature and discovered "a vastly elaborated intellectual tradition which served the purpose of suppressing the truth about incest, a tradition which, like so many others, originates in the works of Freud" (1981, p. 9). This institutionalized skepticism played a major role in fueling the tradition of doubt about allegations of child sexual abuse.

▼   The Legal Literature

The tradition of skepticism is not limited to articles in mental health and medical journals. When we shift our attention to writing by lawyers, we find that the level of skepticism is, if anything, higher. Unless you are an attorney, you may not know that law libraries are filled with thousands of articles written by law professors, law students, and practicing attorneys. These articles are contained in journals called law reviews. Hundreds of new law review articles appear yearly. Recently, I examined law review articles on sexual assault. I went as far back in the legal literature as I could, to the late 1880s. To locate articles, I used one of the major law review indexes and looked under the heading of "rape," because until recently there was no subject heading for child sexual abuse. What I found surprised and dismayed me. Prior to approximately 1975, very little was written in law reviews about rape of adult women and even less was written about child sexual abuse. Out of the hundreds of articles published every year, only four or five a year discussed rape or sexual abuse. By contrast, many articles discussed theft, murder, and other crimes. In the mountains of legal writing, the fact that so few pages were devoted to sexual assault speaks volumes. The very silence of legal scholars on the topics of rape and child sexual abuse are proof of society's blind spot.

As I read the relatively few published articles on rape and sexual assault, I was struck by the uniformity of skepticism directed against women and girls (sexual abuse of boys was rarely discussed). Throughout the pre-1975 legal literature, the level of disbelief in law reviews can only be described as remarkable.

Moving from law review articles to books about law, I'll mention just one. John H. Wigmore was one of the most famous legal writers in the United States. Wigmore was a law professor at Harvard, and in 1904 he published the first edition of his monumental twelve-volume treatise on the law of evidence. Although Wigmore was in many ways a brilliant scholar, his thinking about sex offense victims was remarkably negative. Yet, because Wigmore was so influential among judges and attorneys, he contributed mightily to the tradition of skepticism. Wigmore wrote:

> Modern psychiatrists have amply studied the behavior of errant young girls and women coming before the courts in all sorts of cases. Their psychic complexes are multifarious, distorted partly by inherent defects, partly by diseased derangements or abnormal instincts, partly by bad social environments, partly by temporary physiological or emo-

tional conditions. One form taken by these complexes is that of contriving false charges of sexual offenses by men. The unchaste mentally (let us call it) finds incidental but direct expression in the narration of imaginary sex incidents of which the narrator is the heroine or the victim. On the surface the narration is straight-forward and convincing. The real victim, however, too often in such cases is the innocent man. . . . No judge should ever let a sex offense charge go to the jury unless the female complainant's social history and mental makeup have been examined and testified to by a qualified physician. It is time that the courts awakened to the sinister possibilities of injustice that lurk in believing such a witness without careful psychiatric scrutiny. (1904/1970, pp. 736-737, 740)

As you can see, during much of this century, the legal and mental health literatures contributed to the legacy of disbelief about allegations of child sexual abuse. Then, rather suddenly, in the middle of the 1970s, things changed dramatically.

▼   1975—The Great Divide in the Professional Literature

As far as professional writing about child sexual abuse is concerned, 1975 is the great divide. Prior to that year, professional writing, although not monolithic, was largely skeptical. Beginning in approximately 1975, however, there was a virtual explosion of writing that was more sympathetic to victims of rape and sexual assault. What caused this radical shift for the better in professional writing? I believe the feminist movement of the 1960s and 1970s is largely responsible for the more favorable treatment of victims in professional writing.

Turning to the legal literature, most articles in law reviews are written by law professors, and it's probably no coincidence that in the 1970s a substantial number of women finally broke into the teaching ranks of U.S. law schools. Prior to that time, nearly all law professors were men. Much of the post-1975 legal literature of rape and child sexual abuse has been written by female law professors.

The women's movement was not the only factor influencing the increasingly realistic discussion of child sexual abuse. The modern era of child protection coincides almost perfectly with the women's movement. The modern era of child protection got seriously under way in the mid-1960s and was firmly entrenched by 1975. The 1970s witnessed the first important research aimed at understanding the prevalence and harmful effects of child abuse (see the pioneering research of David Finkelhor, 1979, and Diana Russell, 1983, 1986).

Despite the impressive gains of the 1970s and 1980s, the long tradition of skepticism continues to poison the thinking of some judges, attorneys, doctors, and mental health professionals. Indeed, throughout the United States and Europe, the level of skepticism appears to be on the rise again (Beckett, 1996; Myers, 1994). If you claim your child was sexually abused, you can expect doubt from some and outright disbelief from others. As you can see, this attitude is nothing new. It's a product of years of skepticism and disbelief

Are Doubts About Women's and Children's Credibility Especially Strong in Child Custody Cases?

Skepticism about allegations of child sexual abuse is nowhere greater than in child custody and visitation litigation in family court. Some people automatically assume that a parent who alleges sexual abuse during a custody or visitation battle is lying. Indeed, Richard Gardner, a psychiatrist who devotes considerable energy to criticizing the child protection system, writes, "The vast majority of children who profess sexual abuse are fabricators" (1987, p. 274). Although Gardner's statement lacks empirical support, his statement, and others like it, are common in family court.

Do deliberately false charges of child abuse occur? Of course. Some dishonest or disturbed parents fabricate allegations of abuse to gain an unfair advantage in court or injure the other parent. Such dishonesty appears to be uncommon, but it happens, and it doesn't take very many fabricated claims to undermine the credibility of honest parents trying to protect their children.

What Does Research on Fabricated Allegations of Abuse Show?

Several researchers have investigated the rate of false reports of child sexual abuse. Most of the studies are concentrated on fabricated reports in the general population. A few studies narrow the focus to child custody disputes.

The psychiatrists David Jones and Mel McGraw (1987) evaluated all cases of suspected child sexual abuse reported to the Denver Social Services Department during 1983. Eight percent of the reports were probably deliberate fabrications. Among the small group of fabricated claims, nearly all were made by adults, not children. Recently, Jones, along with the pediatricians Kim Oates and Richard Krugman and others, replicated the Denver study and found similar low rates of fabricated reports of child sexual abuse (Oates, Jones, Denson, Sirotnak, & Krugman, n.d.). Other researchers also find low rates of fabricated allegations. (See Appendix C for further discussion of false allegations.)

When the focus of research turns to false allegations in custody cases, several researchers report higher rates of fabrication. The psychiatrist Arthur Green (1986) evaluated eleven suspected cases of child sexual abuse and concluded that four of the allegations were probably fabricated (36%). The psychiatrists Elizabeth Benedek and Diane Schetky (1985) were unable to document abuse in ten of eighteen cases (55%). Commenting on these studies, the psychiatrist Kathleen Quinn writes, "These are very small clinical samples with a selective pattern of referrals" (1988, p. 181). The social worker Lucy Berliner adds that these and similar studies "describe a limited number of cases referred for evaluation. In most of the cases described, there were multiple evaluations and conflicting opinions among professionals. Ultimately, there is no way of knowing that the authors' assessments are accurate" (1988, p. 52).

David Jones and Ann Seig evaluated twenty cases in which sexual abuse allegations arose in custody disputes (1988). Jones and Seig found that 20% of the allegations probably were fabricated. They concluded, "The setting of the divorce and custody dispute does seem to raise the likelihood that clinicians will find an increased number of fictitious allegations. However, in this study nearly 3/4 (70%) were reliable, arguing strongly against the practice of dismissing allegations in custody disputes as most likely false" (p. 29).

There is little doubt that an increasing number of parents caught up in custody litigation raise the possibility of sexual abuse. There is no evidence, however, that the number of allegations has reached flood stage. Allegations of child sexual abuse occur in a small percentage of custody and visitation cases. Moreover, and this is important, there is no convincing evidence that a substantial portion of the allegations are false. Yet, because fabricated allegations of sexual abuse do arise in custody and visitation cases, there is reason to proceed cautiously. As David Jones and Ann Seig point out, however, the higher percent of fabricated allegations should not lead to exaggerated skepticism about such allegations (1988). Many are true.

Do Mothers Make All the Allegations of Sexual Abuse in Custody Cases?

There is widespread belief that mothers make nearly all allegations of child sexual abuse in custody cases. The perception that allegations of abuse are "women's weapons" undermines the credibility of women in the eyes of some people, especially men. Research does not support the belief mothers are responsible for nearly all charges. The sociologists Nancy Thoennes and Patricia Tjaden conducted research on allegations of sexual abuse in custody cases and found that mothers in their study accused fathers in 48% of the cases (1990). In another 6% of cases, women accused second husbands—stepfathers—of molesting children from the woman's prior marriage. As to other allegations, Thoennes and Tjaden write:

> In 10% of the cases, fathers alleged that a child was sexually abused by the mother's new male partner, while in 6% of the cases the mother herself was accused of abuse. Moreover, nearly 20% involved accusations by mothers (13%) or fathers (6%) against other relatives and family friends. Finally, in 11% of the cases the allegations of sexual abuse originated with someone other than a parent. (p. 154)

Although mothers file the majority of abuse allegations, the belief that women make nearly all such charges is untrue. Moreover, it is not surprising that women make most of the accusations: Most perpetrators are men.

What Is Parental Alienation Syndrome, and Why Is It So Often Used Against Mothers?

A syndrome is a group of medical or psychological symptoms that occur together. For example, posttraumatic stress disorder (PTSD) is a psychological syndrome that is seen in some sexually abused children and adults (see Chapter 3). Rape trauma syndrome describes the psychological aftereffects of rape. Battered woman syndrome helps explain why some abused women remain with their battering partner.

Psychological and medical syndromes play an important role in understanding behavior and providing treatment to victims of abuse. Unfortunately, there is one so-called syndrome that, in my opinion, does tremendous harm to many children and their parents, particularly mothers seeking custody in family court. I speak of the psychiatrist Richard Gardner's *parental alienation syndrome*. Gardner writes:

> One outgrowth of this warfare [over custody] was the development in children of what I refer to as the parental alienation syndrome. Typically, the child viciously vilifies one of the parents and idealizes the other. This is not caused simply by parental brainwashing of the child. Rather the children themselves contribute their own scenarios in support of the favored parent. My experience has been that in about 80 to 90 percent of cases the mother is the favored parent and the father the vilified one. (1989, p. 2)

Gardner is a strident and outspoken critic of certain aspects of the child protection system. Apparently, Gardner believes the United States is in the throes of mass hysteria over child sexual abuse. He writes, "Sex-abuse hysteria is omnipresent" (1992, p. xxv). In his 1991 book titled *Sex Abuse Hysteria: Salem Witch Trials Revisited*, Gardner is harshly critical of an unspecified portion of the mental health professionals, investigators, and prosecutors trying to protect children. For example, Gardner accuses some prosecutors of gratifying their own sexual urges and sadistic tendencies through involvement in sexual abuse cases. Gardner even goes so far as to say that "there is a bit of pedophilia in every one of us" (p. 118). It seems clear that Richard Gardner can't claim to be balanced or objective when it comes to allegations of child sexual abuse.

Gardner's parental alienation syndrome has not, to my knowledge, been subjected to empirical study, research, or testing. Nor, to my knowledge, has his discussion of the syndrome been published in peer-reviewed medical or scientific journals. Rather, the syndrome is little more than Richard Gardner's opinions, based on his clinical experience. Of course, the fact that parental alienation syndrome is based on one man's experience does not imply there is something wrong with the syndrome. Nevertheless, it's clear that the syndrome is not accepted as a scientifically reliable way of telling whether an allegation of sexual abuse is true or false. Moreover, in my opinion, much of Gardner's writing, including his discussion of his parental alienation syndrome, is biased against women. This gender bias infects the syndrome and makes it a powerful tool to undermine the credibility of women who allege child sexual abuse. Because claims of parental alienation syndrome perpetuate and exacerbate gender bias against women, I believe the syndrome sheds much more darkness than light on this difficult issue.

In the final analysis, parental alienation syndrome is little more than a scientific-sounding label for conduct that judges and lawyers have known about for years. In some custody battles, one parent attempts to turn the child against the other parent. The child becomes a pawn in the struggle over custody. Such parental behavior is inexcusable and should not be tolerated. In view of the damage inflicted by parental alienation syndrome and its bias against women, however, the wiser course would be to discard the syndrome and confront unethical behavior head on.

Another term coined by Richard Gardner is *sex abuse legitimacy scale*. Of this scale, Lucy Berliner and Jon Conte write:

A specific and disturbing example of using [behavioral] indicators as determinative of true versus false cases is that of the Sexual Abuse Legitimacy (SAL) Scale. This "scale" claims to be able to discriminate between "bona fide" and "fabricated" cases by indicating the presence or absence of a series of characteristics of cases. There are 26 criteria dealing with the alleged victim, 11 dealing with the accuser (usually the mother), and 13 dealing with the accused (usually the father). Criteria are divided into those which are very valuable (worth 3 points if present), moderately valuable (2 points), and low but potentially valuable (1 point). Separate scores are generated for the child, the accused, and the accuser. Scores in the range of 50% of the maximum or more are highly suggestive of bona fide sexual abuse and those quite low (below 10%) are fabricated. Sample criteria are: for the child, very hesitant to divulge the abuse or if no quality of a litany; for the accuser, appreciates importance of relationship between child and father or initially denies abuse; for the accused, allegation not in the context of divorce or career choice involving children.

The SAL scale suffers many of the problems that all indicator approaches suffer and a number which are unique. It is based entirely on the author's personal observations of an unknown number of cases seen in a specialized forensic practice. Although reference is made to studies carried out "between 1982 and 1987" these are unpublished, not described, and are of unknown value. There are no studies which have determined if the scale can be coded reliably. Many of the criteria are poorly defined. There have been no scientific tests of the ability of the SAL Scale to discriminate among cases. There is no evidence that the numerical scores have any real meaning. Indeed, to our knowledge, the entire scale and parent alienation syndrome upon which it is based have never been subjected to any kind of peer review or empirical test. In sum, there is no demonstrated ability of this scale to make valid predictions based on the identified criteria. (1993, p. 114)

In 1988, Jon Conte wrote that Gardner's sex abuse legitimacy scale is "Probably the most unscientific piece of garbage I've seen in the field in all my time. To base social policy on something as flimsy as this is exceedingly dangerous" (Moss, 1988, p. 26).

If you are a woman and you allege child sexual abuse by your child's father, expect to be attacked with Richard Gardner's parental alienation syndrome. Gardner's writing is popular among attorneys who represent men accused of abuse and among some mental health professionals. Your attorney must be prepared to counteract the misleading and destructive use of parental alienation syndrome and the sex abuse legitimacy scale.

How Reliable Are Children as Witnesses?

Just as there is a long tradition of doubting women who claim rape or sexual assault, there is an equally long tradition of doubting children's credibility. Many people believe children have poor memories, can't tell the difference between reality and fantasy, and are so suggestible that they should not be trusted. Can children be believed?

Children's Memory. During the past ten years, psychologists carried out important research on children's memory. This research confirms that children have good memory ability. The psychologists Robyn Fivush and Jennifer Shukat summarize the research:

> Research over the last decade has amply demonstrated that even quite young children are able to recall personally experienced events accurately over extended periods of time. In fact, 4- and 5-year-old children are able to recall events that occurred 1 to 2 years in the past. . . . Children between the ages of 3 and 6 years are able to give coherent, detailed accounts of past events after long delays. Thus, at least as far as basic memory abilities go, preschool children are competent to testify. (1995, pp. 6, 22)

Of course, children, like adults, forget. No one's memory is perfect. Moreover, children appear to forget some things more quickly than adults. The important point, however, is that children—even young preschoolers—have the ability to remember important events.

Distinguishing Fact From Fantasy. Are young children able to distinguish fact from fantasy? After all, many youngsters believe in Santa Claus, the Easter Bunny, monsters under the bed, and other fanciful creatures. Can a child who thinks Santa is real be trusted? When it comes to some of the finer points of differentiating fantasy from reality, young children are not as accomplished as older children and adults. In the main, however, young children can reliably distinguish fact from fantasy. Moreover, the fact that a young child believes in Santa Claus does not mean the child confuses fact and fantasy. After all, children believe in Santa because their parents tell them he's real!

Suggestibility. The word *suggestible* means easily influenced by suggestion. Are children so suggestible that they can't be trusted? Many people believe children are highly suggestible, especially when questioned by adults. Psychological research discloses, however, that children are not as suggestible as many adults think. By the time children are nine or ten, they appear to be no more suggestible than adults. This is not to say that children approaching adolescence are not suggestible. Given the right circumstances, everyone—children and adults alike—is suggestible. The point is that there is no greater need for concern about suggestibility with older children and adolescents than there is with adults.

Young children, particularly preschoolers, do appear to be more suggestible than older children, at least in some circumstances. Moreover, among preschool-age children, three-year-olds seem to be at the greatest risk of being misled by suggestive questions. At about four years of age, many children's cognitive abilities develop to the point that suggestibility begins to decline.

The fact that young children are suggestible does not mean they can't be trusted. Indeed, young children often are able to resist being misled by suggestive questions. The psychological literature on suggestibility is voluminous, and this is not the place to review the literature in all its complexity. It will suffice to quote briefly from several leading authorities on the subject. The psychologists David Marxsen, John Yuille, and Melissa Nisbet write that the psychological literature "has tended to concentrate on the suggestibility of children and to neglect other topics relevant to those who investigate suspected cases of child sexual abuse" (1995, p. 450). The authors continue:

> That young children are more suggestible than adults is well-established. This does not mean that the investigative interviewing of children is impossible, only that it requires great skill and care. However, the literature's overemphasis on suggestibility can give the police, the judiciary, and media, and the general public the mistaken impression that children are inherently unreliable. . . . The suggestibility problem is a complex one, but the literature . . . give[s] the impression that children are simply untrustworthy witnesses. This is simply not true. . . . Some children (especially very young ones) spontaneously make a false statement in the absence of any risk factors for suggestibility. Conversely, very young children resist suggestion despite the presence of all the factors that might increase suggestibility. (p. 451)

The psychologist Stephen Ceci and his colleagues write:

> Although even adults are suggestible, there appears to be a reliable age-related vulnerability to suggestive postevent questioning, with preschoolers disproportionately more vulner-

able to these forms of suggestion than older children and adults. . . .

In short, there appears to be no useful purpose served by attempting to gainsay what is surely a scientifically robust conclusion, namely, that preschoolers present a special reliability risk if the postevent context has been riddled with repeated, erroneous suggestions. Young children's suggestibility proneness, while probably reduced for bodily events, is by no means nonexistent or negligible.

Having said the above, it is important for the sake of balance to also say that children, no matter how much more suggestible they are than adults, are nevertheless capable of recollecting large amounts of forensically accurate information when the adults who have access to them have not engaged in repeated erroneous suggestions. In many of the studies that have reported age-related differences in suggestibility, young children perform quite well—until and unless an interviewer persists in making repeated erroneous suggestions or subtly rewards the child for inaccurate answers. Short of this, the children do quite well. (Ceci, Huffman, & Smith, 1994, pp. 388-389)

The suggestibility of children is an issue of great concern to professionals who investigate sexual abuse. Children, like adults, can be misled by suggestive questions, and interviewing children requires great skill. When interviews are conducted properly, however, children can provide accurate information. On the other hand, improper interviewing can seriously undermine a child's credibility and lead to inaccuracy.

Experts generally agree that the dangers of suggestive questioning are particularly high with young children. Nevertheless, psychological research reveals that young children are not as suggestible as once believed and can provide accurate and important information when questioned by competent interviewers.

To answer the question asked at the beginning of this section, "Can children be believed?"—Yes, they can. Needless to say, children's statements should not be taken as gospel. Children make mistakes, they forget, they can be misled or coached, and occasionally they lie. The research evidence is clear, however, that children have good memory ability. Children usually can tell the difference between fact and fantasy. Finally, although children are suggestible, adults are too, and children are not so suggestible that their descriptions of abuse should be disregarded. In case after case, children's descriptions of sexual abuse have an undeniable ring of veracity.

12

Sorting Out Your Suspicions,
Controlling Your Emotions

This short chapter covers two potential pitfalls that can ensnare protective parents. First is the danger of misinterpreting innocent behavior as evidence of sexual abuse. Second, there is the unfortunate fact that a woman's natural and appropriate emotions can be used against her.

The Danger of Misinterpretation

Your first suspicion of sexual abuse can arise in several ways. Often, children disclose what happened. Some children come right out with it. Others drop subtle hints that something is wrong. Of course, some children are too confused, frightened, or young to tell, and a parent's suspicion is aroused by changes in the child's behavior. Regardless of how the possibility of sexual abuse appears, you get a terrible sinking feeling. You think, "Oh dear God. This is awful! What if it's true? What should I do?" It's perfectly normal and appropriate to react emotionally to the thought of sexual abuse. Some mothers were victims themselves during childhood, and the idea that their own child could be a victim too is devastating. Whether or not you were sexually abused as a child, your mind floods with thoughts and emotions, including hope that it's not true, fear that it is, outrage, doubt about what to do, and desperation to protect your child. You're on an emotional roller coaster.

The emotions stirred up by sexual abuse have effects that can be both positive and negative. On the positive side, if your child *is* being molested, your emotional reaction gets you started on the road to protection. On the negative side, the emotional reaction that is natural for any loving parent can cloud clear thinking and cause you to jump too quickly to conclusions.

Dealing with the emotions caused by sexual abuse is difficult, and more is said later about the emotional reaction to abuse. For the moment, however, I'd like to ask you put the entire issue of child sexual abuse completely out of your mind. Assume for the moment that you have no suspicion whatever of abuse. Forget child abuse and focus for the moment on the emotions experienced by people who are unhappily married, separated, or divorced. If we are honest, we have to admit that lots of good, decent people who are divorced, separated, or unhappy are, well, not too crazy about each other. And if we are really candid, we have to acknowledge that sometimes unhappily married, separated, or divorced couples hate each other's guts. The negative feelings that sometimes accompany failing and failed marriages cause some people to see only the worst in the spouse. Deep feelings of betrayal and rage cause some people to suspect misbehavior where none exists and to misinterpret the motives and conduct of the spouse. The strong feelings aroused by a bad marriage or divorce do not cloud thinking all the time, but such feelings have the potential to distort objectivity.

Returning now to the subject of child sexual abuse, it's important to understand how the negative emotions generated by an unhappy marriage can lead to unfounded suspicions of child sexual abuse. Consider the case of Brenda and Fred, who were divorced a year ago after Fred had a affair. The divorce was bitter, with Brenda and Fred fighting over the house; spousal support; and, especially, custody of their three-year-old daughter Heather. After a nasty custody battle, Brenda got custody and Fred got weekend visitation. Late one Sunday afternoon, Fred returned Heather from a two-day visit. The little girl seemed unusually quiet. Brenda gave Heather a bath and noticed Heather's genitals were red and irritated. Brenda asked, "How come you're all red down there, honey?" Heather replied, "Owie cause Daddy hurt me." Brenda said, "What did Daddy do?" Heather said, "Finger owie." This was enough to set off alarms. Heather seemed to be saying that her father hurt her genitals with his finger. Heather was red and irritated. Could this be sexual abuse? Brenda got that sinking feeling. She was more than ready to think the worst of Fred, and she quickly concluded that he probably sexually abused their daughter. Brenda's next thought was, "That bastard. He'll never do it again. I'll take his visitation away."

The emotions that flooded over Brenda were a combination of anger from a bitter divorce and Brenda's understandable reaction to what her daughter said. Brenda jumped quickly to the conclusion that Heather was sexually abused. But did she jump too quickly? Was Brenda's thinking clouded by her anger over the divorce? Is there an innocent explanation for Heather's redness and "owie" words? If Brenda rushes to court with accusations of sexual abuse, will she be accusing an innocent man? Suppose Fred *is* innocent. What will the judge think of Brenda?

Brenda's case raises an extremely important issue: Sometimes, well-intentioned parents *misinterpret* innocent behavior as evidence of sexual abuse, and Brenda's case is a perfect example. I'll tell you what really happened at Fred's house: Fred gave Heather a bubble bath. He put too much bubble bath solution in the tub and the solution irritated Heather's genitals. Later, Heather told Fred her "privates" hurt. Fred saw the redness and said, "Daddy's sorry you got an owie. We'll make it better with salve." Fred used his finger to apply soothing ointment to Heather's irritated genitals. By the time Fred returned Heather to Brenda, he'd forgotten the whole thing. Brenda *misinterpreted* what happened. When she saw the redness and heard Heather's words, Brenda's animosity toward Fred kicked in. Sexual abuse was the *only* explanation she could see. Brenda had emotional blinders on that kept her from seeing the possibility of an innocent explanation.

The possibility that innocent behavior will be misinterpreted as evidence of sexual abuse is particularly high when parents are angry and suspicious of each other. The moral of Brenda's story is that parents must avoid jumping too quickly to conclusions. Do not let your worst fears be your only guide. Think of every possible explanation for what you see and hear, and most important, keep an open mind.

Misinterpreting innocent behavior as evidence of sexual abuse can have disastrous consequences. The suspicious parent may come forward too quickly with accusations of abuse, and, once the accusation is made, it's nearly impossible to withdraw. If it turns out there was no abuse, the accusing parent looks at best like a fool and at worst like a malicious liar. In either case, the accuser's credibility is damaged. Everybody's sympathy goes to the falsely accused, and the accuser is branded vindictive or hysterical or both.

With the danger of misinterpretation in mind, what should you do? The best advice is be calm and proceed with caution. Contact the child's pediatrician or a mental health professional who is an expert about sexual abuse. Above all, do not overreact.

Keeping Your Emotions in Check

This book contains a lot of talk about the strong emotions stirred up by child sexual abuse. You may find yourself wondering, "Why so much discussion of emotions? The author is a man. I wonder if he dwells so much on emotions because he thinks emotion is wrong, a sign of weakness, and that women are too emotional?" This is a fair question. Let me be clear. I don't think emotion is wrong, and I don't believe women are "too emotional." I'm the father of two little boys, and there is nothing about which I feel more emotion than my kids. If someone hurt them, I'd be as emotional as any parent, woman or man.

It's not that emotion is wrong or a sign of weakness. The reason it's important to discuss the emotions generated by child sexual abuse is that these emotions can be used against parents, especially mothers. Unfortunately, some judges, lawyers, mental health professionals, and others—mostly men—interpret a woman's emotional reaction as a sign of weakness, instability, and even hysteria or mental illness. Such gender stereotyping is wrong, but it's a fact of life. A mother's perfectly natural emotional response to abuse can be twisted into "evidence" that she is a hysterical woman pursuing a baseless vendetta against her innocent husband. Because your emotional reaction could be turned against you, you must appreciate this possibility and avoid it.

13

The Legal Importance of What Your Child Tells You and Others About the Abuse

The first hint of sexual abuse often comes from something a child says. Telling the secret is not easy. Children are often threatened into silence. Eventually, however, many children find the courage to tell, and when they do, it's vitally important to listen carefully. A child's words are often the most compelling and powerful evidence of sexual abuse. The importance of the child's words raises three critical questions for parents:

- ☐ Should I talk to my child about abuse? (p. 147)
- ☐ What are leading questions, and why should I avoid them? (p. 148)
- ☐ Can my child's words be used in court to prove the abuse? (p. 150)

Should I Talk to My Child About Abuse?

If you suspect abuse, your first impulse is to question your child. This is a terrible moment for any parent and the urge is strong to press the child for details, to talk about it, to question him or her repeatedly. Sexually abused children often are reluctant to describe what happened, and a loving parent feels an almost irresistible impulse to pull the story out of the child—to help the child tell it. Although the urge to press your child for details is understandable, you should know that from a legal perspective questioning your child is sometimes the worst thing you can do. Remember, if you accuse the child's father of molestation, *your* motives will be scrutinized. That's right, your motives for making the accusation will be suspect. The father's lawyer may counterattack with an accusation that you coached the child or asked leading questions that planted a false idea of abuse in the child's mind. Your natural and compassionate act of talking to your child may be portrayed as the cunning plan of a vindictive wife out for revenge or the wild act of a hysterical woman on a witch hunt to frame an innocent man.

The best way to avoid charges of coaching and improper questioning is to *stop questioning* and get your child to a neutral, objective professional as quickly as possible. If you have an attorney, call the attorney. Call the child's pediatrician. The attorney or doctor may advise you to contact the police or another agency. It's important to have the child interviewed by a trained professional *as soon as possible.* Let the professional elicit the story from the child. That is what the professional is trained to do, and it's much more difficult to accuse a professional of coaching than to accuse a parent.

If your child wants to talk to you about abuse, you should listen calmly and patiently. Do not react with strong emotion, and resist the temptation to ask a lot a questions. To the best of your ability, leave the questioning to professionals. Be supportive and loving. Help your child understand that he or she will be talking to adults and should "tell them everything that happened."

I'm not urging you to turn your back on your own child or to squelch a child's efforts to talk to you. My point is simply that there are very real legal dangers in asking too many questions, especially if those questions can be interpreted as leading or suggestive.

What Are Leading Questions, and Why Should I Avoid Them?

Many adults believe children are highly suggestible. Although children are not invariably suggestible, young children—especially preschoolers—are suggestible (see p. 139 for discussion of suggestibility). Because suggestibility is a legitimate concern, you should minimize the number of suggestive questions you ask. The more suggestive questions you ask, the less confidence the legal system is likely to place in your child's answers.

Some suggestive questions are called *leading*. A leading question is a question that suggests to the child that the questioner wants a particular answer. Here are examples of leading questions:

☐ Your daddy put his pee-pee right there on your body, isn't that right?
☐ He hurt you, didn't he?
☐ You didn't want to do that, did you?
☐ It happened in the bedroom, didn't it?
☐ I'll bet he did it lots of times, right?

You can see why these questions are leading. Each question strongly suggests that the adult wants a particular answer. Strongly leading questions like these should never be asked. When talking to children about abuse, it's very important to let them tell their own story in their own words at their own pace. Don't hurry them along, and don't put words in their mouths. Moreover, don't say things like, "So, what you really mean is . . . Isn't that right?" This is highly leading and improper. Here are some examples of what to ask and what to avoid:

☐ Do *not* say, "It happened in the bedroom, didn't it?"
☐ *Do* say, "Where did it happen?"
☐ Do *not* say, "Did he take all your clothes off?"
☐ *Do* say, "Did anything happen to your clothes?"

It's nearly always preferable to ask nonleading, nonsuggestive questions such as:

☐ Can you tell me more about that?
☐ Where were you when that happened?
☐ Tell me everything you can remember.
☐ Let's talk about that a little more. Can you remember anything else?

The more general your questions the better. Of course, it's sometimes necessary to ask specific questions, but keep them as nonsuggestive and nonleading as possible. Remember, when you talk to your child, don't describe what you think happened and then ask your child to agree with your suspicion by asking, "Is that the way it happened?"

It's important to remain calm. You may not feel calm, but your child needs your quiet, reassuring support, not a shocked and emotional reaction. When your child begins disclosing abuse, let him or her know not to pretend, exaggerate, guess, or make things up. You might gently say, "When we talk about this, it's important to say only things that really happened. It's important not to pretend or make up things. Okay? Let's just talk about things that are real, things that really happened."

And finally, remember, when you suspect abuse, it's often best to refrain from questioning your child at all. This applies in all cases of abuse, but especially when mothers suspect abuse by their child's father. Get the child to a professional. I know it sounds absurd to advise a loving parent not to talk to her child about something as important as child abuse. Nevertheless, if you are tempted to press your child for details, remember your ultimate goal: You want to find out what happened and protect your child. In many cases, the best way to achieve that goal is to turn the questioning over to professionals who are trained to interview children.

Can My Child's Words Be Used in Court to Prove the Abuse?

When it comes time to prove abuse in court, your child may have to testify and describe what happened. Unfortunately, however, some children are too young or too frightened to testify. When the child is unable to appear in court and describe what happened, it makes sense for the adults who listened to the child's earlier descriptions of abuse to testify *instead* of the child and to repeat what the child told them weeks or months earlier. Even if the child is able to testify, it's often helpful to reinforce the child's testimony by having adults repeat the child's earlier descriptions of the abuse. When the child's earlier statements are repeated in court, they are used as evidence of the abuse. To fully understand the importance of repeating a child's earlier statements, consider this example: Five-year-old Amanda's mother and father are divorced. The mother has sole custody, and Amanda visits her father on weekends. Shortly after the father returned Amanda to her mother's home following a weekend visit, Amanda blurted out, "Daddy's pee-pee gets big and hard, like a stick, and white stuff comes out that tastes really yucky." What powerful evidence of sexual abuse! Yet, the father states there was no abuse. Following Amanda's disclosure, the mother starts proceedings in family court to terminate father's visitation, and six weeks later everyone is in court. Amanda is unable to testify because she is too frightened to speak. How is the mother's attorney going to prove the abuse? One approach is to put the mother on the witness stand and ask her to repeat Amanda's graphic description of abuse. So, the mother takes the witness stand and answers some preliminary questions from her attorney. Finally, the attorney gets to the point and asks, "What did Amanda tell you when she came home that day?" Before the mother can answer, however, the father's attorney says, "Your honor, I object. If the child said anything to her mother that day it would be hearsay, and hearsay is not admissible." The judge thinks a moment and says, "That is correct, the child's words are hearsay. I'll sustain the objection." Turning to Amanda's mother, the judge says, "You may not repeat what your daughter said." Although Amanda's words are powerful evidence of abuse, the judge is correct: Amanda's statement to her mother is hearsay, and the law in every state says that except in limited circumstances described later, hearsay statements can't be repeated in court.

Although you don't need to become an expert on the highly technical and arcane law of hearsay, it's useful for you to have a good idea of when your child's words are hearsay. Basically, a child's words are hearsay when three requirements are met:

1. The child described something that happened (e.g., sexual abuse)
   and
2. The child's words were spoken before the court proceeding at which an adult proposes to repeat the child's words (e.g., six weeks before the hearing, the child told her mother about sexual abuse and the mother is now in court to repeat what her daughter said)
   and
3. The child's words are used in court to prove that what the child said really happened (e.g., the child's words are repeated in court to prove that the abuse happened as the child said it did).

With these three requirements in mind it's easy to see that Amanda's words to her mother were hearsay, and that the judge was correct in excluding the mother's testimony. First, when Amanda described her father's penis, she described something that happened. Second, Amanda's words were spoken six weeks before the court hearing where her mother proposed to repeat what Amanda said. Finally, the mother's attorney wanted to use Amanda's words to prove that the abuse happened. Amanda's description of the abuse is hearsay, and unless the mother's attorney can convince the judge that Amanda's hearsay statement meets the requirements of one of the exceptions to the rule against hearsay, the mother won't be allowed to repeat what Amanda said that day.

There are numerous exceptions to the rule against hearsay, and several of these exceptions are used in child abuse litigation to allow adults to repeat children's hearsay statements describing abuse. When your child describes abuse, you can take the simple steps outlined below. By following these steps, you preserve for your lawyer the information the lawyer needs to persuade a judge that your child's hearsay statements meet the highly technical requirements of one or more of the exceptions to the rule against hearsay. You should:

1. Write down exactly what your child said. Use the child's own words. Do not summarize or paraphrase.
2. Write down when and where the child made the statements. Make a note of everyone who was there. Document what was going on before and during the time the child described abuse. What led up to the child's statement? Write down what you or others said to the child. For example, if you asked questions, write down your questions and the child's answers.
3. Estimate how much time went by between the abuse and the child's statement.
4. Document how the child was feeling and acting when she described the abuse. For example, was she upset and crying or was she calm?
5. Write down anything you can think of that indicates the child was or was not telling the truth.

When a child's hearsay statements meet the requirements of an exception to the rule against hearsay, the adult who was listening to the child *is* allowed to repeat what the child said and the child's words are evidence of abuse. A child's hearsay statements are not always enough to convince a judge, but children's hearsay is often very powerful. In case after case, hearsay plays a decisive role in proving abuse.

Parents sometimes wonder whether they should audiotape or videotape their child's description of abuse. Recording is sometimes a good idea, but it can backfire. Here is an example: Five-year-old Susie and her mother were at the park when Susie spontaneously blurted out a detailed and powerful description of sexual abuse. The mother rushed home, where she sat Susie in front of a video camera and said, "Tell Mommy what you told me at the park." As often happens with children, Susie would not say a word. The mother pleaded with her and asked many suggestive questions. Finally, Susie gave a watered-down version of what she had said so powerfully at the park. There is a good chance this videotape will come back to haunt Susie's mother. It will be used as evidence that she coached Susie with highly suggestive questions. Susie's original statement in the park will be forgotten and the only thing people will pay attention to is the videotape. So, before videotaping or audiotaping, consult your lawyer.

When your child talks about sexual abuse, you may wonder whether it's wise to ask another adult to be present as a witness. For example, should a friend listen in? This is a delicate issue. On the one hand, you don't want the child to feel intimidated or embarrassed. On the other hand, the odds are high that your motives in talking to your child will be challenged. You may be accused of planting the idea of abuse in your child's mind. A neutral witness can refute this accusation by testifying that you did not coach the child or ask unnecessarily leading questions. There is no clear right or wrong answer to this dilemma. Moreover, having another adult present does not guarantee safety, especially if the adult is your friend or relative. The best advice is to consult your attorney on this issue. And again, get your child to a professional interviewer as soon as possible!

14

Changes in Your Child's Behavior as Evidence of Sexual Abuse

At the beginning of Part IV, I noted that child sexual abuse is often very difficult to prove in court. When you accuse someone of sexual abuse, you have the burden of proof, and you and your lawyer need every scrap of evidence you can find to carry your burden (see p. 108 for discussion of the burden of proof). One source of evidence regarding sexual abuse may be changes in your child's behavior, such as psychological symptoms that are commonly observed in sexually abused children. The use in court of behavior changes and psychological symptoms is extremely complicated and is largely beyond the scope of this book. I've written a highly technical legal treatise on evidence in child abuse litigation (Myers, 1992). In addition, I've written book chapters and articles on the subject (Myers, 1989, 1993, 1996). Your lawyer may find my other writing useful in preparing your case for court.

Although I can't in this little book explore all the details of using behavior changes and psychological symptoms as evidence of abuse, you need to know the basics. Before we get started, however, remember that not all sexually abused children demonstrate behavior changes or psychological symptoms (see p. 28). Thus, the fact that a child's behavior is unchanged does not mean the child was not abused.

In this chapter, I address the following questions:

□ Do symptoms of anxiety provide evidence of sexual abuse? (p. 156)

□ Is sexual behavior or sexual knowledge in young children evidence of sexual abuse? (p. 157)

□ Is a doctor likely to find medical evidence of sexual abuse? (p. 159)

□ How do I avoid falling into the trap of overvaluing the evidence of abuse? (p. 159)

□ Should I try to become an expert on proving abuse? (p. 161)

Do Symptoms of Anxiety Provide Evidence of Sexual Abuse?

As you know from earlier chapters, there is no single psychological symptom or behavior change that is seen in all sexually abused children (see pp. 28, 30). There is no behavioral "smoking gun" for sexual abuse. Moreover, there is no psychological test that identifies sexually abused children. Every child is unique, and every abuse experience is unique. Thus, it's not surprising that children's reactions to abuse vary considerably.

Although no psychological symptom or behavior change provides absolute proof of sexual abuse, certain symptoms and behaviors can provide evidence. Because sexual abuse is often a frightening, traumatic experience, many sexually abused children exhibit symptoms of anxiety and stress. In younger children—especially children under ten—these symptoms include fear, nightmares, difficulty in sleeping, bed-wetting accidents, nervousness, clinginess, and other symptoms. Some sexually abused children lose interest in normal childhood activities such as school or friends, and some children are so depressed that they need psychiatric treatment. Some sexually abused children suffer from posttraumatic stress disorder (see Chapter 3 for a discussion of these symptoms).

What should you do if you observe these or other behavior changes or symptoms in your child? It's vitally important to document the changes and symptoms. Keep a detailed written record of behavior changes and symptoms, along with careful notes describing when they first appear. Document anything that might explain behavior changes or psychological symptoms.

Keep in mind that sexual abuse is not the only trauma that causes nightmares, fear, and other symptoms of stress and anxiety. For example, divorce is traumatic for many children, and some children living through divorce exhibit symptoms of stress and anxiety. Because through divorce exhibit symptoms of stress and anxiety. Because symptoms of anxiety and stress are seen in nonabused as well as in abused children, it's important to avoid reading too much into such symptoms. Symptoms of anxiety and stress are almost never enough by themselves to convince a judge that a child was sexually abused.

Is Sexual Behavior or Knowledge in Young Children Evidence of Sexual Abuse?

Symptoms of stress and anxiety do not provide strong evidence of sexual abuse because such symptoms are found in nonabused as well as abused children. Other symptoms and behaviors have a stronger connection to sexual abuse, particularly when those symptoms or behaviors are observed in young children. In particular, certain types of sexual behavior and sexual knowledge provide relatively strong evidence of sexual abuse in young children. One indicator is detailed knowledge in a young child of adult sex acts. For example, a four-year-old can't invent a detailed description of fellatio and ejaculation unless the child has seen pornography, watched adults perform fellatio, or been the victim of sexual abuse. The likelihood of abuse increases if a child knows details that can't be learned by watching. Thus, a child who provides a description of the texture, taste, and smell of semen is probably a sexually abused child.

Not all sexual behavior or sexual knowledge raises concern about abuse. In Chapter 3, I discuss normal sexual behavior in children. You will recall from that chapter that nonabused children engage in sexual behavior. For example, masturbation is very common among nonabused children and is considered normal.

Although certain sexual behaviors are common in nonabused children, some sexual behaviors are very *un*common in children who have not been abused. In particular, nonabused children seldom engage in aggressive sexual behavior. Nor is it common for young nonabused children to engage in sexual play that imitates adult sexual behavior (Friedrich, 1993; Friedrich et al., 1991, 1992). The psychologist William Friedrich and his colleagues found that the following behaviors are seldom seen in nonabused children:

☐ Placing the child's mouth on a sex part such as a penis
☐ Asking to engage in sex acts

☐ Masturbating with an object
☐ Inserting objects into the child's vagina or anus
☐ Imitating sexual intercourse
☐ Making sexual sounds
☐ French kissing
☐ Imitating sexual behavior with dolls

In research conducted in Sweden, Frank Lindblad and his colleagues reached conclusions similar to those of Friedrich. Lindblad studied sexual behavior in Swedish preschool-age children attending day care centers (1995). While at day care, very few of the Swedish children engaged in the following behaviors:

☐ Attempting to make an adult touch the child's genitals
☐ Attempting to touch an adult's genitals
☐ Attempting to touch the breasts of a female day care center employee
☐ Exhibiting the child's genitals at the day care center
☐ Playing sexually exploratory games like "doctor"
☐ Starting games that imitate adult sex acts

The fact that a young child engages in one or more of the unusual sexual behaviors described by Friedrich and Lindblad does not prove conclusively that the child was sexually abused. Moreover, we know that it's common for young children to engage in age-appropriate sexual behavior. The psychologist Susan Phipps-Yonas and her colleagues remind us, "We are all sexual creatures and sexual learning begins in early infancy" (1993, p. 1). When it comes to more worrisome sexual behaviors, however, the research of Phipps-Yonas and her colleagues dovetails with that of Friedrich and Lindblad:

> Certain behaviors were reported as having a very low probability by the daycare providers, especially for children under age four. These include: efforts to engage in pretend sexual intercourse; French-kissing; requests to have another suck, lick, or kiss their genitals; and attempts to insert objects into their own or another's buttocks or vaginas. (p. 4)

It's important to remember that there is no single behavior or symptom or combination of behaviors or symptoms that always

proves abuse. Moreover, some nonabused children demonstrate unusual sexual behavior. Despite the fact that unusual sexual behavior
does not definitively prove abuse, unusual sexual behavior in a young
child is a good indicator of sexual abuse and, along with other evidence, goes a long way toward proving abuse.

Is a Doctor Likely to Find Medical Evidence of Sexual Abuse?

Most sexual abuse does not leave medical evidence that a doctor can
find. For example, gently fondling a little girl's breasts and genitals
leaves no marks. Putting a finger or penis inside a child's vagina or
bottom sometimes causes injury but not always. When a child's genitals are injured, the tissues heal quickly, and in a few days or weeks
the injury may disappear.

   If your young child's genitals are red and irritated, you may wonder whether this is evidence of abuse. Of course, sexual abuse is one
explanation for such symptoms, but usually not the most likely explanation. Redness and irritation is a nonspecific sign, and typically
provides very weak, if any, evidence of abuse. "Redness (erythema)
appears to be as common among nonabused children as among
abused children" (Lyon & Koehler, in press).

   Even though medical evidence is seldom found, if sexual abuse
is suspected, the child should be examined as quickly as possible by
a physician or nurse with training and expertise in child sexual
abuse. I advise you to begin with a call to your child's pediatrician. The doctor will advise you who to contact for an expert medical
evaluation.

How Do I Avoid Falling Into the Trap of Overvaluing the Evidence of Abuse?

Parents who suspect sexual abuse are desperate to protect their children, and when they find evidence they grab onto it and hold tight.
Unfortunately, in my experience, it's common for protective parents
to *over*value the evidence of abuse. Because most parents—and many
professionals—don't understand the strengths and weakness of various kinds of evidence, parents often think their evidence is stronger

than it really is. This mistake—overvaluing the evidence—can lead to disaster. An example will illustrate the problem: Ms. Jones suspects that her ex-husband is molesting their four-year-old daughter Jenny on weekend visits. Jenny has not said anything about abuse, but she is reluctant to go to her father's house, and when she returns from visits, she is upset for hours. Recently, Jenny started having nightmares in which she is chased by monsters. In addition, she started masturbating. Ms. Jones read in a magazine that behavior changes can be signs of sexual abuse. Worried, Ms. Jones talked to the therapist she had been seeing for several years. The therapist said, "Oh yes, those symptoms are definitely consistent with abuse. Maybe you should take Jenny to the doctor." By this time, Ms. Jones was really frightened. You see, Ms. Jones had been molested by her own father at about Jenny's age.

The following day, Ms. Jones took Jenny to the pediatrician. The doctor examined Jenny and found what looked like irregularities in Jenny's hymen—irregularities that might have been evidence of penetration by a finger. The doctor did not say Jenny was abused, but she did not rule out abuse either. As far as Ms. Jones was concerned, *she had evidence.* Jenny's behavior had changed, she didn't like going to her father's house, the therapist said her symptoms were "consistent" with abuse, and the pediatrician found medical "evidence."

Ms. Jones telephoned the attorney who had represented her in her divorce and described the evidence. Ms. Jones asked if she could go to court and cut off the father's visitation. Unfortunately, the attorney knew nothing about sexual abuse and said, "The evidence sounds good to me. I'll get a court hearing to stop visitation." The attorney got a court date a week later and telephoned the father's attorney with the news. At the appointed hour, the mother, the father, and their attorneys were in court. The mother described the evidence to the judge. The father testified and denied any sexual abuse. The judge ruled there was not enough evidence of abuse to suspend father's visitation. Ms. Jones was devastated! She couldn't believe it. She said, "But what about the evidence?"

The problem here is that Ms. Jones *overvalued* the evidence of sexual abuse which, in Jenny's case, is actually very weak. It's important to remember that Ms. Jones was the accuser and she had the burden of proving that the abuse happened. Her evidence simply was not strong enough to convince the judge. (The burden of proof is discussed at p. 108.)

Now consider Ms. Jones's predicament. If there was no abuse, Jenny's father will be mad as a hornet. Even if there *was* abuse, Ms. Jones failed to prove it and in the eyes of the law, the father is innocent. Whether the father is guilty or innocent, he may decide to retaliate by asking the judge to take custody away from Ms. Jones because "she is a hysterical false accuser." He just might win!

Overvaluing the evidence of sexual abuse is a trap you simply must avoid. I've talked to many mothers who fell into this deadly snare and paid the ultimate price: They lost their child to the man they believe is a molester! It breaks my heart when this happens. Don't let it happen to you. How can you avoid it? The best advice is to make sure you don't react too quickly, don't jump to conclusions, don't overvalue the evidence. Most important, put your case in the hands of attorneys and mental health professionals who are *experts* on child sexual abuse. They are the ones who know how to gather and evaluate the evidence to build a strong case.

Should I Try to Become an Expert on Proving Abuse?

When you finish this book, you'll know a lot about the legal system and about child sexual abuse. You won't be an expert, however. Nor should you to try to become one. Neither this nor any other book can equip you with the knowledge and experience required to decide whether a child's symptoms and behaviors prove sexual abuse. This book is certainly not a substitute for a good lawyer. I urge you to focus your energy on being a loving protective parent, not an amateur lawyer or psychologist. If this book has value, it's in helping you avoid the pitfalls that lie hidden along the rocky road to protecting your child. If you suspect sexual abuse, you need a knowledgeable lawyer and advice from a mental health professional who is a true expert on child sexual abuse. This book gives you the information you need to help these professionals do their job as effectively as possible.

Part V

Summing It All Up

Plan for Victory,
Prepare for Defeat

The title of Part V sounds more like advice from a military commander than advice to protective parents. It's important to remember, however, that when you step into court, you step into the adversary system, and in that system, as in warfare, there are winners and losers. Moreover, the military flavor of the title is apropos because some contested custody cases really are battles, with parents locked in legal warfare. To the victor go the spoils, the child; to the vanquished goes heartache. Of course, not all custody cases resemble military confrontations. Nevertheless, contested custody cases often boil over with hostility, especially when one parent accuses the other of child abuse. If you accuse your spouse of sexual abuse, you're in for the fight of your life.

Part V contains two short chapters, summaries really, of what you learned in previous chapters. Chapter 15, "Plan for Victory, " gives you a concise ten-point plan for building a successful case in court.

Chapter 16 bears the ominous title "Prepare for Defeat." This final chapter offers guidance on what to do if disaster strikes and you lose your battle for custody.

15

Plan for Victory

If you believe your child has been sexually abused, you need a plan, a blueprint for action. As you learned from earlier chapters, your plan should be worked out with great care and well in advance of going to court. The following ten-point action plan is drawn from the discussion in earlier chapters:

1. Do Not Overreact or Act Too Quickly

Once you accuse your spouse of child sexual abuse, you are committed to the accusation. It's extraordinarily difficult to withdraw such an accusation without looking like a fool. If it turns out there was no abuse, you are almost guaranteed to look terrible, and you should expect the other attorney to label you "hysterical," "vengeful," "unstable," and "a classic example of parental alienation syndrome."

So, if you charge sexual abuse, you've got to make it stick or risk being branded a false accuser. If you keep this very real danger in mind, it will be easy to see the importance of not overreacting and not going to court too quickly.

2. Get a Good Lawyer

It's impossible to overestimate the importance of a good lawyer (see Chapter 6). Going to court without a competent lawyer is like scuba diving without oxygen.

3. Get a Psychosocial Assessment by an Expert on Child Sexual Abuse

Chapter 7 covers the importance of a thorough psychosocial assessment by a mental health professional who is an expert on child sexual abuse. If you need more than one psychosocial assessment, don't forget the problem of "too much assessment" (see p. 80).

4. Document the Evidence, Build the Case, But Don't Overvalue the Evidence

To repeat a constant drumbeat of this book, child sexual abuse is often extremely difficult to prove in court. In Part IV, I discuss the kinds of evidence you need to prove abuse. As you work with your lawyer to build your case, you may find it useful to keep a written record of your child's behavior and statements that support your suspicions.

Although you may want to go to court quickly, your attorney may advise that the best strategy is to postpone making an accusation of abuse until more evidence accumulates. Needless to say, if you suspect molestation, you are anxious to proceed, and waiting seems intolerable. Nevertheless, waiting is sometimes essential, even if it means you have to send your child on additional visits. This critical question—how long to wait—has to be answered through careful consultation with your attorney. Always remember, however, that if you strike too soon the legal system could backfire on you. Of course, there is also danger in waiting too long. If you fail to bring your suspicions of abuse to the judge's attention, you could be accused of neglect. It seems that no matter what they do, protective parents leave themselves open to criticism.

Please keep in mind the tendency of so many protective parents to overvalue the evidence of abuse (see p. 159). You may think you have a solid case, but if your evidence doesn't hold up in court, you won't be able to convince the judge and you run the decided risk of looking like a false accuser. If that happens, the stage is set for the legal system to backfire against you. (See p. 108 for discussion of your burden of proving sexual abuse.)

5. Limit Your Questioning of the Child

Your first instinct when you suspect your child has been sexually abused is to talk to the child. Unfortunately, this perfectly natural and normal instinct can damage or destroy your ability to prove abuse in court. Don't lose sight of the fact that your motives for talking to your child are *automatically* suspect. As I discuss on page 147, the best advice usually is to keep your questioning to a minimum. Leave the questioning to professionals whose motives are above suspicion.

6. Emotions Are Used Against Women, So Guard Your Emotions

I discussed the long and deeply ingrained tradition of doubting women who allege sexual abuse and attributing such allegations to hysteria and emotional instability (see Chapter 11). This shameful legacy of skepticism continues to this day and is an obstacle for many women trying to protect their children.

7. The Goal Is to Protect Your Child, to Find the Truth; the Goal Is Never to Hurt the Father or Get Revenge

If your child is sexually abused, you're angry. No, you're outraged. It's completely natural to react with moral indignation to evidence of abuse. Yet, women must take care how they express their anger. If you can't prove abuse, your anger can be turned against you. The other lawyer may accuse you of being vengeful and "out to destroy this innocent man with false charges and outrageous lies." You are likely to be accused of manipulating the child to injure the father.

How can you avoid such an attack on your motives? The most important thing is to realize that it can happen to you. In everything you do and say you must send one clear message: "All I care about is the truth. My only goal is to find out what is best for my child. I'm not out for revenge, and I'm not acting because of spite or hurt feelings."

If professionals get the impression that you are interested more in hurting your spouse than protecting your child, the professionals may conclude that your accusations are fabricated. Keep your focus on your child, not on yourself.

8. Consider Raising Faults Other than Child Sexual Abuse— for Example, Does the Father Abuse Drugs? Does He Beat You or the Children?

When a judge decides who should have custody, the judge considers each parent's strengths and weaknesses (see Chapter 9 for a discussion of factors judges consider in deciding custody). If you lack strong evidence of sexual abuse, your lawyer may decide to focus on the father's other faults and avoid any mention of sexual abuse. This is sometimes a good strategy because the father's other faults may be easier to prove. The decision to focus on other faults and avoid accusations of sexual abuse is one of the most important decisions you and your lawyer will make. Moreover, the decision to remain silent about sexual abuse has highly technical legal implications that the attorney must consider. Careful planning is necessary.

9. Always Consider the Possibility That There Was No Abuse: Remember the Danger of Misinterpreting Innocent Behavior as Evidence of Abuse

In Chapter 12, I discuss the danger of misinterpreting innocent behavior as evidence of abuse. If your child says or does something that raises suspicion of sexual abuse, it's critical that you examine *all* the possibilities and ask, "Is there some innocent explanation for what my child said or did?" Often, there is an innocent explanation. It's vitally important to keep an open mind and resist jumping to conclusions about abuse.

10. Find Emotional Support, Be Strong, and Never Give Up

If your child is sexually abused, the only thing you think about is protecting him or her. In the fight to protect your child, however, do not forget yourself. You are your child's most important source of love, support, and protection. Your battle may be long and draining. You need adults who love you and who will be there for you with emotional support. You must be strong for your child, and no matter what you must never give up. Your friends and family are your allies. Lean on them when the going gets rough.

Summary

Most of the time, the legal system works well to protect children, and I sincerely hope it works for you. There are times, however, when the system fails and children are not protected. In some cases, the system backfires on mothers who are trying to protect their children, and these cases are unspeakable tragedies. This book gives you tools to avoid this tragedy for the child you love so much.

16

Prepare for Defeat

The most important point I want to make in this chapter is that I hope the chapter *never* applies to you. If your child has been sexually abused, I hope you succeed every step of the way. But I have to be honest. I wrote this book because I've talked to so many women who did not succeed. Across the United States, there are wounded women who tried desperately to protect their children and who saw the legal system turn against them like an angry tiger. If the sad day comes when the system turns against you, the information that follows may help.

What Happens If I Fail to Prove Abuse?

If you accuse your child's father of sexual abuse and you win, the legal system will probably do a good job protecting your child. You will get custody, and the father's visitation will be limited or denied. But if you fail to prove abuse, several things can happen. The best you can hope for is a judge who protects the child even though you didn't prove abuse. The judge may share your suspicion even though the evidence is lacking, and find a way to protect your child.

If the judge does not share your suspicion about abuse, however, several things can happen. If you already have custody and you are trying to limit or stop the father's visitation, the judge may leave custody with you but refuse to limit or stop the visits. In this case, the judge will order you to continue visitation. The judge's order puts you in a terrible dilemma: You know you should obey the judge's order, but what mother can send her child to a man she believes is molesting the child?

The worst-case scenario is one in which you fail to prove abuse and the judge takes custody away from you and gives it to the father. What are you left with? All you have is visits with your child, and if the judge thinks you are a false accuser or an unstable, hysterical woman, your visits may be severely limited. For some women the ultimate disaster strikes: They are not allowed to see their children at all! That's right. Some mothers are denied any contact with the child they adore. How utterly tragic. Yet, it happens.

What should you do if you fail to prove abuse and the judge makes a decision against you? The remainder of this chapter offers some options.

Don't Let It Drive You Crazy

Losing custody of your child to a man who may be sexually abusing her is enough to drive you crazy. The same is true if you are ordered to send your child on visits with the father. But you can't afford to become irrational. The more irrationally you behave, the more you'll be labeled a hysterical woman. It doesn't matter that you're acting irrational because you are desperate to protect your child. Remember, the judge has already decided there was *no* abuse. To other people you are a sore loser, a vindictive woman who won't take no for an answer, or a woman who refuses to accept the truth. A woman who fails to prove abuse is in a terrible catch-22. She tries to protect her child in court but fails. The failure in court drives her to distraction and her distraction is used as further evidence that she is unstable!

If this nightmare happens to you, you have to keep your wits about you. You can't allow your natural emotions to be turned against you. Somehow, in the face of unbearable suffering, you have to pluck up your courage and forge ahead with strength, stability, and dignity. This may sound impossible, but when you doubt your ability to carry on, remember: Your child needs you now *more than ever.* You can't afford to do anything to jeopardize whatever contact you still have with your child.

Examine Your Legal Options

When a parent loses in court, several legal options should be considered. Let me note at this point that losing in court doesn't mean your lawyer was incompetent. The best attorneys lose cases, and child sexual abuse is often very difficult to prove.

Request a New Trial. Every state has procedures to request a judge to grant a new trial, or in effect, to reexamine the judge's decision. These procedures have different names, including "motion for new trial," "motion for reconsideration," and "motion to set aside a judgement." Unfortunately, the chances are small of persuading the judge to grant a new trial.

The Judge's Final Custody Decision Is Res Judicata. Once the judge's decision regarding child custody is final and the time expires to request a new trial, the losing parent can't go back to court and ask the judge for another trial based on the same evidence. You will remember from Chapter 9 that the final custody decision is just that, final, or res judicata.

Appeal to a Higher Court. If you lose a custody trial, you may appeal to a higher court. The appeal process is described in Chapter 9. It's important to note, however, that the likelihood of success on appeal is not high. Moreover, an appeal can take years and cost many thousands of dollars.

If Circumstances Change Substantially in the Future, You May Be Able to Modify the Custody Decision. If a judge makes a custody decision you disagree with, you have to live with it. You can't to go court to change the judge's decision unless at some time in the future circumstances change substantially. Suppose, for example, that you accuse your husband of sexually abusing your son. In court, your attorney is unable to prove the sexual abuse and the judge gives custody to the father. The judge's decision at the time of the trial is final; it's res judicata. But if circumstances change substantially in the future, you may be able to go back to court and request the same or a different judge to modify the original custody decision. By "in the future," I don't mean next week or next month. Judges don't modify custody and visitation decisions unless circumstances change substantially, and major changes usually don't happen overnight. Of course, when sexual abuse is an issue, a substantial change could occur at any time. Thus, suppose that a month after you lose custody, the abuse happens again, and this time you've got the evidence to prove it. Armed with this new evidence, you can seek modification.

Should You Disobey a Judge's Custody or Visitation Decision?
Should You Escape With Your Child Into the Underground?

If a judge makes a custody or visitation decision that you believe harms your child, you wonder whether you can obey. You are in a terrible dilemma. On the one hand, you've been taught to respect the law. On the other hand, your child's safety is at stake and the law has let you down.

Should you disobey a judge's order if disobedience is the only way you can protect your child? I can't make this terrible decision for you. I'll say this, however. I believe you should obey. In my experience, disobeying a judge's order is more likely to harm than help your ability to protect your child.

Some desperate mothers decide they simply can't turn their child over to a man they believe is a molester, and these mothers take their child and run away. Some women find their way into the loose network of individuals across the United States who hide parents on the run from family court. Before you consider running away or going underground, however, consider this: If the father has legal custody, you can be charged with the *crime* of kidnapping your own child. Moreover, it's both a state crime and a federal crime for parents to "kidnap" their own child. You will be pursued not only by the local police but by the FBI. If you are caught, and the odds are you will be, you can be prosecuted and sent to prison. Once you are caught, your chances of getting custody are practically nil.

Never Forget, You Are Your Child's Safe Harbor

If you try but fail to protect your child, remember always that you are still the most important person in the child's life. No matter how bad things get, no matter how little you are allowed to see your own child, you are still the child's mother, and your love will give the child strength. Children who receive their mother's love can cope with the horror of abuse even though their mother doesn't have custody. So, if the legal system turns against you, don't despair. Try to put the past behind you and look to the future. Think of ways—no matter how small—to keep the love alive. One mother who lost custody sent cards and little gifts every week. These tokens of her mother's love meant everything to her child. Your love is a safe harbor for your little one as he or she struggles through the storm. Someday—maybe next month, maybe next year, maybe years from now—your child will come back to you.

Appendix A

Guidelines for Psychosocial Evaluation of Suspected Sexual Abuse in Young Children

AMERICAN PROFESSIONAL SOCIETY
ON THE ABUSE OF CHILDREN

Statement of Purpose

These Guidelines for mental health professionals reflect current knowledge and an emerging consensus about the psychosocial evaluation of suspected sexual abuse in children. They are not intended as a standard of practice to which practitioners are expected to adhere in all cases. Evaluators must have the flexibility to exercise clinical judgment in individual cases. Laws and local customs may also influence the accepted method in a given community Practitioners must be prepared to justify their decisions about particular practices in specific cases. As experience and scientific knowledge expand, further refinement and revision of these Guidelines are expected.

These Guidelines are specific to psychosocial evaluations. Psychosocial evaluations are a systematic process of gathering information and forming professional opinions about the source and meaning of statements, behavior, and other evidence that are the basis of concern about possible sexual abuse. The results of such evaluations may be used to direct treatment planning and to assist in legal decision making.

Psychosocial evaluators should first establish the purpose of the evaluation and their role in the evaluation process. Psychosocial evaluations may be conducted for purely clinical reasons or be forensic in nature. These Guidelines pertain to both situations.

Clinical evaluations may be requested by parents, guardians or other professionals to determine whether there is reason to be concerned about possible abuse. It is also customary for clinicians to precede treatment for the effects of sexual abuse with an assessment of the sexual abuse history.

Forensic evaluations have the explicit purpose of contributing to legal decision making or legal proceedings. Such evaluations may be requested by parents or guardians, public child protective services (CPS) agencies, attorneys, guardians ad litem (or court appointed special advocates), or other professionals. The results may be used in civil or criminal proceedings. As noted in these Guidelines, forensic evaluations are different from clinical evaluations in generally requiring a different professional stance and additional components.

In all cases, evaluators should be aware that any interview with a child regarding possible sexual abuse may be subject to scrutiny and have significant implications for legal decision making and the child's safety and well-being.

GUIDELINES

I.   The Evaluator

     A. Characteristics

         1. The evaluator should possess a graduate level mental
            health degree in a recognized discipline (e.g., psychiatry,

psychology, social work, nursing, child development) or be supervised by a professional with a graduate level degree.

2. The evaluator should have professional experience assessing and treating children and families, and professional experience with sexually abused children. A minimum of two years of professional experience with sexually abused children is expected; three to five years is preferred for forensic evaluators. If the evaluator does not possess such experience, supervision is essential.

3. The evaluator must have had specialized training in child development and child sexual abuse. This training should be documented in terms of formal course work, supervision, or attendance at conferences, seminars, and workshops.

4. The evaluator should be knowledgeable about the dynamics and the emotional and behavioral consequences of sexual abuse experiences. The evaluator should be familiar with the professional literature and with current issues relevant to understanding and evaluating sexual abuse experiences.

5. The evaluator should be familiar with different cultural values and practices that may affect definitions of sexual abuse, child and/or family comfort with the evaluation process, child and/or family willingness to provide complete and accurate information, and the evaluator's own interpretation of responses.

6. If the purpose of the evaluation is forensic, the evaluator should have experience in conducting forensic evaluations and providing expert testimony. If the evaluator does not possess such experience, supervision is essential.

7. The evaluator should approach the evaluation with an open mind to all possible responses from the child and all possible explanations for the concern about sexual abuse. The evaluator should recognize that all sources of information have limitations and may contain inaccuracies. In forming an opinion, the evaluator should consider plausible alternative hypotheses.

II. Components of the Evaluation

    A. Protocol

        1. A written protocol is not necessary; however, evaluations should ordinarily involve reviewing those materials considered relevant for the type of evaluation; conducting collateral interviews when necessary; establishing rapport; assessing the child's developmental status, cognitive capacity, level of functioning and level of distress; and specifically evaluating the possibility of abuse. The evaluator may use discretion in the order and method of assessment.

           Forensic evaluations differ from evaluations conducted for purely clinical reasons in that they generally involve reviewing relevant materials and conducting collateral interviews.

        2. If information is available prior to the evaluation that meets the respective state's definition of reasonable suspicion for a CPS report, but no CPS report has yet been made, the evaluator should make the report and may choose to defer the evaluation until the CPS investigation has been conducted.

        3. When possible, unsupervised contact between the child and the suspected offender should be strongly discouraged during the evaluation process.

    B. Employer of the Evaluator

        1. Evaluation of the child may be conducted at the request of a legal guardian prior to court involvement. When only one parent has requested the evaluation, evaluators should give careful consideration to informing the other parent about the evaluation whether or not that parent is the focus of concern. When the other parent is the focus of concern, that parent is likely to request another evaluation; evaluators should consider whether it would be in the child's best interest to have a mutually agreed upon or court appointed evaluator to avoid unnecessary evaluations.

        2. If the evaluation is specifically requested or intended for use in a legal proceeding or a court is already involved, the

preferred practice is a court-appointed or mutually agreed upon evaluator of the child. In some circumstances exceptions to this practice are acceptable or are customary practice (e.g., contractual arrangements with child protective services, civil damage suits, when one party refuses to cooperate).

3. Discretion should be used in agreeing to conduct an evaluation of a child when the child has already been evaluated. Additional evaluations should be conducted only if they clearly further the best interests of the child. When a second opinion is required, a review of the records may eliminate the need for re-interviewing the child.

C. Number of Evaluators

1. The evaluation may be conducted by a single evaluator or by a team of professionals.

D. Collateral Information Gathered as Part of the Evaluation

1. Evaluators may seek and review background materials or conduct interviews as part of the evaluation process. The amount and nature of information reviewed depends on the purpose of the evaluation and the extent to which such information will be helpful in addressing the referral question and understanding the child's presenting problems or concerns. For clinical evaluations, clinical judgment should determine the necessity for additional records, materials, or interviews. Evaluators should request that background material be made available and collateral interviews be permitted for forensic evaluations.

2. The evaluation report should reflect an objective review of collateral information relied upon in the evaluation or opinion forming process.

E. Interviewing the Accused or Suspected Individual

1. It is not necessary to interview the accused or suspected individual in order to form an opinion about possible sexual abuse of the child.

2. An interview with or review of the statements from a suspected or accused individual may provide additional relevant information (e.g., alternative explanations, admissions, insight into relationship between child and accused individual).

3. If the accused or suspected individual is a parent who seeks to participate in the evaluation and there are no contraindications (e.g., criminal investigation or charges pending, civil suit), interviewing of the accused or suspected parent should be given strong consideration.

F. Releasing Information

1. Suspected abuse should always be reported to authorities as dictated by state law. Except as specified by law, clinical evaluators have no affirmative duty to disclose confidential clinical information.

2. Permission should be obtained from legal guardian(s) to request collateral materials and for release of information about the evaluation to relevant medical or mental health professionals, other professionals (e.g., schoolteachers), and involved legal systems (e.g., CPS, law enforcement, lawyers, courts). Discretion should be used in releasing sensitive individual and family history that does not directly relate to the purpose of the assessment.

3. Feedback about the results of the evaluation should usually be offered to parent(s) or legal guardian(s) and may be offered to the child, except where doing so would not be in the best interests of the child.

III. Interviewing

A. Recording of Interviews

1. Written documentation is the minimum requirement. Verbatim quotation of significant questions and answers is desirable. Forensic evaluations should contain specific documentation of questions and responses (verbal and nonverbal) regarding possible sexual abuse.

2. Audio or video recording may be preferred practice in some communities. Professional preference, logistics, or clinical considerations may contraindicate recording of interviews. Professional discretion is permitted in recording policies and practices.

3. When audio and video recording are used, the child and legal guardian should be informed. It is desirable to obtain assent from the child (when age appropriate) and consent from legal guardian(s).

B. Observation of the Interview

1. Professional discretion is permitted in observation policies and practices. Observation of interviews by involved professionals (CPS, law enforcement, etc.) may be indicated if it reduces the need for additional interviews and will not compromise the evaluation process.

2. Observation by non-accused and non-suspected primary caregiver(s) may be indicated for particular clinical reasons; however, great care should be taken that the observation is clinically appropriate, does not unduly distress the child, and does not affect the validity of the evaluation process.

3. If interviews are observed, the child must be informed. It is desirable to obtain assent from the child(when age appropriate) and consent from legal guardian(s).

C. Number of Interviews

1. The evaluator determines the number of interviews necessary to address the referral question and assess the child's presenting problems or concerns. This does not imply that all sessions must include specific questioning about possible sexual abuse. The evaluator may decide, based on the individual case circumstances, to adopt a less direct approach and reserve questioning about possible sexual abuse for subsequent interviews. Repeated direct questioning of the child regarding sexual abuse when the child is not reporting or is denying abuse is usually contraindicated.

2. If the child does not report abuse and further direct questioning is judged to be counterproductive, but the evaluator has continuing concerns about the possibility of abuse, the child may be referred for an extended evaluation or therapy that is less directive, but diagnostically focused. Recommendations regarding conditions necessary to insure the child's protection from possible abuse should be made.

D. Format of Interview

1. When possible, interviewing the primary caregiver and reviewing other collateral data first to gather background information may facilitate the evaluation process.

2. The child should be seen individually, except when the child refuses to separate from a parent/guardian. Discussion of possible abuse with the child in the presence of the caregiver during evaluation interviews should be avoided except when necessary to elicit information from the child. In such cases, the interview setting should be structured to reduce the possibility of improper influence by the caregiver on the child's behavior or statements.

3. In some cases, joint sessions with the child and the non-accused caregiver or accused or suspected individual might be helpful to obtain information regarding the overall quality of the relationships. Such joint sessions should not be conducted for the purpose of determining whether abuse occurred based on the child's reactions to the participating adult. Joint sessions should not be conducted if they will cause significant distress for the child.

4. Joint sessions with a child and an accused or suspected individual should only be considered when the individual is a parent or primary caregiver. In making a decision about conducting a joint session with a child and the accused or suspected parent, the evaluator should carefully weigh the possibility of gaining valuable information against the significant potential for negative consequences for an abused child and for the evaluation process. A child should never be asked to discuss the possible abuse in front of an accused or suspected parent.

IV. Child Interview

A. General Principles

1. The evaluator should create an atmosphere that enables the child to talk freely, including providing physical surroundings and a climate that facilitates the child's comfort and communication.
2. The evaluator should convey to all parties that no assumptions have been made about whether abuse has occurred.
3. Language and interviewing approach should be developmentally and culturally appropriate.
4. The evaluator should take the time necessary to perform a complete evaluation and should avoid any coercive quality to the interview.
5. Interview procedures may be modified in cases involving very young, minimally verbal children or children with special problems (e.g., developmentally delayed, electively mute, non-native speakers).
6. The difference between the evaluation phase and a treatment phase should be articulated. Under certain circumstances, (e.g., disputed custody cases) it may be preferable to obtain agreement from the parties before proceeding with treatment following evaluation.

B. Questioning

1. It may be helpful to preface questioning with specific statements designed to reduce misunderstandings during the interview(s), and promote accuracy and completeness.
2. It may be helpful to begin the interview with open-ended questions about neutral topics (e.g., family, school, recent event) so that the child has an opportunity to practice providing free recall responses.
3. Initial substantive questioning should be open-ended and as non-directive as possible to elicit free recall responses. More focused or specific questioning should follow. Once information is provided in response to a specific question, open-ended prompts should again be used.

4. The child should be questioned directly about possible sex-ual abuse at some point in the evaluation if less directive approaches have not yielded adequate information to an-swer the referral question.

5. The evaluator may use the form of questioning deemed necessary and justified to elicit information on which to base an opinion. Highly specific questioning should only be used when other methods of questioning have failed, when previous information warrants substantial concern, or when the child's developmental level precludes more non-directive approaches. However, responses to these questions should be carefully evaluated and weighed ac-cordingly. Coercive or intimidating questioning is never justified.

C. Use of Dolls and Other Devices

1. A variety of non-verbal tools may be used to assist young children in communication, including drawings, toys, doll-houses, dolls, puppets, etc. Since such materials have the potential to be distracting or misleading they should be used with care. They are discretionary for older children.

2. Anatomical dolls are accepted interview aids. Evaluators using anatomical dolls should be knowledgeable about the functions they may serve and should conform to accepted practice. (Refer to the APSAC Guidelines on the Use of Anatomical Dolls in Child Sexual Abuse Assessments.)

3. Anatomical dolls should not be used as a diagnostic test for sexual abuse. Definitive conclusions about a history of sex-ual abuse should not be based solely on interpretation of behavior with the dolls. Unusual behavior with the dolls may suggest further lines of inquiry that should be pur-sued. The unusual behavior and the responses to further questioning should be noted in the evaluation report.

4. Story books, coloring books or videos that contain explicit descriptions of abuse situations are potentially suggestive and are primarily teaching tools. They are typically not appropriate for evaluation purposes.

D. Psychological Testing

1. Formal psychological testing of the child is not necessary for the purpose of proving or disproving a history of sexual abuse.

2. Psychological testing may useful when the clinician has questions about the child's intellectual or developmental level. Psychological tests can also provide helpful information regarding a child's emotional status and general functioning.

3. Psychological testing of parents is not a routine component of child evaluations. An evaluation that includes assessment of parents may involve psychological tests.

V. Conclusions/Report

A. General Principles

1. The evaluation report should document the sources of information and/or data relied on in forming an opinion and making recommendations.

2. The evaluator may state an opinion that abuse did or did not occur, an opinion about the likelihood of the occurrence of abuse or simply provide a description and analysis of the gathered information.

3. Opinions should include supporting information (e.g., the child, parent(s)/guardian(s) and/or the accused individual's statements, behavior, psychological symptoms). Possible alternative explanations should have been considered. The evaluator should not suggest that mental health professionals have any special ability to detect whether an individual is telling the truth.

4. The evaluation may be inconclusive. If so, the evaluator should cite the information that causes continuing concern but does not enable confirmation or disconfirmation of abuse. If inconclusiveness is due to such problems as missing information or an untimely or poorly-conducted investigation, these obstacles should be clearly noted in the report.

5. Recommendations should be made regarding therapeutic or environmental interventions to address the child's emotional and behavioral functioning and to ensure the child's safety.

Acknowledgments

These Guidelines are the product of APSAC's Task Force on the Psychosocial Evaluation of Suspected Sexual Abuse in Children, chaired by Lucy Berliner, MSW. The initial version was the result of a lengthy, iterative process. These revisions are the result of a similar process conducted in 1996.

Appreciation goes to the many APSAC members who contributed their time and expertise to produce these Guidelines.

The Guidelines will be updated periodically. Any comments or suggestions about them should be directed to Lucy Berliner through APSAC, 332 South Michigan Avenue, Suite 1600, Chicago, Illinois, 60604.

Appendix B

Crime Victim Compensation Programs

Alabama Department of Economic and Community Affairs

Law Enforcement Planning Division
401 Adams Avenue
P.O. Box 5690
Montgomery, AL 36103-5690
Telephone (205) 242-5100

Alaska

Department of Public Safety
Council on Domestic Violence and Sexual Assault
P.O. Box 111200
Juneau, AK 88911-1200
Telephone (907) 465-4356

American Samoa

American Samoa Department of Human Resources
American Samoa Government
Pago Pago, AS 96799
Telephone (011)(684) 633-4485

Arizona

Department of Public Safety
P.O. Box 6638
Phoenix, AZ 85005
Telephone (602) 223-2000

SOURCE: Adapted from Saldaña, R. H. (1994) *Crime Victim Compensation Programs: A Reference Guide to the Programs in the U.S.* Bountiful, Utah: QuartZite.

Arkansas

> Prosecutor Coordination's Office
> 323 Center Street, Suite 750
> Little Rock, AR 72201
> Telephone (501) 682-3671

California

> Office of Criminal Justice Planning
> 1130 K Street, Suite 300
> Sacramento, CA 95814
> Telephone (916) 324-9140

Colorado

> Colorado Dept. of Public Safety
> Division of Criminal Justice, Suite 1000
> 700 Kipling Street
> Denver, CO 80215
> Telephone (303) 239-4402 or (303) 239-4442

Connecticut

> Office of Policy and Management
> Policy and Planning Division
> 80 Washington Street
> Hartford, CT 06106
> Telephone (203) 566-4298

Delaware

> Criminal Justice Council
> Carvel State Office Building
> 820 North French, 4th Floor
> Wilmington, DE 19801
> Telephone (302) 577-3437

District of Columbia

> Department of Human Services
> 801 North Capitol Street, NW
> Washington, D.C. 20002
> Telephone (202) 279-6002

Florida

> Office of the Attorney General
> Bureau of Victim Compensation, PLO1
> The Capitol
> Tallahassee, FL 32399-1050
> Telephone (904) 488-0848

Georgia

> Criminal Justice Coordinating Council
> 503 Oak Place, Suite 540
> Atlanta, GA 30349
> Telephone (404) 559-4949

Guam

> Office of the Attorney General
> Department of Law, Suite 2-200E
> Guam Judicial Center
> 120 West O'Brien Drive
> Agana, GU 96910
> Telephone (011)(671) 475-3406

Hawaii

> Office of the Attorney General
> 425 Queen Street
> Honolulu, HI 96813
> Telephone (808) 586-1282

Idaho

> Department of Health and Welfare
> Council on Domestic Violence
> 450 West State Street
> Boise, ID 83720-9990
> Telephone (208) 334-5580

Illinois

> Criminal Justice Information Authority
> 120 South Riverside Plaza
> 10th Floor, Suite 1016
> Chicago, IL 60606
> Telephone (312) 793-8550

Indiana

> Criminal Justice Institute
> 302 West Washington Street, E209
> Indianapolis, IN 46204
> Telephone (317) 232-1233

Iowa

> Department of Justice
> Crime Victim Assistance Division
> Compensation Program
> Old Historical Building
> Des Moines, IA 50319
> Telephone (515) 281-5044 or (800) 373-5044

Kansas

> Department of Social and Rehabilitation Services
> Crime Victim Assistance Program
> Docking State Office Building, Room 600 North
> 915 Harrison
> Topeka, KS 66612
> Telephone (913) 296-3271

Kentucky

> Kentucky Justice Cabinet
> Bush Building
> 403 Wapping Street, 2nd Floor
> Frankfort, KY 40601
> Telephone (502) 564-7554

Louisiana

> Crime Victims Reparations Board
> Louisiana Commission on Law Enforcement
> 1885 Wooddale Boulevard, Room 708
> Baton Rouge, LA 70806-1442
> Telephone (504) 925-4437

Maine

> Department of Human Services
> Bureau of Social Services
> State House, Station #11
> Augusta, ME 04333
> Telephone (207) 287-5060

Maryland

> Community Services Administration
> State of Maryland Department of Human Resources
> 311 West Saratoga Street, Room 272
> Baltimore, MD 21201
> Telephone (410) 333-0059

Massachusetts

> Victim and Witness Assistance Board
> 100 Cambridge Street, Room 1104
> Boston, MA 02202
> Telephone (617) 727-5200

Michigan

> Criminal Justice Center
> Lansing Community College
> P.O. Box 40010
> 419 North Capitol
> Lansing, MI 48901
> Telephone (517) 483-1570

Minnesota

> Minnesota Crime Victims Reparations Board
> N 465 Griggs Midway Building
> 1821 University Avenue
> St. Paul, MN 55104
> Telephone (612) 282-6256 or (800) 247-0390

Mississippi

> Department of Public Safety
> Division of Public Safety and Planning
> 301 West Pearl Street
> Jackson, MS 39203
> Telephone (601) 949-2225

Missouri

> Department of Public Safety
> Truman Building, Room 870
> P.O. Box 749
> Jefferson City, MO 65102-0749
> Telephone (314) 751-4905

Montana

> Crime Victims Unit
> 303 N. Roberts, 4th Floor
> Helena, MT 59620-1408
> Telephone (406) 444-3653

Nebraska

> Nebraska Crime Commission
> 301 Centennial Mall South
> P.O. Box 94946
> Lincoln, NE 68509
> Telephone (402) 471-2828 or (402) 471-2194

Nevada

> Department of Human Resources
> Kinkead Building
> Capitol Complex
> 505 East King Street, Room 600
> Carson City, NV 89710
> Telephone (702) 687-4400

New Hampshire

> U.S. Department of Justice
> Victim/Witness Program
> 55 Pleasant Street
> P.O. Box 480
> Concord, NH 03302-0480
> Telephone 225-1552

New Jersey

> Department of Law and Public Safety
> Division of Criminal Justice
> Office of Victim/Witness Advocacy
> 25 Market Street, CN 085
> Trenton, NJ 08625-0085
> Telephone (609) 984-3880

New Mexico

> State of New Mexico
> Crime Victims Reparation Commission
> 8100 Mountain Road NE, Suite 106
> Albuquerque, NM 87110
> Telephone (505) 841-9432; Fax (505) 841-9435

New York

> Crime Victims Board
> 270 Broadway, Room 200
> New York, NY 10007
> Telephone (212) 417-5133

North Carolina

> Governor's Crime Commission
> Department of Crime Control and Public Safety
> 3824 Barrett Drive, Suite 100
> Raleigh, NC 27609
> Telephone (919) 571-4736

North Dakota

> Crime Victim Reparations
> Workers Compensation Bureau
> P.O. Box 5521
> Bismarck, ND 58502-5521
> Telephone (701) 221-6195 or (800) 445-2322

Northern Mariana Islands

> Northern Mariana Islands
> Criminal Justice Planning Agency
> P.O. Box 1133, Saipan MP
> Saipan, CM 96950
> Telephone (011)(670) 322-9350

Ohio

> The Court of Claims of Ohio
> Capitol Square Office Building
> Victims of Crime Division
> 65 East State Street, Suite 1100
> Columbus, OH 43215
> Telephone (614) 466-6480 or
>   Victims Hotline (800) 824-8263

Oklahoma

> State of Oklahoma
> District Attorney's Council
> Crime Victims Compensation Board
> 2200 Classen Boulevard, Suite 1800
> Oklahoma City, OK 73106-5811
> Telephone (405) 557-6704

Oregon

> Office of the Attorney General
> Special Compensation Program
> 100 Justice Building
> Salem, OR 17101
> Telephone (503) 378-5348

Palau

> Palau Juvenile Justice Planner
> Ministry of Justice
> P.O. Box 100
> Koror, Palau 96940

Pennsylvania

> Commission on Crime and Delinquency
> P.O. Box 1167
> Federal Square Station
> Harrisburg, PA 17108-1167
> Telephone (717) 787-8559

Puerto Rico

> Puerto Rico
> Department of Justice
> P.O. Box 192
> San Juan, PR 00902
> Telephone (809) 723-4949

Rhode Island

> Governor's Justice Commission
> Executive Department
> 222 Quaker Lane, Suite 100
> Warwick, RI 02886
> Telephone (401) 277-2620

South Carolina

> Division of Public Safety
> Office of the Governor
> 1205 Pendleton Street
> Columbia, SC 29201
> Telephone (803) 734-0425

South Dakota

> Community Assistance Programs
> 910 East Sioux
> c/o 500 East Capitol
> Pierre, SD 57501-5070
> Telephone (605) 773-3178

Tennessee

> Department of Human Services
> Citizens Plaza Building, 15th Floor
> 400 Deaderick Street
> Nashville, TN 37219
> Telephone (615) 741-3241

Texas

> Criminal Justice Division
> Office of the Governor
> P.O. Box 12428
> Capitol Station
> Austin, TX 78711
> Telephone (512) 463-1919

Utah

> State of Utah
> Office of Crime Victim Reparations
> 350 East 500 South, Suite 200
> Salt Lake City, UT 84111
> Telephone (801) 533-4000 in Salt Lake City
>   (800) 621-7444 for all other areas in Utah

Vermont

> Vermont Center for Crime Victim Services
> P.O. Box 991
> Montpelier, VT 05601-0991
> Telephone (802) 828-3374 or
>   (800) 750-1213 toll free in Vermont

Virgin Islands

> Virgin Islands
> Law Enforcement Planning Commission
> 8172 Submarine Base, Suite 3
> St. Thomas, VI 00802-5803
> Telephone (809) 774-6400

Virginia

> Department of Criminal Justice Services
> 805 East Broad Street, 10th Floor
> Richmond, VA 23219
> Telephone (804) 786-4000

Washington

> Department of Social and Health Services
> Mail Stop OB-41C
> Olympia, WA 98504-0095
> Telephone (206) 753-3395

West Virginia

Criminal Justice and Highway Safety Office
Governor's Office of Community and Industrial Development
1204 Kanawha Boulevard, East
Charleston, WV 25301
Telephone (304) 558-8814

Wisconsin

Wisconsin Department of Justice
Crime Victim Compensation
P.O. Box 7951
Madison, WI 53707-7951
Telephone (608) 266-6470 in Madison
    (800) 446-6564 for all other areas in Wisconsin

Wyoming

Wyoming Crime Victims Compensation Commission
Office of the Attorney General
1700 Westland Road
Cheyenne, WY 82002
Telephone (307) 635-4050; Fax (307) 638-7208

Appendix C

Research on False Allegations of Sexual Abuse in Divorce

KATHLEEN COULBORN FALLER
DAVID L. CORWIN
ERNA OLAFSON

The statement, "There is an epidemic of false allegations of sexual abuse in divorce cases," is regarded by some as a truism. The argument is that women seeking to win custody of their children, to cut off the father's visitation, or to wreak vengeance on former spouses, falsely accuse them of child sexual abuse (Mantell, 1988; Renshaw, 1985, 1987). Such is the assertion of accused fathers, their attorneys (Gordon, 1985), and their expert witnesses (Blush & Ross,

SOURCE: Copyright © 1990, 1996 by the American Professional Society on the Abuse of Children. All rights reserved. This article is reproduced with permission of the American Professional Society on the Abuse of Children (APSAC), the nation's largest interdisciplinary professional society for those who work in the field of child maltreatment. APSAC's aim is to ensure that everyone affected by child maltreatment receives the best possible professional response. APSAC provides ongoing professional education in the form of publications and conferences and, through the media and legislative advocacy, educates the public about the complex issues involved in child maltreatment. For further information contact APSAC at 407 South Dearborn St., Suite 1300, Chicago, IL 60605. Phone (312) 554-0166; fax (312) 554-0919; or e-mail: APSACPubls@aol.com.

1986; Gardner, 1989). Moreover, the media have supported and broadcast these views, and many professionals with mandated responsibility for these cases, including child protection workers, law enforcement personnel, and, most importantly, judges, have come to believe that abuse allegations during divorce are likely to be false.

Are there any empirical findings that lend credibility to the view that most allegations of child abuse in divorce are false? In this article, literature addressing this issue will be critically reviewed, looking specifically at data cited, sample size, any sample biases, and the criteria employed to determine the veracity of the allegation.

"STUDIES" PROVIDING NO DATA

Writers holding the most extreme positions and promulgating new "syndromes" provide no data to support their statements (Blush & Ross, 1986; Gardner, 1987).

Blush and Ross have propounded the Sexual Allegations in Divorce, SAID Syndrome, the overwhelming majority of which they assert are false. These false allegations are fostered by mothers, whom Blush and Ross label psychotic or hysterical (dominated, dominating, or "justified vindicators"). They advise that almost no weight should be given to any statement made by the child, and in practice they may not even interview the child. However, Blush and Ross maintain, great weight should be given to the fact that these allegations are made by mothers who wish to restrict their ex-partners' access to their children (Ross, 1988). Blush and Ross find fathers much less likely to make false allegations, and describe those who do as rigid and hypercritical of their estranged wives. Falsely accused men are also described as inadequate, dependent, and passive, descriptors the authors also apply to incest perpetrators.

Since no data are provided, there is no way to evaluate the SAID Syndrome, other than to note that the admonition to put little weight on children's accounts is contrary to general practice (see Conte, Sorenson, Fogarty, & Dalla Rosa, 1991).

Perhaps even stronger views are held by Gardner (1987, 1989, 1991, 1992), who has defined the Parental Alienation Syndrome (PAS), which is manifest in children who "view one parent as all good and the other as all bad." These children have been "programmed by their mothers to hate their father and to subject him to a campaign of denigration" (Gardner, 1992, p. 160). Among the material the mother some-times also programs the child to believe is that the father has sexually abused him/her. When an allegation arises after a dispute over cus-tody, Gardner believes it possesses a "high likelihood of being false" (Gardner, 1991, p. 4).

A companion to the PAS is the Sexual Abuse Legitimacy Scale (SALS) (Gardner, 1987). The present version (Gardner, 1992) contains 84 differentiating criteria, 24 of which apply to the alleged offender, 30 to the child, and 30 to the mother. Many of these criteria relate specifically to allegations of abuse in divorce. For example, if one finds, in examining the mother, "the presence of a child custody dis-pute and/or litigation," "enlistment of the services of a 'hired gun' attorney or mental health professional," or "history of attempts to destroy, humiliate, or wreak vengeance on the accused," her allega-tions are less likely to be true, according to Gardner.

Gardner presents no data to validate either the PAS or the SALS. Therefore, the utility of the scales cannot be evaluated. Most of Gard-ner's writing on these topics is not peer reviewed and is published through his own press.

STUDIES INVOLVING SMALL SAMPLES

The first and oft-cited clinical study of false allegations of sexual abuse in divorce involved a single case and reference to a second one (Kaplan & Kaplan, 1981). In the case described in detail, an 11-year-old boy and his 5-year-old sister made allegations against their father and paternal grandparents. Both children had testified numerous times in court about the abuse and persisted in their accusations when chal-lenged. Indeed, the Kaplans describe one particularly stormy session in which the boy is confronted simultaneously by the paternal grand-parents and one of the Drs. Kaplan. Because, during this session, the boy partially recanted and said he had only been anally penetrated once instead of numerous times, the Kaplans conclude that his allega-tion is false. His partial recantation also led them to doubt the sister's account even though, in addition to her statements, she had a number of behavioral and emotional symptoms of sexual victimization. The Kaplans propose the possible dynamic of *folie à deux* as an explanation for the children's allegations, despite the fact there was no delusional thinking diagnosed in either child, the mother, or the maternal grandparents, who were supportive of the allegations, and despite the fact that the allegations originated with the children rather than a dominant adult.

Another frequently quoted study is that of Schuman (1986), who cites seven cases determined to be false on the basis of "psychodynamic formulation" and court determinations, out of an unknown number seen in his practice of probate and family court cases. Six of these were sexual abuse allegations against a father or stepfather; the seventh was a physical abuse case. The psychodynamic explanation for the false allegations was regression by the child and the accusing adult; in addition, in some instances (Schuman does not say how many) this adult retracted the allegation. This study is limited by its small sample size and by the lack of an empirical basis for the criteria Schuman uses to determine that allegations are false.

A study that has excited quite a lot of controversy is one reported by Green (1986) involving 11 cases from his practice, four of which (36%) he believed to be false. From these four cases, he generates criteria indicative of a false allegation, including easy disclosure, no evidence of negative affect, use of adult sexual terminology, checking with the accusing parent (mother) during the interview, and an ability to confront the father with the accusation. Falsely accusing mothers are described as hysterical and paranoid.

Green's conclusions were challenged because of the size and bias of his sample, and because one of his "false" cases was deemed possibly valid by two other experts in child sexual abuse (which would reduce his rate of false cases to 27%). His paper occasioned a rebuttal article (Corwin, Berliner, Goodman, Goodwin, & White, 1987) as well as a letter to the editor of the journal that published the original article, challenging its findings (Hanson, 1988). Among other things, Corwin and colleagues point out that there is a difference between a false (no abuse) and an unsubstantiated case (a null finding). In addition, they note that marital dissolution may increase the risk of sexual abuse and increase the likelihood of disclosure of pre-existing incest.

Benedek and Schetky (1985) also present findings from their private practices. They were interested in studying the characteristics of false allegations in divorce, and Benedek (1987) reports screening at intake to include suspected false cases and to exclude ones that appeared to be true. Fourteen of the 18 cases they assessed involved custody or visitation disputes in the context of divorce (four involved other issues related to custody). The authors thought that 10 of their cases were false (71% of 14 and 56% of 18). Not surprisingly, since they screened for false cases, this is the highest false allegation rate reported by any author presenting case data. All but one of the allegedly false allegations were made by mothers. It is not clear what criteria Benedek and Schetky used to determine that allegations were false; among the explanatory factors they cited were that the mother suffered from psychiatric disturbance ("paranoia" was the diagnosis most frequently mentioned by the authors), or wished to exclude their ex-spouses from their lives, were being vindictive, or were "crying wolf."

A much larger study (576 cases) of sexual abuse cases referred to child protective services provided findings relevant to the issue of sexual abuse and divorce (Jones & McGraw, 1987). Criteria employed in classifying the cases as likely true or likely false consisted of source of report, vindictiveness of parties, emotional disturbance in the ac- cuser or the accused, abnormal parent/child relationships, timing of report, child's emotional state, physical evidence, confessions, poly- graph results, and court role. Of the 5% of cases which a team of sexual abuse experts determined were "fictitious" allegations by adults, a large proportion involved contested custody or visitation. These find- ings suggest that false accusations are very rare generally, but may be more common in the context of custody disputes.

In a subsequent study by Jones and Seig (1988), 20 divorce cases involving accusations of sexual abuse from the Kempe Center were evaluated using the Jones and McGraw (1987) criteria to ascertain the rate of fictitious allegations. Four cases (20%) were determined to be fictitious, 14 (70%) reliable, and 2 (10%) uncertain. In this study, the authors observed that factors thought to be characteristic of false al- legations were noted in the reliable cases, and characteristics expected in reliable cases were noted in the fictitious ones.

Using the criteria developed by Jones and McGraw (1987) and used by Jones and Seig (1988), McGraw and Smith (1992) re-examined 18 cases referred to Boulder County Protective Services involving sex- ual abuse allegations in the context of divorce, all but one of which had been unfounded after CPS investigation. The results of this re-ex- amination were that eight cases (44.4%) were founded, seven cases (39%) had insufficient information or unsubstantiated suspicion, and three (16.5%) were fictitious (one from a child and two from adults). The authors admonish investigators and clinicians to keep an open mind when investigating such cases, rather than assuming that they will be false.

STUDIES COMPARING DIVORCE CASES TO
OTHER SEXUAL ABUSE CASES

Two studies compare results from divorce and non divorce cases. Paradise, Rostain, and Nathanson (1988) examined 31 cases (25 from Children's Hospital of Philadelphia and six from the first author's private practice), 12 of which involved divorce. Those cases involving divorce were significantly less likely to be substantiated: 67% substantiation rate in divorce cases vs. 95% substantiation rate in cases not involving divorce. In addition, children in the divorce group were significantly younger (5.4 years vs. 7.8); this age difference may have affected substantiation rates, since cases involving younger children may be generally more difficult to substantiate (Thoennes & Tjaden, 1990).

Hlady and Gunter (1990) examined the records of 370 children seen at the Child Protection Service Unit at British Columbia Children's Hospital. One hundred seventeen children were primarily referred for alleged physical abuse, and 253 for alleged sexual abuse. Forty-one children were the objects of custody disputes. Surprisingly, children involved in custody disputes were more likely to exhibit physical findings (71% had findings of physical abuse, 17.6% had findings of sexual abuse) than were children not involved in custody disputes (43.6% showing findings of physical abuse, 15% of sexual abuse). Generalizations from these data must be cautious, since the number of custody cases with allegations of physical abuse was small, and the difference on sexual abuse cases was not significant. However, these data suggest that sexual abuse allegations made in the context of divorce are at least as likely to have the corroboration of medical findings.

More studies comparing commonly evaluated characteristics of sexual abuse cases in divorce and other contexts would be very useful.

STUDIES INVOLVING LARGER SAMPLES

To date, there are two pieces of research with samples larger than 100 cases. Faller (1988) studied 136 cases involving divorce that were referred to the University of Michigan Interdisciplinary Project on

Child Abuse and Neglect, which includes a tertiary care program for evaluation of child maltreatment cases. Using criteria derived from a study of confessed cases, Faller determined the likelihood of sexual abuse in her sample. These criteria included (1) description of the sexual abuse; (2) details about the context; and (3) affect congruent with allegations and circumstance. Faller categorized these cases into six groups: cases in which disclosure of apparently true abuse leads to divorce (N=11; 8.1%); cases in which divorce leads to disclosure of apparently true abuse by the child or belief by the parent (N=26; 19.1%); cases in which divorce leads to sexual abuse (N=52; 38.2%); cases in which apparently false allegations arise in an atmosphere of acrimony surrounding the divorce (N=19; 14%); cases in which false allegations may have been made (N=12; 8.8%); and cases in which other dynamics were at work (N=16; 11.8%). Of the 19 cases involving apparently false allegations, three appeared to be consciously made, and two of these intentionally false allegations were made by fathers.

By far the most important study to date is that conducted by the Association of Family and Conciliation Courts Research Unit (Thoennes, Pearson, & Tjaden, 1988; Thoennes & Tjaden, 1990). The researchers surveyed 9,000 divorce cases involving custody/visitation disputes from 12 domestic relations courts to determine how many such disputes involve allegations of sexual abuse. The researchers found allegations of child sexual abuse in less than two percent (169) of these cases. In 129 cases, the question of sexual abuse was addressed by the domestic relations court. Accusations were made by mothers (67%), fathers (28%), and third parties (11%). Fewer than half of cases involved mothers making accusations against the fathers of children.

Using the Child Protective Services determination and/or the report of a court-appointed mental health evaluator as the criteria for substantiation, the researchers found that 50% of cases were likely, 33% were unlikely, and 17% were uncertain (which included cases in which two evaluators held different opinions). They also attempted to discern the motivation for unlikely reports and found 58 cases in which the case material addressed that issue. In eight cases, child protective service workers thought the allegation was maliciously made. Factors associated with cases being classified as unlikely or uncertain were younger age of the child, a single incident alleged, non-intrusive sexual behavior, a single report, a report less than two years since the filing for divorce, and animosity between the parents.

CONCLUSIONS

On the basis of the research that has been conducted so far, it is difficult to support an assertion that there are high rates of false allegations of sexual abuse consciously made by mothers in divorce situations.

There is no way to evaluate authors' opinions not supported by data. Thus all that can be said about the SAID Syndrome and the Parental Alienation Syndrome is that they express the authors' opinions. Moreover, the language used in both suggests a bias against mothers concerned about sexual abuse of their children.

The remainder of the research can be evaluated regarding possible sample biases, sample size, and criteria used to determine that the allegation is false.

With the exception of the research supported by the Association of Family and Conciliation Courts (Thoennes et al., 1988; Thoennes & Tjaden, 1990) and that by Paradise and colleagues (1988), all of the studies cited rely on cases from a single source. A single site or source may introduce biases based upon geography, the authors' selection criteria, and the reputation of the clinician or the site. Selection criteria include such factors as Benedek's screening for cases she thought might be false, or Faller's taking cases referred by another agency. Payment source for the service may also determine the sorts of cases seen at a particular site. In addition, cases seen in private practices are likely to differ from those seen at an agency or at a hospital.

Sample size is also very important in weighing the utility and potential validity of findings. It is very difficult to draw any conclusions from samples smaller than 20 cases. Particularly problematic is the situation in which the writer draws conclusions about characteristics of false allegations from a subset of a small sample, as does Green (1986).

The most difficult problem in evaluating research on allegations of child sexual abuse is evaluating the criteria researchers use to assess the veracity of allegations. To test these criteria, researchers need to see if they are in fact reflected in a sample of cases proven false or true by some independent measure (for example, that the offender never had access to the victim, or, alternatively, that the offender gave a complete, detailed confession). Since such samples are hard to find and indeed may be unrepresentative, research on the veracity of child sexual abuse allegations cannot draw upon them. Most writers use their clinical judgment, the consensus of several clinicians or experts, or a legally supported decision, such as the disposition of the child protection agency, the conclusion of a court-appointed expert, or a judge's opinion. All of these have limitations. Jones and Seig's (1988) determination that cases thought to be reliable had characteristics of false reports and vice versa is illustrative. So is the Association of Family and Conciliation Courts' classification of cases as "uncertain" when two opinions disagreed.

Moreover, there is a fair amount of disagreement among writers about characteristics of false allegations. Indeed, one professional's indicator of a false allegation may be another's indicator of a true one. In addition, some criteria lend themselves to a variety of interpretations, either in the context of a single case, or depending upon the case.

When the research is examined critically, the strongest study is that conducted by the Association of Family and Conciliation Courts, because of its large sample, its use of multiple sites, and the fact that cases are fairly representative of the total population of divorce cases with disputes over custody and visitation. Its findings indicate that sexual abuse allegations do occur in the context of divorce, but the overwhelming majority (98%) of disputed custody cases do not involve sexual abuse accusations. Moreover, although the majority of charges are brought by mothers, by no means all are. The predominance of women as accusers and men as accused is consistent with the finding that the majority of offenders are men. This study and that of Faller contradict the assertion by others that most adults who make false reports do so knowingly (e.g., Benedek & Schetky, 1985; Blush & Ross, 1986; Gardner, 1987; Renshaw, 1987).

Where the Association of Family and Conciliation Courts may be weaker than other studies is in the criteria it used to judge the veracity of an allegation: the child protective services determination or a court-appointed mental health professional's opinion. Perhaps criteria such as those based on a consensus of experts or a collaborative decision (Jones & McGraw, 1987; Jones & Seig, 1988; McGraw & Smith, 1992) or derived indirectly from cases substantiated by confession (Faller, 1990) are more accurate. Interestingly, substantiation rates tend to be higher in such studies and uncertainty rates lower.

Altogether 11 data-based articles about sexual abuse allegations in divorce are cited here. This number is too small to draw more than tentative conclusions. Moreover, characteristics of allegations in divorce may be influenced by increased public education and experience regarding sexual abuse, so that samples that are just five years old may not reflect current caseloads. Perhaps the likelihood of a parent making a false allegation in a divorce has increased because of greater awareness of sexual abuse and of the potential power of an allegation. Conversely, adults may be cognizant of the recent outcomes in such cases. These include disbelief by the court or refusal to hear evidence of sexual abuse, incarceration of the parent who refuses visitation, loss of custody by the parent alleging sexual abuse, and negative experiences of parents, who with their children may go so far as to enter the "underground" to avoid court decisions. This knowledge may result in parents becoming less likely to raise a legitimate concern about sexual abuse because the legal consequences may further traumatize a child and family without stopping the abuse.

REFERENCES

Benedek, E. (1987). Court testimony. *E. Morgan v. E. Foretich, V. Foretich, & D. Foretich*. Alexandria, VA: United States District Court, February 18.

Benedek, E., & Schetky, D. (1985). Allegations of sexual abuse in child custody cases. In E. Benedek & D. Schetky (Eds.), *Emerging issues in child psychiatry and the law* (pp. 145-156). New York: Brunner/ Mazel.

Blush, G., & Ross, K. (1986). *Sexual allegations in divorce: The SAID syndrome*. Unpublished manuscript available from the Psychodiagnostic Clinic, Macomb County Circuit Court, Mt. Clemens, MI.

Conte, J., Sorenson, E., Fogarty, L., & Dalla Rosa, J. (1991). Evaluating children's reports of sexual abuse: Results from a survey of professionals. *American Journal of Orthopsychiatry, 61,* 428-437.

Corwin, D. L., Berliner, L., Goodman, G., Goodwin, J., & White, S. (1987). Child sexual abuse and custody disputes: No easy answers. *Journal of Interpersonal Violence, 2,* 91-105.

Faller, K. (1988). Criteria for judging the credibility of children's statements about their sexual abuse. *Child Welfare, 67*(5), 389-401.

Faller, K. (1990). *Understanding child sexual abuse*. Newbury Park, CA: Sage.

Gardner, R. (1987). *The parental alienation syndrome and the differentiation between fabricated and genuine child sexual abuse*. Cresskill, NJ: Creative Therapeutics.

Gardner, R. (1989). Differentiating between bona fide and fabricated allegations of sexual abuse of children. *Journal of the American Academy of Matrimonial Lawyers, 5,* 1-25.

Gardner, R. (1991). *Sex abuse hysteria: Salem witch trials revisited.* Cresskill, NJ: Creative Therapeutics.

Gardner, R. (1992). *True and false allegations of child sex abuse.* Cresskill, NJ: Creative Therapeutics.

Gordon, C. (1985). False allegations of abuse in child custody disputes. *Minnesota Family Law Journal, 2*(14), 225-228.

Green, A. (1986). True and false allegations of sexual abuse in child custody disputes. *Journal of the American Academy of Child Psychiatry, 25,* 449-455.

Hanson, G. (1988). The sex abuse controversy [Letter to the editor]. *Journal of the American Academy of Child and Adolescent Psychiatry, 27,* 258.

Hlady, L., & Gunter, E. (1990). Alleged child abuse in custody access disputes. *Child Abuse & Neglect, 14,* 591-594.

Jones, D., & McGraw, M. (1987). Reliable and fictitious accounts of sexual abuse to children. *Journal of Interpersonal Violence, 2,* 27-45.

Jones, D., & Seig, A. (1988). Child sexual abuse allegations in custody or visitation cases: A report of 20 cases. In B. Nicholson & J. Bulkley (Eds.), *Sexual abuse allegations in custody and visitation cases.* Washington, DC: American Bar Association.

Kaplan, S., & Kaplan, S. (1981). The child's accusation of sexual abuse during a divorce and custody struggle. *Hillside Journal of Clinical Psychiatry, 3,* 1, 81-95.

Mantell, D. (1988). Clarifying erroneous child sexual abuse allegations. *American Journal of Orthopsychiatry, 58*(4), 618-621.

McGraw, J., & Smith, H. (1992). Child sexual abuse allegations amidst divorce and custody proceedings: Refining the validation process. *Journal of Child Sexual Abuse, 1,* 49-62.

Paradise, J., Rostain, A., & Nathanson, M. (1988). Substantiation of sexual abuse charges when parents dispute custody or visitation. *Pediatrics, 81,* 6, 835-839.

Renshaw, D. (1985). When sexual abuse is wrongly charged. *Medical aspects of human sexuality, 19,* 116-121.

Renshaw, D. (1987). Child sexual abuse: When wrongly charged. *Encyclopedia Britannica Medical and Health Annual,* 301-303.

Ross, K. (1988, May). *SAID syndrome: Fact or fallacy.* Workshop at Grand Valley State University, Grand Rapids, MI.

Schuman, D. (1986). False allegations of physical and sexual abuse. *Bulletin of the American Academy of Psychiatry and the Law, 14*(1), 5-21.

Thoennes, N., Pearson, J., & Tjaden, P. (1988). *Allegations of sexual abuse in custody and visitation cases.* Denver: Association of Family and Conciliation Courts.

Thoennes, N., & Tjaden, P. (1990). The extent, nature, and validity of sexual abuse allegations in custody/visitation disputes. *Child Abuse & Neglect, 14,* 151-163.

Appendix D

Psychosocial Evaluation of Suspected Psychological Maltreatment in Children and Adolescents

AMERICAN PROFESSIONAL SOCIETY
ON THE ABUSE OF CHILDREN

I.   Statement of Purpose

The purpose of these Guidelines is to provide guidance for professionals evaluating children to determine whether they are or have been victims of psychological maltreatment. The results of such evaluations may be used to assist in case planning, legal decision making, and treatment planning. The Guidelines concern psychological maltreatment that occurs in isolation as well as psychological maltreatment that occurs in conjunction with other forms of abuse and neglect.

The Guidelines apply primarily to forensic assessments of psychological maltreatment. Professionals providing treatment and performing nonforensic assessments may also find the Guidelines helpful.

The Guidelines will be modified as research and practice evolve. Because each child is unique, the Guidelines will not apply equally or exactly to all children. Assessment of psychological maltreatment is complex, and professionals must have the flexibility to exercise clinical judgment in individual cases.

The Guidelines are not intended to serve as a rigid blueprint for practice, nor are they intended to establish a legal standard of care to which professionals must adhere. Rather, the Guidelines provide a model of desirable professional practice.

II. Meaning of Key Terms

This section defines some key terms employed in the Guidelines. The definitions should be read in conjunction with definitions provided in applicable Federal and State laws.

"Child maltreatment" means the physical or mental injury, sexual abuse or exploitation, negligent treatment, or maltreatment of a child by a person who is responsible for the child's welfare under circumstances which indicate harm or threatened harm to the child's health or welfare. This definition is drawn from the Federal Child Abuse Prevention and Treatment Act. 42 United States Code § 5106g(4). See also, 45 C.F.R. § 1340.2(d). "Child maltreatment" includes child abuse and child neglect. Definitions specific to a particular state will generally be found in one or more of its civil or criminal statutes.

"Forensic assessment," for the purpose of these Guidelines, means a psychosocial assessment that is conducted wholly or in part for use in legal proceedings. For example, a psychosocial assessment conducted at the request of a juvenile court judge for use in legal proceedings is a "forensic assessment." Psychosocial assessments that are not conducted for use in legal proceedings may nevertheless be relevant to such proceedings.

"Intervention," in this context, means action on behalf of a child who may be psychologically maltreated. Intervention is a broad concept. Some forms of intervention involve official action by government agencies such as child protective services and juvenile courts. Examples of official intervention include investigations conducted by child protective services agencies and juvenile court orders designed to protect children from psychological mal-treatment. Some official intervention is taken over the objection of caregivers, and represents the legal authority of government to intervene in families. Other official intervention can be received on a voluntary basis. In addition to official action on behalf of children, intervention includes a wide range of acts by profession-als in public and private sectors. Examples of non-official inter-vention include providing therapy for children and referring care-givers to appropriate agencies.

"Psychological maltreatment" means a repeated pattern of caregiver behavior or extreme incident(s) that convey to children that they are worthless, flawed, unloved, unwanted, endangered, or only of value in meeting another's needs. The term "psycho-logical," instead of "emotional," is used because it better incorpo-rates the cognitive, affective, and interpersonal conditions that are the primary concomitants of this form of child maltreatment. Pro-fessionals should be aware of legal definitions of psychological maltreatment that are applicable in their community. Psychologi-cal maltreatment includes acts of commission (e.g., verbal attacks by a caregiver) as well as acts of omission (e.g., emotional unavail-ability of a caregiver). Definitions specific to a particular state will generally be found in one or more of its civil or criminal statutes.

"Psychosocial assessment" means a systematic process of gathering information and forming a professional opinion re-garding whether or not a child has been or is being subjected to psychological maltreatment. Psychosocial assessments are broadly concerned with understanding developmental, familial, and historical factors that might be associated with psychological maltreatment. The results of a psychosocial assessment might be used to assist in legal decision making and in treatment planning. In the Guidelines, the terms "assessment" and "evaluation" are used interchangeably, and have the same meaning. Some psy-chosocial assessments are "forensic assessments" as that term is defined in the Guidelines.

III. Prevalence of Psychological Maltreatment

Psychological maltreatment can occur alone, without co-occur-rence of other forms of child abuse or neglect. Approximately 10% of reports to child protective services are for psychological maltreatment alone. Although psychological maltreatment occurs in isolation, it is often associated with other forms of maltreatment and is commonly considered to be embedded in all forms of child abuse and neglect. Thus, children who are physically abused, sexually abused, or neglected, in most cases are also be psychologically maltreated.

Psychological maltreatment, in stand-alone occurrences, is the third most common form of maltreatment reported in the United States. Although there are no fully accurate national statistics on the prevalence of psychological maltreatment, this form of maltreatment is likely to be underreported and widespread.

IV. Short- and Long-Term Effects of Psychological Maltreatment

Psychological maltreatment produces both acute and long-term negative effects. Research establishes a connection between psychological maltreatment and attachment disorders, limitations in cognitive ability and problem solving, poor academic achievement, poor peer relationships, behavior problems, anxiety disorders (especially PTSD), and anti-social behavior (see Hart, Brassard, & Karlson, in press, for extensive references).

Other forms of child maltreatment are also associated with the foregoing effects (see Briere, Berliner, Bulkley, Jenny, & Reid, in press). An assessment of suspected psychological maltreatment should attempt to differentiate effects caused primarily by psychological maltreatment from effects caused by other factors, including other forms of maltreatment.

V. Confidentiality and Privilege

Professionals conducting forensic assessments should be aware of basic legal principles in their jurisdictions governing confidentiality and privileged communications with caregivers, children, and others. Professionals should maintain confidentiality and privilege to the extent reasonably possible.

In the forensic context, confidentiality and privilege are often limited. For example, when a professional conducts an assessment at the request of a judge, the professional's findings and report may not be confidential, and communications between the professional and the subject of the assessment may not be privileged from disclosure in legal proceedings. Professionals should be aware of applicable limitations on confidentiality and privilege, and should inform appropriate individuals of such limitations.

VI. Informed Consent

Professionals conducting forensic assessments should be aware of legal and ethical principles governing informed consent. Informed consent should be obtained unless such consent is unnecessary because of the forensic nature of the assessment. Whether or not informed consent is obtained, the professional should advise persons being assessed of the purposes of the assessment and the intended uses of any report or testimony resulting from the assessment.

In forensic situations where informed consent is required but the person being assessed is incapable of giving such consent, the professional should consult with legal counsel or the judge regarding the appropriate way to proceed.

VII. Training and Experience of Professionals Conducting Assessments

Professionals conducting a forensic assessment should possess an advanced mental health degree in a recognized discipline or an advanced health services degree with training and substantial experience in mental health. The professional should hold the licensure or credentials required to practice in the jurisdiction. Child protective service employees who meet the experience standards set forth in this section, but who are not licensed or credentialed in a mental health discipline, may carry out forensic assessment functions under the supervision of a mental health professional meeting the criteria outlined in this paragraph.

The professional should have broad experience in evaluation and treatment of both functional and dysfunctional children and families. The professional should possess a minimum of two years of experience with abused and neglected children. Two or more years of experience with non-maltreated children is desirable. The professional should also have specialized training in or knowledge of child development and psychological maltreatment.

The professional should be familiar with current literature on psychological maltreatment. If the professional lacks the experience described in this paragraph, appropriate supervision by someone with such experience is required.

The professional should have experience conducting forensic assessments and testifying in court. The professional should be familiar with the forensic implications of interviews of children and adults, including the importance of proper interviewing and documentation. If the professional lacks the experience described in this paragraph, appropriate supervision is required.

The professional should approach the assessment with an open mind regarding what, if anything, might have happened to the child.

If a multidisciplinary team of specialists conducts an assessment, it is advisable for one member of the team to assume the responsibility to coordinate the assessment process, integrate findings, and develop any report. Where the opinions of team members differ, it is recommended that this be identified in reports provided.

VIII. Assessment Considerations

A. Global Assessmen Considerations

Psychological maltreatment is often accompanied by or embedded in other forms of child abuse and neglect. Thus, when professionals evaluate possible physical abuse, sexual abuse, or neglect, it is recommended that psychological maltreatment also be considered.

The goal of forensic assessments is often to determine for a court of law whether a caregiver has maltreated or is psychologically maltreating a child and, if so, the severity of maltreatment and the degree to which maltreatment is related to existing or future harm to the child. Acts of maltreatment are in themselves deplorable regardless of the degree to which a child is damaged by them or is coping with them; however, depending on the cause of action or type of proceeding, laws and practices of many states require evidence of both acts and harm (extant or predicted) for case determinations. Therefore, these Guidelines deal with both acts and harm.

Psychological maltreatment is a repeated pattern or extreme incident(s) of caregiver behavior that convey the message that a child is worthless, flawed, unloved, unwanted, endangered, or only valuable in meeting someone else's needs. Virtually every caregiver, at some point, sends such unfortunate messages. There are few perfect caregivers. Most psychological maltreatment occurs when such negative messages pass from isolated incidents to a consistent caregiving style.

Psychological maltreatment can occur as part of a one-time incident, such as a painful divorce. For example, a parent who is depressed and traumatized by a bitter custody battle might terrorize a child with threats about the child's future.

In some cases, psychological maltreatment occurs only when some specific, recurring triggering event occurs. For example, with an alcoholic or drug addicted caregiver, psychological maltreatment may occur only when the caregiver is intoxicated.

Some psychological maltreatment is chronic, regular, and embedded in the child's daily existence. An example is a caregiver who levels a daily barrage of verbal abuse at a child.

Child behavior often provides evidence of psychological maltreatment. One must be cautious, however, about inferring causation from behavior. Multiple pathways lead to particular behaviors. When considering the possibility of psychological maltreatment, the professional should rule out other factors such as psychological trauma unrelated to maltreatment, inherited or congenital vulnerabilities, and various forms of mental illness.

Professionals should understand the influence of base rates on the diagnostic value of specific behaviors. For example, post-traumatic stress disorder is more prevalent in inner city neighborhoods with high crime rates than in most suburban and rural areas. Thus, children living in dangerous neighborhoods may have a higher incidence of PTSD than children living in safer environments (Osofsky & Jackson, 1994). Presence of PTSD symptoms in a child living in a dangerous neighborhood may be the result of environmental influences rather than caregiver-perpetrated psychological maltreatment.

Although child behaviors can yield useful information, behavior alone is not a sufficient basis to determine whether psychological maltreatment has occurred. Moreover, some victims of psychological maltreatment demonstrate no detectible signs or symptoms. Evaluators should consider various influences on caregiver-child and family interaction, and should investigate as many sources of information as possible.

B.   The Child's Developmental Level

An assessment for possible psychological maltreatment should include consideration of the child's developmental level. The caregiver-child relationship should be considered within a developmental framework that takes into account the primary developmental tasks of the child and the related tasks placed upon the caregiver. For example, one of an infant's primary developmental tasks is to form a secure attachment with an adult caregiver, learning in the process to trust others to provide a stable, loving, nurturing, responsive environment, and to believe in his/her own ability to solicit that care. A caregiver who predominantly rejects a child's bids for attention (for comfort, play, or assistance) negatively shapes a child's sense of self, worthiness, competence, efficacy, and trust in others. Professionals may use the list of "Developmental Tasks" contained in Table A.1 to assist in the assessment process.

C.   Forms and Severity of Psychological Maltreatment

This subsection discusses forms and severity of psychological maltreatment.

Table A.1 Developmental Tasks

Infancy	–Attachment –Assistance in the regulation of bodily states, emotion
Toddlerhood	–Development of symbolic representation and further self-other differentiation –Problem-solving, pride, mastery motivation
Preschool	–Development of self-control—the use of language to regulate impulses, emotions, store information, predict and make sense of the world –Development of verbally mediated or semantic memory –Gender identity –Development of social relationships beyond immediate family and generalization of expectations about relationships –Moral reasoning
Latency age	–Peer relationships –Adaptation to school environment –Moral reasoning
Adolescence	–Renegotiation of family roles –Identity issues (sexuality, future orientation,, peer acceptance, ethnicity) –Moral reasoning
Young adult	–Continued differentiation from family –Refinement and integration of identity with particular focus on occupational choice and intimate partners –Moral reasoning

Table A.2 Psychological Maltreatment Forms

A repeated pattern or extreme incident(s) of the conditions described in this Table constitute psychological maltreatment. Such conditions convey the message that the child is worthless, flawed, unloved, endangered, or only valuable in meeting someone else's needs.	
SPURNING (Hostile Rejecting/ Degrading) includes verbal and non-verbal caregiver acts that reject and degrade a child. SPURNING includes: –belittling, degrading, and other nonphysical forms of overtly hostile or rejecting treatment –shaming and/or ridiculing the child for showing normal emotions such as affection, grief, or sorrow –consistently singling out one child to criticize and punish, to perform most of the household chores, or to receive fewer rewards –public humiliation	EXPLOITING/CORRUPTING includes caregiver acts that encourage the child to develop inappropriate behaviors (self-destructive, anti-social, criminal, deviant, or other maladaptive behaviors) EXPLOITING/CORRUPTING includes: –modeling, permitting, or encouraging antisocial behavior (e.g., prostitution, performance in pornographic media, initiation of criminal activities, substance abuse, violence to or corruption of others) –modeling, permitting, or encouraging developmentally inappropriate behavior (e.g., parentification, infantilization, living the parent's unfulfilled dreams) –encouraging or coercing abandonment of developmentally appropriate autonomy through extreme over-involvement, intrusiveness, and/or dominance (e.g., allowing little or no opportunity or support for child's views, feelings, and wishes; micromanaging child's life) –restricting or interfering with cognitive development

Table A.2 (Continued)

TERRORIZING includes caregiver behavior that threatens or is likely to physically hurt, kill, abandon, or place the child or child's loved ones/objects in recognizably dangerous situations. TERRORIZING includes: –placing a child in unpredictable or chaotic circumstances –placing a child in recognizably dangerous situations –setting rigid or unrealistic expectations with threat of loss, harm, or danger if they are not met –threatening or perpetrating violence against the child –threatening or perpetrating violence against a child's loved ones or objects	DENYING EMOTIONAL RESPONSIVENESS (Ignoring) includes caregiver acts that ignore the child's attempts and needs to interact (failing to express affection, caring, and love for the child) and showing no emotion in interactions with the child. DENYING EMOTIONAL RESPONSIVENESS includes: –being detached and uninvolved through either incapacity or lack of motivation –interacting only when absolutely necessary –failing to express affection, caring, and love for the child

continued on p. 220

1. Forms of Psychological Maltreatment

Table A.2 describes six forms of psychological maltreatment. These forms find support in research and clinical experience. The forms are intended to help professionals analyze cases. A child's maltreatment experiences may be categorized by one or more of these forms and will not necessarily fit simply or completely within one form. The six forms of psychological maltreatment are: (a) spurning, (b) terrorizing, (c) isolating, (d) exploiting/corrupting, (e) denying emotional responsiveness, and (f) unwarranted denial of mental health care, medical care, or

Table A.2 (Continued)

| ISOLATING includes caregiver acts that consistently deny the child opportunities to meet needs for interacting/communicating with peers or adults inside or outside the home.

ISOLATING includes:

–confining the child or placing unreasonable limitations on the child's freedom of movement within his/her environment
–placing unreasonable limitations or restrictions on social interactions with peers or adults in the community | MENTAL, HEALTH, MEDICAL, AND EDUCATIONAL NEGLECT include unwarranted caregiver acts that ignore, refuse to allow, or fail to provide the necessary treatment for the mental health, medical, and educational problems or needs of the child.

MENTAL, HEALTH, MEDICAL, AND EDUCATIONAL NEGLECT include:

–ignoring the need for, failing or refusing to allow or provide, treatment for serious emotional/behavioral problems or needs of the child
–ignoring the need for, failing or refusing to allow or provide, treatment for serious physical health problems or needs of the child
–ignoring the need for, failing or refusing to allow or provide, treatment for services for serious educational problems or needs of the child |

SOURCE: Office for the Study of the Psychological Rights of the Child, Indiana University–Purdue University at Indianapolis, 902 West New York Street, Indianapolis, Indiana 48202-5155.

education. These forms are recommended for consideration as complements to legal and regulatory definitions of psychological maltreatment particular to the state.

2. Levels of Severity

In determining the level of severity of psychological maltreatment, consideration should be given to: (a) Inten-
sity/extremeness, frequency, chronicity; (b) The degree to
which psychological maltreatment pervades the caregiver-child relationship; (c) Number of forms of psychological maltreatment which have been or are being perpetrated; (d) Influences in the child's life that may buffer
the child from psychological maltreatment. For example,
does the maltreating caregiver also provide nurturance
for the child? Does the child have regular access to a nurturing, nonmaltreating adult? (e) Salience of the maltreatment given the developmental period(s) in which it occurs and the developmental periods that will follow; and
(f) Extent to which negative child developmental outcomes exist, are developing, or are predicted.

3. "Severe Emotional Disturbance" Defined in the Federal
Individuals With Disabilities Education Act

This subsection of the Guidelines draws on the Federal
Individuals with Disabilities Education Act, commonly
known as 94-142, and formerly titled the Education of the
Handicapped Act. Regulations implementing 94-142 define "severe emotional disturbance." (See 34 Code of Federal Regulations 300.7(9).) The 94-142 definitions incor-
porate psychological criteria for: (a) major mental
disorders and (b) interpersonal, cognitive, and emotional
behavior problems. Professionals assessing children for
possible psychological maltreatment will find these definitions of severe emotional disturbance and the standards included in the American Psychiatric Association's
Diagnostic and Statistical Manual(s) of Mental Disorders
(i.e., DSM III-R and DSM IV) useful to guide determinations of extant or predicted harm related to psychological
maltreatment. The 94-142 definitions provide:

"Serious emotional disturbance" is defined as follows:

(i) The term means a condition exhibiting one or more of the following characteristics over a long period of time and to a marked degree that adversely affects a child's educational performance—

(A) An inability to learn that cannot be explained by intellectual, sensory, or health factors;

(B) An inability to build or maintain satisfactory interpersonal relationships with peers and teachers;

(C) Inappropriate types of behavior or feelings under normal circumstances;

(D) A general pervasive mood of unhappiness or depression; or

(E) A tendency to develop physical symptoms or fears associated with personal or school problems.

D.   Assessment Techniques and Sources of Information

1. The Child-Caregiver Relationship

Psychological maltreatment consists primarily of messages a child receives about him- or herself and about important interpersonal relationships. When feasible, the professional should observe the child-caregiver relationship. Because of the chronicity of much psychological maltreatment, repeated observations may be necessary to obtain a representative sample of behavior and to provide grounds on which to recognize patterns of child-caregiver interaction. Although direct observation of the child-caregiver relationship is often useful, such observation is not always necessary to form an opinion regarding psychological maltreatment. Observations of caregiver-child interaction have limitations because parents may not behave in their usual manner when being observed. The child-caregiver relationship can also be assessed through interviews of the caregiver and the child, review of pertinent records, observation, consultation with other professionals, and collateral reports from siblings, grandparents, school and daycare personnel, neighbors, and others.

2. Child Characteristics

Psychological evaluation procedures such as observations, interviews, questionnaires, and projective techniques, with due consideration of their reliability and validity, can provide clarifying and corroborative information about patterns of interaction, care, and treatment, and their impact on the child. Deviance or delay in the child's functioning are assessed through direct observation by the evaluator, testing, the observations of others, and available reports and records (e.g., school, health, therapy).

3. Caregiver/Family Competencies and Risk Factors

Evaluation of caregiver competencies and risk factors assists in determining the existence of psychological maltreatment, in developing a prognosis for improvement in the child-caregiver relationship, and in identifying issues to address in treatment. Relevant areas of functioning include: (1) Caregiver's representational models or attitudes toward past attachment figures, current partner, and child(ren); (2) Personal resources (intelligence, job skills, social skills, personality variables, mental health); (3) Social support/resources (marital status, family, friends, financial status, community involvement); and (4) Life stresses or transitions in the family.

Assessment of the caregiver usually includes one or more interviews, review of collateral reports and records, and psychological testing.

Interaction with caregivers or members of the extended family should normally be carried out so as to increase the likelihood of voluntary involvement in the assessment and any intervention.

4. Consideration of Societal and Cultural Context

A family's community context and immediate social and economic circumstances should be taken into consideration when evaluating caregiver behavior. The psychological conditions jeopardizing a child's development may not be under the control of a caregiver. Homelessness, poverty, or living in a violent neighborhood can have an adverse impact on quality of and child development. Caregivers are not responsible for conditions over which they have no control.

Professionals should be knowledgeable about and sensitive to cultural and ethnic differences in caretaking styles and customs. If the evaluator is not familiar with the cultural context of the child and family, consultation with appropriate experts is required.

IX. Reporting Findings

Professionals conducting forensic assessments typically prepare reports that contain findings and recommendations.

A. Findings of Assessment

The report of a forensic assessment should document all sources of information considered by the professional during the assessment. The report should state the professional's findings. In appropriate circumstances the report may set forth the professional's opinion concerning whether a child has or is suffering from psychological maltreatment or other forms of child abuse or neglect. The report may indicate findings consistent or inconsistent with psychological maltreatment.

If the professional concludes that psychological maltreatment has or is occurring, the report should: (a) State the form(s) of psychological maltreatment; (b) Describe specific occurrences of caregiver behavior that constitute psychological maltreatment; (c) Document the severity through reference to intensity/extremeness, frequency, chronicity, pervasiveness, multiplicity of forms, counterbalancing positive treatment, developmental saliency, and probable short- and long-term effects of the maltreatment; and (d) Describe the relations between the psychological maltreatment and harm to the child.

In some cases the assessment is inconclusive. In such cases the professional should state the reasons for the inconclusive finding, and should indicate whether, in the professional's judgment, the child is at risk of harm.

B.   Recommended Interventions

The report should contain recommendations for appropriate intervention.

X.   Testifying in Court

Professionals should always be prepared for the possibility that they will be required to testify in court. Professionals should only provide expert testimony on matters for which they possess special competence that can assist the legal system, and should always acknowledge the limits of their competence.

When called upon to testify in court, professionals have an obligation to testify in a manner that is accurate and fair to all parties. Although straightforward and forceful presentation of findings and recommendations is proper, professionals reporting the results of forensic evaluations should avoid the temptation to become advocates for one side or the other in litigation.

XI. Related Guidelines and References

GUIDELINES

Professionals conducting forensic assessments and testifying in court should consult guidelines and ethical codes that apply to their particular specialty. The following list is provided as a reference:

• Specialty Guidelines for Forensic Psychologists (1991). *Law & Human Behavior, 15,* 655-665.

- American Professional Society on the Abuse of Children (1990). *Guidelines for Psychosocial Evaluation of Suspected Sexual Abuse in Young Children.* Chicago: Author.
- National Association of Social Workers. *Code of Ethics of the National Association of Social Workers.* Washington, DC: Author.
- American Association for Marriage and Family Therapy (1991). *AAMFT Code of Ethics.* Washington, DC: Author.
- American Academy of Psychiatry and the Law (1989). *AAPL Ethical Guidelines for the Practice of Forensic Psychiatry.* Chicago, IL: Author.

REFERENCES

The following references provide clarification and supportive information for the statements and recommendations presented in these Guidelines.

American Psychologist. (1987). Psychology in the public forum (subsection theme: psychological maltreatment). *42,* 157-175.

American Psychiatric Association. (1987). *Diagnostic and statistical manual of mental disorders: Third edition-revised (DSM-III-R).* Washington, DC: Author.

American Psychiatric Association. (1994). *Diagnostic and statistical manual of mental disorders: Fourth edition (DSM-IV).* Washington, DC: Author.

Baily, F. T., & Baily, W. H. (1986). *Operational definitions of child emotional maltreatment.* Augusta: Maine Department of Social Services.

Brassard, M. R., Germain, R., & Hart, S. N. (Eds.). (1987). *Psychological maltreatment of children and youth.* Elmsford, NY: Pergamon.

Briere, J., Berliner, L., Bulkley, J. A., Jenny, C., & Reid, T. (Eds.). (1996). *The APSAC handbook on child maltreatment.* Thousand Oaks, CA: Sage.

Development and Psychopathology. (1991). [Theme issue on psychological maltreatment]. *3.*

Garbarino, J., Guttman, E., Seeley, J. (1986). *The psychologically battered child: Strategies for identification, assessment and intervention.* San Francisco: Jossey-Bass.

Hart, S. N., Brassard, M. R., & Karlson, H. (1996). Psychological maltreatment. In J. Briere, L. Berliner, J. A. Bulkley, C. Jenny, T. Reid (Eds.), *The APSAC handbook on child maltreatment.* Thousand Oaks, CA: Sage.

Individuals With Disabilities Education Act. 34 Code of Federal Regulations 300.7(9). Washington, DC: Government Printing Office.

O'Hagan, K. (1993). *Emotional and psychological abuse of children.* Toronto: University of Toronto Press.

Osofsky, J., & Jackson, B. R. (1994, April). Parenting in violent environments. *Zero to Three,* pp. 8-11.

School Psychology Review. (1987). Mini-theme issue: Psychological maltreatment of children. *16,* 126-211.

Wolfe, D. (1991). *Preventing physical and emotional abuse of children.* New York: Guilford.

ACKNOWLEDGMENTS

These Guidelines are the product of the National Psychological Maltreatment Consortium and APSAC's Task Force on Psychological Maltreatment, chaired by Stuart Hart, Ph.D., and Marla Brassard, Ph.D. Seventy professionals commented on the first draft of these Guidelines at the San Diego Conference on Responding to Child Maltreatment in January, 1993. Members of the Consortium and the Task Force, and all APSAC members who participated, are thanked for the significant contributions they have made to the development of these Guidelines. John E. B. Myers, JD, is recognized particularly for provision of extensive editorial support. The Guidelines will be updated periodically. Any comments or suggestions about them should be directed to APSAC, 407 S. Dearborn, Suite 1300, Chicago, IL 60605.

List of Further Reading

James, Beverly. (1989). *Treating Traumatized Children: New Insights and Creative Inventions.* New York: Free Press.

Friedrich, William N. (1990). *Psychotherapy of Sexually Abused Children and Their Families.* New York: Norton.

Friedrich, William N. (1991). *Casebook of Sex Abuse Treatment.* New York: Norton.

Friedrich, William N. (1995). *Psychotherapy With Sexually Abused Boys: An Integrated Approach.* Thousand Oaks, CA: Sage.

Monahon, Cynthia. (1995). *Children and Trauma: A Parent's Guide to Helping Children Heal.* New York: Free Press.

Landry, Dorothy B. (1991). *Family Fallout: A Handbook for Families of Adult Sexual Abuse Survivors.* Brandon, VT: Safer Society Press.

Sanford, Linda. (1992). *Strong at the Broken Places: Overcoming the Trauma of Childhood Abuse.* New York: Avon.

Gil, Eliana. (in press). *Trauma, Children, and Treatment.* Walnut Creek, CA: Launch Press.

Gil, Eliana. (1996). *Treating Abused Adolescents.* New York: Guilford.

References

Abel, G. G., Becker, J. V., Cunningham-Rathner, J., Mittelman, M., & Rouleau, J. L. (1988). Multiple paraphilic diagnosis among sex offenders. *Bulletin of the American Academy of Psychiatry and the Law, 16,* 153-168.

Abel, G., Mittelman, M., & Becker, J. (1985). Sex offenders: Results of assessment and recommendations for treatment. In J. Ben-Aron, S. Hucker, & C. Webster (Eds.), *Clinical criminology: Current concepts.* Toronto: M & M Graphics.

American Psychiatric Association. (1994). *Diagnostic and statistical manual of mental disorders* (4th ed.). Washington DC: American Psychiatric Association.

Becker, J. V. (1994). Offenders: Characteristics and treatment. *The Future of Children, 4,* 176-197.

Becker, J. V., & Quinsey, V. L. (1993). Assessing suspected child molesters. *Child Abuse & Neglect, 17,* 169-174.

Beckett, K. (1996). Culture and the politics of signification: The case of child sexual abuse. *Social Problems, 43,* 57-76.

Bender, L., & Blau, A. (1937). The reactions of children to sexual relations with adults. *American Journal of Orthopsychiatry, 7,* 500-518.

Bender, L., & Grugett, A. E. (1952). A follow-up report on children who had atypical sexual experience. *American Journal of Orthopsychiatry, 22,* 825-837.

Benedek, E. P., & Schetky, D. H. (1985). Allegations of sexual abuse in child custody and visitation disputes. In D. H. Schetky & E. B.

Benedek (Eds.), *Emerging issues in child psychiatry and the law* (pp. 145-156). New York: Brunner/Mazel.

Berliner, L. (1988). Deciding whether a child has been sexually abused. In B. Nicholson & J. Bulkley (Eds.), *Sexual abuse allegations in custody and visitation cases* (pp. 48-69). Washington, DC: American Bar Association.

Berliner, L., & Conte, J. R. (1993). Sexual abuse evaluations: Conceptual and empirical obstacles. *Child Abuse & Neglect, 17,* 111-125.

Berliner, L., & Elliott, D. M. (1996). Sexual abuse of the child. In J. Briere, L. Berliner, J. A. Bulkley, C. Jenny, & T. Reid (Eds.), *The APSAC handbook on child maltreatment* (pp. 51-71). Thousand Oaks, CA: Sage.

Black's Law Dictionary. (1979). (Ed.). H. C. Black. St. Paul, MN: West.

Blumer, H. (1969). Social movements. In B. McLaughlin (Ed.), *Studies in social movements: A social psychological perspective* (pp. 8-29). New York: Free Press.

Brassard, M. R., Germain, R., & Hart, S. N. (1987). *Psychological maltreatment of children and youth.* New York: Pergamon.

Briere, J. N. (1992). *Child abuse trauma: Theory and treatment of the lasting effects.* Newbury Park, CA: Sage.

Brunhold, H. (1964). Observations after sexual trauma suffered in childhood. *Excerpta Criminologica, 11,* 5-8.

California Penal Code. (1996). Various sections.

California Welfare and Institutions Code. (1996). Various sections.

Ceci, S. J., Huffman, M. L. C., & Smith, E. (1994). Repeatedly thinking about a non-event: Source misattributions among preschoolers. *Consciousness and Cognition, 3,* 388-407.

DeMott, B. (1980, March). The pro-incest lobby. *Psychology Today, 13*(10), 11-12, 15-16.

Ferenczi, S. (1955). The sexual passion of adults and their influence on the character development and sexual development of children. (Title of article in book is "Confusion of tongues between adults and the child: The language of tenderness and passion"). In M. Balint (Ed.), *Final contributions to the problems and methods of psycho-analysis* (pp. 156-167). (E. Mosbacher, Trans.). New York: Basic Books. (Original work published in 1932)

Finkel, M. A., & DeJong, A. R. (1994). Medical findings in child abuse. In R. M. Reece (Ed.), *Child abuse: Medical diagnosis and management* (pp. 185-247). Philadelphia: Lea & Febiger.

Finkelhor, D. (1979). *Sexually victimized children.* New York: Free Press.

Finkelhor, D. (1986). *A sourcebook on child sexual abuse.* Beverly Hills, CA: Sage.

Finkelhor, D. (1994). Current information on the scope and nature of child sexual abuse. *The Future of Children, 4,* 31-53.

Finkelhor, D., & Berliner, L. (1995). Research on the treatment of sexually abused children: A review and recommendations. *Journal of the American Academy of Child and Adolescent Psychiatry, 34,* 1408-1423.

Finkelhor, D., & Browne, A. (1985). The traumatic impact of child sexual abuse: A conceptualization. *American Journal of Orthopsychiatry, 55,* 530-541.

Fivush, R., & Shukat, J. R. (1995). Content, consistency, and coherence of early autobiographical recall. In M. S. Zaragoza, J. R. Graham, G. C. N. Hall, R. Hirschman, & Y. S. Ben-Porath (Eds.), *Memory and testimony in the child witness* (pp. 5-23). Thousand Oaks, CA: Sage.

Friedrich, W. N. (1993). Sexual behavior in sexually abused children. *Violence Update, 3*(1), 7-10.

Friedrich, W. N., Grambsch, P., Broughton, D., Kupier, J., & Beilke, R. L. (1991). Normal sexual behavior in children. *Pediatrics, 88,* 456-464.

Friedrich, W. N., Grambsch, P., Damon, L., Hewitt, S. K., Koverola, C., Lang, R. A., Wolf, V., & Broughton, D. (1992). Child sexual behavior inventory: Normative and clinical contrasts. *Psychological Assessment, 4,* 303-311.

Garbarino, J., Guttmann, E., & Seeley, J. (1986). *The psychologically battered child.* San Francisco: Jossey-Bass.

Gardner, R. A. (1987). *The parental alienation syndrome and the differentiation between fabricated and genuine sex abuse.* Cresskill, NJ: Creative Therapeutics.

Gardner, R. A. (1991). *Sex abuse hysteria: Salem witch trials revisited.* Cresskill, NJ: Creative Therapeutics.

Gardner, R. A. (1992). *True and false allegations of child sex abuse.* Cresskill, NJ: Creative Therapeutics.

Green, A. H. (1986). True and false allegations of sexual abuse in child custody disputes. *Journal of the American Academy of Child Psychiatry, 25,* 449-456.

Groth, A., Longo, R., & McFadin, J. (1982). Undetected recidivism among rapists and child molesters. *Crime & Delinquency, 28,* 450-458.

Henderson, D. J. (1975). Incest. In A. M. Freedman, H. I. Kaplan, & B. J. Sadock (Eds.), *Comprehensive textbook of psychiatry*. Baltimore: Williams & Wilkins.

Herman, J. L. (1981). *Father-daughter incest*. Cambridge, MA: Harvard University Press.

Herman, J. L. (1990). Sex offenders: A feminist perspective. In W. L. Marshall, D. R. Laws, & H. E. Barbaree (Eds.), *Handbook of sexual assault: Issues, theories, and treatment of the offender* (pp. 177-193). New York: Plenum.

In re K. S., 737 P2d 170 (Utah 1987).

Jenny, C. (1996). Medical issues in sexual abuse. In J. Briere, L. Berliner, J. A. Bulkley, C. Jenny, & T. Reid (Eds.), *The APSAC handbook on child maltreatment* (pp 195-205). Thousand Oaks, CA: Sage.

Jones, P. H., & McGraw, M. J. (1987). Reliable and fictitious accounts of sexual abuse to children. *Journal of Interpersonal Violence, 2,* 27-45.

Jones, P. H., & Seig, A. (1988). Child sexual abuse allegations in custody or visitation cases: A report of 20 cases. In B. Nicholson & J. Bulkely (Eds.), *Sexual abuse allegations in custody and visitation cases* (pp. 22-36). Washington, DC: American Bar Association.

Kendall-Tackett, K. A., Meyer Williams, L., & Finkelhor, D. (1993). Impact of sexual abuse on children: A review and synthesis of recent empirical studies. *Psychological Bulletin, 113,* 164-180.

Kempe, H. (1978). *Sexual abuse, another hidden pediatric problem* (The 1977 C. Anderson Aldrich Lecture). *Pediatrics, 62,* 382-389.

Kinsey, A. C. (1953). *Sexual behavior in the human female*. Philadelphia, PA: Saunders.

Lindblad, F., Gustafsson, P. A., Larsson, I., & Lundin, B. (1995). Preschoolers' sexual behavior at daycare centers: An epidemiological study. *Child Abuse & Neglect, 19,* 569-577.

Lyon, T. D., & Koehler, J. J. (in press). The relevance ratio: Evaluating the probative value of expert testimony in child sexual abuse cases. *Cornell Law Review*.

Marxsen, D., Yuille, J. C., & Nisbet, M. (1995). The complexities of eliciting and assessing children's statements. *Psychology, Public Policy and Law, 1,* 450-460.

Masson, J. M. (1984). *The assault on truth: Freud's suppression of the seduction theory*. New York: Farrar, Straus & Giroux.

Moss, D. C. (1988). Abuse scale: Point system for abuse claims. *American Bar Association Journal, 74,* 26.

Murphy, W. D. (1994). Offender treatment: The perils and pitfalls of profiling child sex abusers. *The APSAC Advisor, 7,* 3-4, 28-29. (Newsletter of the American Professional Society on the Abuse of Children)

Murphy, W. D., & Smith, T. A. (1996). Sex offenders against children: Empirical and clinical issues. In J. Briere, L. Berliner, J. A. Bulkley, C. Jenny, & T. Reid (Eds.), *The APSAC handbook on child maltreatment* (pp. 175-191). Thousand Oaks, CA: Sage.

Myers, J.E.B. (1992). *Evidence in child abuse and neglect cases.* New York: John Wiley.

Myers, J.E.B. (1993). Expert testimony regarding child sexual abuse. *Child Abuse & Neglect, 17,* 175-185.

Myers, J.E.B. (1994). The literature of the backlash. In J.E.B. Myers (Ed.), *The Backlash: Child Protection Under Fire.* (pp. 86-103). Thousand Oaks, CA: Sage.

Myers, J.E.B. (1996). Expert testimony. In J. Briere, L. Berliner, J. A. Bulkley, C. Jenny, & T. Reid (Eds.), *The APSAC handbook on child maltreatment* (pp. 319-340). Thousand Oaks, CA: Sage.

Myers, J.E.B., Bays, J., Becker, J., Berliner, L., Corwin, D. L., & Saywitz, K. J. (1989). Expert testimony in child sexual abuse litigation. *Nebraska Law Review, 68,* 1-145.

Myers, J.E.B., Berliner, L., Murphy, W. D., Pithers, W. D., & Prentky, R. (1991). *Brief of amicus curiae American Professional Society on the Abuse of Children.* Filed in the United States Supreme Court case of *State of Montana v. Donald Glenn Imlay.* October Term.

Nicholas, H. R., & Molinder, I. (1984). *Multiphasic sex inventory manual.* Tacoma, WA: Author.

Oates, R. K., Jones, D.P.H., Denson, D., Sirotnak, A., & Krugman, R. D. (n.d.). *Erroneous accounts of child sexual abuse.* Manuscript in preparation.

Pennsylvania v. Ritchie, 480 U.S. 39 (1987).

People v. D. A. K., 596 P2d 747 (Col. 1979).

Phipps-Yonas, S., Yonas, A., Turner, M., & Kauper, M. (1993). Sexuality in early childhood: The observations and opinions of family daycare providers. *Center for Urban and Regional Affairs Reporter, 23,* 1-5.

Pomeroy, W. B. (1976, November). A new look at incest. *Forum,* pp. 9-13.

Quinn, K. M. (1988). The credibility of children's allegations of sexual abuse. *Behavioral Sciences & the Law, 6,* 181-199.

Reid, T. (1995). *Father-daughter incest in contemporary fiction*. Unpublished manuscript.

Russsell, D.E.H. (1983). The incidence and prevalence of intrafamilial and extrafamilial sexual abuse of female children. *Child Abuse & Neglect, 7*, 133-146.

Russell, D.E.H. (1986). *The secret trauma: Incest in the lives of girls and women*. New York: Basic Books.

Saldaña, R. H. (1994). *Crime victim compensation programs: A reference guide to the programs in the U.S.* Bountiful, UT: QuartZite.

Salter, A. C. (1995). *Transforming trauma: A guide to understanding and treating adult survivors of child sexual abuse*. Thousand Oaks, CA: Sage.

Shengold, L. L. (1979). Child abuse and deprivation: Soulmurder. *Journal of the American Psychoanalytic Association, 27*, 533-559.

Simon, W. T., & Schouten, P.G.W. (1993). The plethysmograph reconsidered. Comments on Barker and Howell. *Bulletin of the American Academy of Psychiatry and Law, 21*, 505-512.

Summit, R. C. (1988). Hidden victims, hidden pain: Societal avoidance of child sexual abuse. In G. E. Wyatt & G. J. Powell (Eds.), *Lasting effects of child sexual abuse* (pp. 39-60). Thousand Oaks, CA: Sage.

Summit, R. C., Olafson, E., & Corwin, D. L., (1993). Modern history of child sexual abuse awareness: Cycles of discovery and suppression. *Child Abuse & Neglect, 17*, 7-24.

Tardieu, A. A. (1873). *Etude medicale-legale sur les attentats aux moeurs* [A medico-legal study of assaults on decency] (6th ed.). Paris. (Original work published in 1857)

Thoennes, N., & Tjaden, P. G. (1990). The extent, nature and validity of sexual abuse allegations in custody/visitation disputes. *Child Abuse & Neglect, 14*, 151-163.

Waterman, J. (1986). Developmental considerations. In J. Waterman & K. MacFarlane (Eds.), *Sexual abuse of young children* (pp. 15-29). New York: Guilford.

Wigmore, J. H. (1970). *Evidence in trials at common law*. Boston: Little, Brown. (Original work published 1904).

Index

About the Author

John E. B. Myers, JD, Professor of Law at the University of the Pacific, McGeorge School of Law in Sacramento, California, is nationally recognized as an expert on investigation and litigation of child abuse and neglect.

He is the author of numerous books and articles discussing legal issues in child abuse and neglect. His writing has been cited by more than seventy courts, including the U.S. Supreme Court and numerous state supreme courts. In addition, he is a regular speaker at conferences on child abuse.